£5.99

Free Tir

To Julia
from Father
with love.

Can research be leisure?
(see pp. 34 and 57-8)

June 30th 2004

To J., A. and H.
who have enriched my leisure

# Free Time
# Towards a Theology of Leisure

## Graham Neville

**THE UNIVERSITY
OF BIRMINGHAM**

**UNIVERSITY PRESS**

First published in the United Kingdom by The University of Birmingham Press, University of Birmingham, Aitchison Building, Edgbaston, Birmingham, BI5 2TT, UK.

ISBN 1 902459 21 0

British Library Cataloguing in Publication Data

A CIP catalogue record for this book is available from the British Library

Printed in Great Britain by
Lightning Source

# Contents

# Preface

If the intention of Christian theology is to examine and reflect on the whole of human experience in the light of the Christian revelation, there must be a place for theological reflection on our contemporary experience of leisure in Western society. The essays presented here are offered as a contribution to that task of reflection. It is proper, however, to declare at the outset some of the writer's assumptions underlying what is written.

I take for granted that theology is never 'timeless', but constantly changing, and that its changes are related to the changes of its social setting. There must, therefore, always be a historical, and even a biographical, element in the description of any coherent theological scheme. And since leisure as it is now experienced in Western society has nothing exactly corresponding to it in previous cultures, it is also assumed that we cannot expect theological voices from the past to speak directly to our present situation. Nor is it likely that there will emerge a single, agreed message which can be elicited from the many voices of theology. As if these problems were not enough, there is the additional problem that those who consider leisure from a sociological viewpoint are as little agreed about it as theologians are likely to be when they consider leisure.

This book, then, is offered simply as a number of essays towards the understanding of leisure, not as any kind of definitive statement. It arises, as do all attempts at theology (however little that is acknowledged), out of an individual's experience, which it is only right to indicate. Back in the 1970s the author became involved, like so many others, in the stresses of educational reorganization. The particular aspect of it which is relevant to the present theme was the merger of a college of physical education (PE) with a college of general (or multi-specialist) teacher training. It was an interesting experience for those who had not had much previous experience of PE colleges to discover that for some of their colleagues physical education was seen as a possible basis for a complete humanistic education. That conviction did not really carry the day; but at least it raised the profile of what it had been easy to see as 'mere leisure'. Unfortunately the subsequent development of university courses in 'leisure management' and related topics has tended to commercialize the subject and so to distance it from any ideal of humanistic education. The next stage along a path of discovery was taken in sermons and discussions at the parish level when two things became clear: that lay people were deeply interested in the nature of leisure, and that they had not been encouraged to think about it. The final stage (in more senses than one) was the experience of extended retirement.

These details are only of use as indicating a particular viewpoint, with its inevitable limitations. It might be characterized as academic or élitist, the typical position of one whose leisure does not include watching 'Coronation Street'. The reader's own position might be identified by testing his or her response to the following comic passage from Coleridge's *Biographia Literaria*, relating to those who used circulating libraries, the first part of which is a prophetic analysis of the condition of the modern couch-potato.

> I dare not compliment their pass-time, or rather kill-time, with the name of reading. Call it rather a sort of beggarly day-dreaming, during which the mind of the dreamer furnishes for itself nothing but laziness and a little mawkish sensibility; while the whole *matériel* and imagery of the doze is supplied *ab extra* by a sort of mental camera obscura manufactured at the printing office, which *pro tempore* fixes, reflects and transmits the moving phantasms of one man's delirium, so as to people the barrenness of an hundred other brains afflicted with the same trance or suspension of all common sense and all definite purpose. We should therefore transfer this species of amusement ... from the genus, reading, to that comprehensive class characterized by the power of reconciling the two contrary yet coexisting propensities of human nature, namely, indulgence of sloth, and hatred of vacancy. In addition to novels and tales of chivalry in prose or rhyme, (by which last I mean neither rhythm nor metre) this genus comprises as its species, gaming, swinging or swaying on a chair or gate; spitting over a bridge; smoking; snuff-taking; tête-à-tête quarrels after dinner between husband and wife; conning word by word all the advertisements of the Daily Advertizer in a public house on a rainy day, etc. etc. etc.[1]

To which we may add the remark of George Steiner: 'Given a free vote, the bulk of humankind will choose football, the soap opera or bingo over Aeschylus. To pretend otherwise is cant.'[2]

One other limitation, beside those of a personal nature, should be mentioned. It would be tempting to take a predominately moralistic approach in discussing leisure from a Christian point of view, and to criticize the life-style of a particular social class. But that is not the main line of thought followed in this study, because the intention is to begin with theology, or with doctrine, rather than moralism. Moral questions cannot be entirely excluded; but, as will appear, leisure is in some sense or other 'beyond morality'.

I gratefully acknowledge advice and criticism which has helped to shape this essay in applied theology. In particular, I am grateful to Professor Duncan B. Forrester for his criticism of an earlier draft, which initiated its fundamental revision, and to Professor Hugh McLeod for his constructive comments at a later stage of its development. The present text would be much the poorer without their help, though its defects remain, of course, my responsibility. I have also appreciated the help of my friend, Dr Glyn Tegai Hughes, who extracted and translated for me the article 'Musse' in *Historisches Wörterbuch der Philosophie*; and of the Revd Dr J. Wesley Parfitt, for lending me his unpublished Ph.D. thesis on COPEC; and I should like to record my thanks for the help of the late Canon Iain Mackenzie, former Canon Librarian of Worcester Cathedral, in making its treasures of seventeenth-century books available to me, although he is, sad to say, beyond receiving thanks. I am indebted to the Managing Editor of the University of Birmingham press, Alec McAulay, for his encouragement and advice, and to my daughter, Anstice Hughes, for copy-editing the typescript. The quotation on pages 37–8 is reproduced by permission of Penguin Books Ltd and the estate of J.A.K. Thomson. Thanks are due, also, to the Golsoncott Foundation and its administrator, Hal Bishop, and the Somerset Museums Service for the use of the wood engraving 'Siesta', by the late Rachel Reckitt.

Graham Neville

## Notes

1 *Biographia Literaria* (London 1956 [1817]), ch. 3 (footnote).
2 George Steiner, *Real Presences: Is There Anything in What We Say?* (London 1989), 67.

# Introduction

Although the purpose of this enquiry is to look for a theological understanding of leisure, it must not be assumed that leisure itself is a thing easily identified. We need to take into account some of the changes of the last hundred years which have already transformed the meaning of leisure or are likely to do so in the near future. Indeed, these changes began to take effect as long ago as the eighteenth century.[1] The result has been a dramatic reduction in the hours of work for the general population. The demands of trade unions have been almost as much directed to reduction of working hours as to increase of wages. The creation of the so-called Welfare State has helped to prolong life expectancy and to provide the basic standard of living in unemployment and retirement which is needed to give meaning to the idea of leisure for all and not just for the privileged class. In Western society that idea is near to realization, and we can expect that pattern to be more widely disseminated as time passes. For many people in our society leisure is no longer confined to evenings and weekends. Leisure time (if that is the right description) often occupies prolonged periods during unemployment or redeployment, and there may be twenty years or more after retirement.

Clearly we need to come to terms with this change. A book about *The Problem of Leisure* published in 1938 could refer to 'the preaching by every denomination in Western Europe of the Gospel of Work' and quoted Zwingli as declaring 'Labour is a thing so good and god-like... In the things of this life, the labourer is most like God'.[2] Is the senior citizen, then, not a god-like figure? Most of us will need, at some stage, a theological rationale of leisure, not a life-line from over-work. But when we begin to look into the subject seriously the horizons seemed to recede. There is an enormous landscape which it would take years to explore. If we make a list of some of the fields in that landscape it must include things like these: the nature of man as worker and artist; worship as leisure and leisure as worship; creation and procreation; recreation and rebirth; happiness and utopia; Sunday and feast day; grace and gift; music and meditation; nature mysticism ... and so on and so on.

The need to give theological consideration to the understanding of leisure seems to be gaining recognition only slowly. There was a time during the last century when the question was asked, Can anyone be a Christian at work? A small number of priests in England, and far more in France, took jobs in factories and mines, looking for an answer to that question.[3] The changing condition of Western society now poses the question, Can anyone be a Christian in leisure? The question has a certain kind of inevitability. Priests and others who may ask that question only have to wait to find out, as lengthy retirement becomes the norm. They may be challenged to do some thinking about their own leisure.

It is, however, just this kind of concern over the debasement of leisure that demands an enquiry whether there is a truer understanding of its place in the purposes of God. If there is such a place it cannot be simply as an adjunct or accessory of work. Christian writers, where they have not made work the be-all and end-all of human life, have generally treated leisure as an inseparable appendix to work, or at least something which cannot be understood except in relation to work. A recent book written from a Christian perspective claims to be distinctive in treating work and leisure together, whereas other books treat the topics separately.[4] This is not true about books written from a secular standpoint.[5] On the contrary, in the past, work and leisure have been considered in relation to each other; though there is now a tendency, at least in research in the USA, to relate leisure studies to the family rather than to work, in response to the development of feminist concerns.[6] In the case of Christian books, there are not many about leisure as such.[7] Leisure only features commonly in Christian discourse either as relaxation from work, or in recent explorations of the idea of 'play'[8] (which is only a particular kind of leisure or else not leisure at all), or when it assumes a more serious guise in discussions of the arts or of beauty in general, which are categories transcending divisions between work and worship and leisure.

We cannot altogether avoid some attempt to define what, in these essays, leisure is taken to mean; though inevitably different writers, as they are quoted, will use the word differently. In distinguishing relaxation from leisure there is the danger of doing what T.S. Eliot, in another context, called producing 'an artificial distinction, peculiar to the book, which the reader would have difficulty in retaining; and which, after closing the book, he would abandon with a sense of relief'.[9] It will be more entertaining to refer to various types of definition and offer the reader a choice, even if that choice proves, on consideration, to be heavily loaded. To begin with a description which is less than helpful, the Methodist Statement on the Christian Use of Leisure (1974) tried to distinguish that part of life which is regulated by external disciplines from that which is at our own disposal, but then proceeded: 'We are at leisure when we ourselves determine the use of our time – even when we accept the internal disciplines of faith, family and social responsibilities'.[10] That seems to locate things like voting or nappy changing or praying equally in the area of leisure. Some implied definitions are clearly hostile. 'Work is the sole human dignity: man is a spirit precisely because he does not resemble the birds of the air who sow not, neither do they reap.'[11] Evidently Jesus did not want us to study them too closely. There is, fortunately, a more favourable tradition which goes back to Josef Pieper: 'The soul of leisure, it can be said, lies in "celebration". Celebration is the point at which three elements of leisure emerge together: effortlessness, calm and relaxation, and its superiority to all and every function.'[12] In this way of thinking, leisure is seen as something rather mysterious, a cultural inheritance related to worship. Two brief statements carry on this religious strain. 'Leisure is a kind of time, whereas work is a kind of action.'[13] Leisure is 'an internship for the eternal'.[14] Even outside a religious context it can be called 'a divergent form of being'.[15]

It would be possible to extend this list of varied definitions of leisure beyond the limits of the reader's patience. It may be enough at this point to propose a simple classification of areas of human life, and to draw attention to an essential factor in any definition of leisure. Setting aside complications, such as the proposal to call some things 'semi-leisure',[16] we may divide human activities (and passivities) three ways. Work is that by which we make a living. Duty is that which social life imposes on us. Leisure is all that we choose to do or experience beyond the limits of work and duty. Some of that is simply relaxation; but some of it is longer lasting, and it is this more extensive kind of activity or inactivity which merits serious consideration. The range of things people actually regard as leisure is very great. In one particular Christian congregation an enquiry conducted by the author elicited over ninety responses to questions about their leisure occupations. Many of them were what we recognize as hobbies, but some were not. They included words like thinking, dreaming, appreciating – 'appreciating the wondrous works of our Creator' – and even silence, the particular shared silence of a father with his children as they patiently watched small animals in the wild. All in their different ways were freely chosen.

In the extended kind of 'free time' which retirement provides and in short-term times of leisure, most people simply adopt patterns of behaviour from their social environment. There is nothing wrong with that. But a reflective person will want to understand the significance of the chosen pattern. For every kind of action or inaction takes its meaning from the way it is understood by the agent, and its meaning can be changed by choosing a different kind of intention. Take tourism for instance. It has been analysed into three different kinds.[17] There is 'recreational tourism', in which responsibilities are left behind, but the tourist's social values are carefully retained. There is 'experiential tourism', in which there is a deliberate meeting with another culture, though the traveller's central social values are preserved. There is 'existential tourism', in which the traveller makes a deliberate attempt to enter an alien culture and adopt its values. Alongside this three-fold division, there is the kind of tourism which qualifies as pilgrimage, in which the traveller carries one form of belief to a chosen destination where that belief may be in some way modified. Neither existential tourism nor pilgrimage (in its true meaning) qualify as leisure. Only self-examination can tell anyone which kind of travelling is in question. The essays in this book do not try to answer that kind of question, or to commend particular ways of using free time, but only to offer a reflective basis for self-assessment.

The fundamental implication of leisure, then, seems to be freedom. This idea will be explored in more detail in a later chapter, but a brief consideration of it may help with our initial definition. Etymologically leisure means 'that which is permitted' (though etymological arguments in theology are always suspect). It cannot include anything which is demanded or enforced. Because work is done under some kind of necessity, leisure is the proper antithesis of work. It includes all that is freely chosen, all that is done for its own sake, all that could be left undone without endangering the life of the individual or the life of society. Perhaps we may take at least as a working definition of leisure 'those activities (and passivities) which are chosen freely, in the sense that they might just as freely have been left undone'. Certainly we should avoid any attempt to define leisure in terms of enjoyment, for it is obviously possible to enjoy at least some kinds of work, even though that work is done under the compulsion of earning a living.

Presumably those who reject the notion of human freedom will have to define leisure some other way. We certainly need to recognize that all human choices are conditioned, though not determined, by all sorts of extraneous factors. But if human actions are assumed to be free in this restricted sense, there is an additional element of free choice in leisure as compared with work. Perhaps for some rare souls the most free moment in their lives may be when they commit themselves with loving abandon to the work which gives significance to their whole being, even though it is also the means of earning their daily bread. That kind of freedom may even be enjoyed on a smaller scale whenever we undertake a particular kind of employment as the result of deliberate choice. But once the work has been accepted and the commitment made, then duty takes over. Work depends on discipline. The world of work is the world of regularities, and things go badly wrong if duty is replaced by caprice. But it is not so with leisure. The freedom which permits someone to choose a particular kind of leisure activity permits that person to abandon it too. The choice is made without commitment, and can be unmade just as freely. In leisure no one should be reproached for a change of mind.

In actual experience, however, this complete freedom from accountability is seldom to be had. In discussing different kinds of equality, Michael Walzer has argued that the organization of leisure in a pre-industrial society, being related to special feast days, made it part of a corporate activity, and to that extent an obligation on the members of the participating community.[18] Those who opted out would be seen as eccentric. Even in the modern, individualized Western world many leisure activities are co-operative, and if only one other person is involved, the freedom of the individual is to that extent limited. Nothing can be done without agreement, if a companion is involved. But the agreement can be brought to an end without reproach. Because two people play tennis together today, as a leisure activity, it does not follow that they have any obligation to do so tomorrow. As the group involved in a leisure activity becomes larger, and as its members develop specialized functions within it, for example in an amateur dramatic group, it becomes more difficult for the individual to exercise this theoretical freedom to withdraw without reproach. Having made an initial choice to join the group, each member feels increasingly obliged to sustain its existence, at least until the point where withdrawal will not create great problems for its other members. Each member is properly aware that his or her own freedom to enjoy the chosen activity depends upon the same patience and tolerance being shown all round. It would be very insensitive not to restrain the exercise of freedom until an appropriate moment. It is also true (though perhaps this is not strictly relevant to the definition of leisure) that groups at leisure, like groups at work, easily tyrannize over their members, and even set about recruiting new members with arguments which suggest that the outsiders have a kind of duty to enjoy themselves in a particular way. Probably we all know the keen bathers or dancers who react in this indefensible way to the sight of others whose happiness consists, at least for the time being, in not bathing or not dancing. But this is a question of group dynamics; it does not bear directly on the definition of leisure in terms of freedom.

Another limitation on the freedom of the individual lies in the nature of the activity chosen. If the activity is simple and short, in the units of action which make it up, then it hands back to the agent the freedom of choice at frequent intervals. You can stop skipping every time the rope comes round. You can stop drinking pints of beer (subject to the conventions of treating) at the bottom of every glass. But there are other chosen activities which are made up of much larger units. If you choose to build a cathedral out of match-sticks, it will be a long time before you can choose what to do next. Of course you are free to abandon the attempt, and there is not the slightest reason why anyone else should blame you for doing so. But in that case leisure may become a source of frustration where it was intended to be an opportunity for self-fulfilment. Freedom, it seems natural to suppose, is directed towards fulfilment and not frustration.

The most serious limitation, however, on the freedom of the individual in leisure arises in practice from the unwillingness of many human beings to exercise freedom; indeed, from the unwillingness of all human beings, to some degree, to exercise freedom. However much we pay lip-service to the idea of individual freedom, we actually want it only in limited quantities. For freedom, which brings a feeling of strength, also brings the awareness of isolation; and that can engender doubt and even anxiety.[19] The result is that many people, because they lack inner security, are tempted to respond to an increase in leisure by filling it with activities which minimize their responsibility for decision. These activities range from a second paid job, through group activities which submerge the individual, down to the simple imposition of a rigid and unvarying pattern on theoretically spontaneous pastimes.

Traditional Christian views of the world have represented it either as a vale of soul-making or as the arena of the active life from which an élite might escape into the life of contemplation which is nearest to the life of heaven. There was little room in either scheme for what we now call leisure. It was often dismissed as mere idleness or even sloth. Biblical writers are not friendly to those who are 'at ease in Sion'. But the meaning of leisure has been transformed in Western society. It is no longer a class privilege. For an increasing number it is a third of life. Perhaps this is only the restoration of a pre-industrial situation, in which the routine of work, not yet dominated by the machine, was frequently interrupted by traditional feasts. But the difference lies in the incidental benefits conferred by post-industrial society, including freedom of thought and action, access to physical and electronic communications, and the consequent huge range of choice available. The leisure revolution in the Western world requires a theological response, or at least a response informed by theological ideas.

It is almost a hundred years since the American sociologist Thorstein Veblen wrote what he called 'an economic study of institutions' with the title *The Theory of the Leisure Class*. Its impact has been kept alive, even when the book itself has not been read, by the memorable phrase 'conspicuous consumption'. That phrase does indeed conveniently sum up its main emphasis. He argued (and who can deny his argument?) that when a group or class in society emancipates itself from the need to spend all its time in productive work, it asserts its superiority by flaunting its freedom in the face of those who are not emancipated in the same way. This involves the deliberate use of time or money or both in non-productive ways, either personally or through the women-folk of the so-called leisure class. This situation, which faces us every day, might indeed be subjected to Christian criticism of a moral kind. We might criticize the inequity of any society which distributes the rewards of labour in such a way as to create a minority 'leisure class'. We might inveigh against its vanity and its wastefulness. We might hold up the model of stewardship which such behaviour denies. We might propound a feminist critique of an arrangement which marks out women as intentionally useless members of the leisure class.

But we need to begin with some kind of positive evaluation of leisure, and with an important distinction. A useful starting-point in understanding Christian attitudes to leisure in the modern world is provided by the 1924 Conference on Christian Politics, Economics and Citizenship (COPEC). This will be considered in more detail later. Here it is enough to note that the report of its commission on Leisure draws a distinction which will be apparent or implied in much of the rest of this book.[20] It distinguishes between 'recreation', which effects the restoration of poise by such things as pleasure and laughter, and 'leisure', which is a growing time of the human spirit through the employment of spare time creatively.[21]  But still the members of the Commission thought that leisure could not be considered apart from work. They concluded that the achievement of happy leisure depended on the prior achievement of happiness at work, though they hoped to point to ways in which leisure might be made more satisfying in 'the world as we know it to-day'.[22] It is obvious that work and leisure often have reciprocal effects on each other, and, where leisure is only a minor part of life, it may rightly consist for the most part in what the report called the 'delightful irresponsibility of spontaneous fun and nonsense'. But our Western society was already beginning to move into the post-industrial phase. For 'men of leisure', for the unemployed, for the retired, it is only a small part of the truth to say now that the nature of work determines the nature of leisure.

And so to the experience of retirement, which is often both desired and feared. It poses for many people in an acute form the question about the meaning of leisure. There is little enough in the Bible to help us interpret retirement. It has been observed that the only reference to the condition of old age in the recorded teaching of Jesus is his description of the destiny of Peter (John 21.18). In the Hebrew scriptures old age, with its wisdom drawn from the experience of a long life, was a time to be respected, and yet old people were afraid that they would be despised (Proverbs 23.22). That could happen even when society was comparatively static. Now in an age of rapid social and technological change there is much more likelihood that old people will find themselves relegated to the status of mere spectators on the margins of life. 'Old men and old women shall again sit in the streets of Jerusalem, each with staff in hand because of their great age. And the streets of the city shall be full of boys and girls playing in its streets' (Zechariah 8.4–5). The best prospect for those who lived beyond the limits of a fully active life was that they should devote themselves to religion, like Simeon and Anna (Luke 2.25–38). When their messianic expectation had been fulfilled and the eschatological hope had faded in the Christian church, the last phase of inactivity was regarded, if it occurred, as a time to prepare for death, or rather, for individual judgment. The weak and the sick and the aged, near their journey's end, faced the crisis in which they were 'so speedily to appear before the most Holy God, and be used for ever as [they had] lived here'.[23]

In this generation it does not seem appropriate to spend perhaps twenty years in so self-regarding a way. Retirement looks like the time of leisure *par excellence*. But it has a forbidding appearance for those who miss the stimulus of a work-discipline and regret the loss of those personal relationships which grew out of their daily work. There are those who advocate a second career, not in the line of duty, but for the love of people.[24] That kind of advice brings home the fact that retirement is not a single stage on the way. It may be begun like a prolonged holiday, an extended time of relaxation. Then perhaps there will be the period of active retirement, with time for something like that second career. Beyond that, what? We hope to escape 'that specially self-indulgent mindlessness of old age which is its most intolerable aspect', described by Ronald Blythe.[25] Certainly retirement comes often as a challenge, perhaps especially to those who are not used to having their partner about the house all day long.[26]

The challenge for the Christian believer is to discover a way of understanding retirement as a gift of God. It is not the most important thing in human life, but it will become part of the lifetime of increasing numbers of people. No one has done more to provide a way of understanding this stage of life than W.H. Vanstone.[27] In his study of the Gospels he came to see a moment of transition in the life of Jesus, at the point at which he was 'betrayed', or as

Vanstone prefers, 'handed over'. It is the moment of transition from active to passive, from action to 'passion' (in the liturgical sense). In Mark's Gospel Jesus falls silent, and we have no further indication of his thoughts until his cry from the cross. He is no longer the doer, but the sufferer. In John's Gospel the change is shown in a different way, and chiefly in John's use of words. It is the end of day (when people work); it is the beginning of night (when no-one can work). It is the end of Jesus' freedom. He is bound, and surrenders his authority. But also, very strangely, it is the completion of the Father's work and the fulfilment of his own glory (John 17.1). Vanstone sees here a possible analogy with a stage in retirement.

The public attitude to leisure is that it should be 'creative', full of activities. But 'it is not necessarily the case that man is most fully human when he is achiever rather than receiver, active rather than passive, subject rather than object'. Perhaps it is even true that this passive role is, in its own way, creative.

> Without man's receptivity the world exists simply as physical fact... Beauty, as opposed to physical fact, appears within the world when a butterfly's wing is seen by a human eye. ... so when a man receives and recognizes the beauty of a butterfly's wing he is no less enriching the totality of the world than when, by art and skill, he creates – if that were possible – a thing of equal beauty. A man who receives and recognizes the beauty of a garden is no less enriching the totality of the world than a man who works and creates a garden.[28]

There are certainly other ways of describing the value of inactive retirement, but all depend, like Vanstone's way, upon awareness of the corporate nature of human experience. To make retirement what it really is, in the divine intention, we need insight; and insight itself requires leisure to bring imagination to bear upon the richness of our free time.

If leisure is 'free time', it can have its own dignity. It is like the life of heaven – free from self-seeking, often binding its participants in fellowship, and at its best utterly absorbing. Perhaps it achieves the third love enshrined in Jesus' summary of the Law. Worship expresses love of God. The active life is where we show our love of our neighbour. We love ourselves in leisure. Christian theology needs to come to terms with this revelatory change – revelatory, because it discloses a new dimension of human life, or at any rate emphasizes a dimension which has been neglected.

# NOTES

1. See Roy Porter, *England in the Eighteenth Century* (London 1998), ch. 6: 'Having & Enjoying', 199–232.
2. Henry Durant, *The Problem of Leisure* (London 1938) 17.
3. See e.g. John Mantle, *Britain's First Worker-Priests* (London 2000).
4. Leland Ryken, *Work and Leisure in Christian Perspective* (Leicester 1989), 15.
5. E.g. Stanley Parker, *Leisure and Work* (London 1983); and note the long article 'The Catholic Doctrine of Work and Play' by F. Gavin in *Theology*, XXI (July 1930), 14–40; also the references to COPEC (1924) below.
6. See Nicole Samuel (ed.),*Women, Leisure and the Family in Contemporary Society: A Multinational Perspective,* (Wallingford 1996), 164.
7. Exceptions are *In Praise of Leisure* (Scottdale, Pa. 1974) by the Mennonite scholar Harold D. Lehman and Robert Lee, *Religion and Leisure in America* (Nashville, Tenn. 1964).
8. See below, Chapter 7.
9. T.S. Eliot, *Notes towards the Definition of Culture* (London 1948), 13.
10. Reprinted in Methodist Church, *Statements on Social Responsibility 1946–1995* (London 1995), 2.
11. Etienne Borne and François Henry, *A Philosophy of Work,* trs. F. Jackson (London 1938), 20.
12. Josef Pieper, *Leisure: The Basis of Culture* (London 1952), 71.
13. Bennett Berger, quoted in Lee, *Religion and Leisure in America*, 29.
14. Lehman, *In Praise of Leisure*,134f.
15. Martin Davies, 'Another Way of Being: Leisure and the Possibility of Privacy', in T. Winnifrith and C. Barrett (eds) *The Philosophy of Leisure* (Basingstoke 1989), 111.
16. Lee, *Religion and Leisure in America*, 31.
17. E. Cohen, 'Pilgrimage and Tourism' in A. Morinis (ed.) *Sacred Journeys* (Westport, Conn. 1992) 53–5, quoted in J. Stopford (ed.) *Pilgrimage Explored* (York 1999), 46.
18. Michael Walzer, *Spheres of Justice* (Oxford 1984), ch. 7: 'Free Time', 184ff.
19. See e.g. Erich Fromm, *The Fear of Freedom* (London 1991), esp. 40.
20. The report is considered further in Chapter 4.
21. COPEC, *Commission Reports*, Vol.V – Leisure (London 1924), xiii, 6, 8.
22. Ibid. 16.
23. Richard Baxter, *A Christian Directory* (London 1673), 292.
24. Paul Tournier, *Learning to Grow Old* (London 1972), 130.
25. Ronald Blythe, *The View in Winter: Reflections on Old Age* (London 1979), 36.
26. See Erica Wimbush and Margaret Talbot (eds), *Relative Freedoms – Women and Leisure* (Milton Keynes 1988), ch. 6.
27. W.H. Vanstone, *The Stature of Waiting* (London 1982).
28. Ibid. 113–14.

# 1

# Beginning with Aquinas

*Leisure does not figure greatly in the Christian tradition, but a theological inquiry may begin from Aquinas's teaching about the sabbath, and the contrast between the active life and the contemplative life. The figures of Mary and Martha suggest this contrast, but have been variously interpreted. Aquinas's dependence on Aristotle is suspect, suggesting that leisure is only a kind of inactivity. But it raises significant issues. Is leisure a foretaste of heaven? Is leisure beyond morality?*

There is very little traditional Christian teaching about leisure. Perhaps that is due in large part to the absence of leisure itself in the past, though we may exaggerate the continuous, unremitting toil of working people in pre-industrial society. It has been estimated that in the thirteenth century about one day in three was a holiday of some kind.[1] But holidays did not necessarily make a complete separation between work and leisure. Farm work and housework cannot simply be set aside because of a holiday, and most workers on farms and in houses would have to work on most days, whether holidays or not. There was certainly not enough leisure as we now understand it to make theologians see much significance in it. Holidays were regarded as religious celebrations rather than as free time. To find any relevant theology in traditional sources, we have to search for implications rather than gather conclusions. We have to read between the lines. The lines of mediaeval theology were themselves written almost entirely by those who lived, worked and thought within the limitations of the monastic or academic context; and they were not much helped by the scriptures.

There are, indeed, two particular topics in the Torah which might be taken up by Christian interpreters looking for a theology of leisure: the seventh day of creation (Genesis 2.1–3), and the commandment concerning the sabbath (Exodus 20.8–11). But they offer uncertain grounds for a theological critique. Indeed, they have always been contentious, because they raise fundamental questions about the status of Old Testament law in the Christian church. The attitude of Jesus himself is not sufficiently clear from the Gospels. Not a jot or tittle was to pass away until all should be fulfilled; yet laws were made for man, not man for the laws. There is the same ambiguity in Paul's writings. His experience of liberation through Christ set him free from law, yet left him with an ineradicable reverence for the law in which he had been nurtured. Authorities in the growing churches, when later they faced difficult moral issues about the use of time, needed more help than they could find in the New Testament and turned to the scriptures of the older dispensation. Yet much of it too was firmly attached to the community of the old Israel and could not be taken as valid for the new community of faith. So a distinction was drawn between the moral law and the ceremonial law, between the moral commandments which were part of God's immutable demands upon humankind and the ceremonial rules which were only provisional, in the sense that they foreshadowed better things to come.[2]

Where, then, did the commandment concerning the sabbath stand? Did it belong to the moral law or the ceremonial law? In what ways should time be given to God, and was there a special way of giving it on the holy day? The Gentile churches had never tried to observe the seventh day by refusing to do any work on it. Their attention was focused on the risen Lord, and his rising on the first day of the week. Sunday was the day to be observed, not Saturday. But how was it to be observed? The unquestioned answer of the church throughout the centuries was that it was a time for worship, for eucharist. So even when the emperor Constantine had determined that the Lord's Day should be set apart from the work which filled all ordinary days, there was still the contentious question about other uses to which time could rightfully be devoted on the holy day. On that question the scriptures seemed to be silent. The commandment spoke only of keeping the seventh day holy by refraining from work. Because that day commemorated God's rest from the work of creation and his contemplation of its goodness (Genesis 1.31), it might be argued that the whole day should be devoted to the kind of restful contemplation of God and his works which was the central meaning of worship. With sufficient ingenuity it was possible to claim that the command had been transferred from the seventh day to the first.[3] But there must be a difference between the old sabbath and the new. Some writers tried to dissociate the Christian teaching about the Lord's Day from the sabbath command by speaking of the Sunday as the 'eighth day' on which the redeemed entered by anticipation into the final rest of the age to come.[4] But this eschatological reference left open questions about the use of time in the present age.

The Jewish tradition had come to associate the sabbath rest with the commemoration of deliverance from slavery in Egypt, a weekly memorial of the Exodus comparable with the annual Passover; but that was no longer relevant, in a literal sense, to the Christian church. It was, in Jeremy Taylor's words, 'external, ritual, national, relative and temporary, and abused by tradition' and consequently abrogated. The moral rules which were to govern Christian behaviour every day obviously applied just as much on the holy day. 'Idleness and luxury and pride are the worst ceremonies of the religion of the sabbath'.[5] But should there be even more exacting standards, so that some things acceptable in times of relaxation on weekdays were not to be allowed on Sunday? During the Reformation period the question was debated with acrimony. Some of those who believed that the whole day must be devoted to worship and pious reading were forced to the expedient of finding other times for proper recreation.[6]

That is to anticipate a long process of social change and theological adaptation. In the mediaeval period, theological critique of the use of time was overshadowed by the development of the monastic life. This exalted the ideal of withdrawal from the activities of the world for the practice of contemplation. It was, however, obvious that such an ideal was irrelevant to the general run of Christian believers. So the idea of a 'mixed life' of action and contemplation came to be discussed in Christian circles from the time of the Fathers. Augustine had spoken of three kinds of life – the contemplative, the active, and the mixed – any one of which might merit an everlasting reward, provided that the contemplative life did not make someone forget the welfare of neighbours, nor the active life rule out contemplation. But Augustine had no intention of commending the kind of thing which passes for leisure today. For him, leisure was a serious business.

> The charm of leisure must not be indolent vacancy of mind , but the investigation or discovery of truth, that thus every man may make solid attainments without grudging that others do the same... Accordingly no one is prohibited from the search after truth, for in this leisure may most laudably be spent... And therefore holy leisure is longed for by the lover of truth.[7]

The 'mixed' life consisted in a kind of alternation between active benevolence and the serious search for truth. There was to be no separate area of the good life which allowed for occupations which were neither charitable nor serious.

If we move on to the culmination of mediaeval Christian thought in the *Summa Theologiae* of Thomas Aquinas, to see what he has to say, however obliquely, about the Christian understanding of leisure, we might expect some useful observations in the discussion either of the seventh day of creation,[8] or of the commandment to observe the sabbath.[9] In both cases we are disappointed. The former focuses on asking in what sense the creation was already complete at its very beginning and in what sense God rested from creation on the seventh day. The answers given throw no light on human rest; indeed God's rest is expressly contrasted with the rest of any of his creatures. The other discussion, about the sabbath, is slightly more relevant. When Aquinas faced there the dilemma concerning the status of Old Testament law in the church, he managed to have the best of both answers by saying that the giving of time to God belonged to the moral law, which was permanent, but the fixing of the particular time was only a ceremonial matter, and could be changed.[10] So we are left with little more than the broad generalizations that man must set aside time to celebrate God's act of creation, the chief of divine blessings, and learn to repose his mind in God now by grace as an anticipation of the future life in which he will repose his mind in God by glory.[11]

Not surprisingly, Thomas sees the world with a clerical eye. If you tried to build up a picture of contemporary Christian life on the evidence of the *Summa*, you might think that men and women divided their time between three things: worship, work and the gratification of bodily needs. The sports and pastimes, and even the arts and crafts, which engaged their energy and attention in the thirteenth century did not seem a suitable subject in a handbook for clergy. But then the same could probably be said of all such handbooks down to the present day. The application of doctrine to practical life is always governed by particular social conditions of time and place. Aquinas viewed human life from within his religious order and his academic calling.

In Protestant thought the reaction against the proliferation of saints and holy days, with attendant superstitions, concentrated the sacredness of time upon the Christian sabbath, which must then be totally given to worship and pious thoughts. Yet the strictest moralist could hardly deny the human need of relaxation. It was only wrong when it usurped the place of spiritual things on the holy day. If there is any relevance here to the consideration of leisure in the modern world, it is in making the obvious point that the time given consciously to God in prayer and worship must be safeguarded from erosion. There is nothing inherently better about any particular way of dividing up the time which is free from work and social duties. To quote Jeremy Taylor again: 'One day in seven is not a piece of natural religion any more than one in ten.'[12] The same reasoning could also question the need for dividing time by whole days. 'Why should the ordering of work and leisure depend on days and weeks? Can it not much more suitably be arranged merely by counting hours?'[13] For lay people the mediaeval pattern of life had interspersed work, worship and leisure in a rather haphazard way. The modern world which was coming into existence at the Reformation required a more disciplined arrangement. This brief consideration of Christian teaching about the sabbath leads only to the conclusion that the Christian life should make room for a variety of activities and passivities outside work.

To return to the *Summa Theologiae*, there is another relevant discussion concerned with sloth or 'accidie', which will be taken up in a later chapter, but the most suggestive topic for the consideration of leisure is the comparison of the active life and the contemplative life. Aquinas certainly has nothing like twenty-first century questions in mind, but we can try to find pointers towards a contemporary rationale, although our present conception of leisure does not really enter into the scholastic scheme of things. It does, however, present a difficulty that what we mean by leisure today includes a great deal of activity as well as inactivity; and so modern leisure occupies territory on either side of the boundary running between action and contemplation. Nevertheless the contrast between the two 'ideal types' of life may help in discussing something which includes elements of both.

Aquinas offers a list of reasons for the superiority of the contemplative life over the active life, eight avowedly derived from Aristotle and one derived from Jesus' saying, 'Mary has chosen the better part'.[14] The contemplative life is superior to the active life because it:

1.   uses the best in man, namely his intellect;
2.   can be exercised more continuously;
3.   affords greater delight;
4.   is less dependent on circumstances;
5.   is its own reward;
6.   consists in leisure and rest
7.   is occupied with divine, not human, things;
8.   distinguishes man from the animals; and
9.   will never end.

Some of the values implied in this list seem questionable today. (1) We are less sure that the intellect is man's best part. The more we exalt imagination and creativity, or even physical activity, the less we feel inclined to set the intellect on a pedestal. It is not necessary to set one part of human capability against another. (2) Again, it is not clear that an alternation of functions is necessarily inferior to the continuous exercise of a single function, even if that were possible; and Aquinas himself admits that contemplation cannot be long sustained at its highest pitch. (7) Nor does it seem self-evident to all Christians today that it is possible to grade the divine, the human and the animal in a simple scale of values, such as is implicit in Aquinas's argument. Some would maintain that the highest activity of man lies precisely in being fully human and not attempting to transcend the limitations of humanity through union with the non-human divine. Such, it might be argued, is implied in a doctrine which claims finality for revelation through incarnation. (8) Others, on the contrary, would argue that a human being loses an important element in true humanity when alienated from non-human partners in the created order. The animal world is not to be regarded as inferior to the human, but simply as different. To be occupied with animals may enrich someone's humanity. So, for example, Nicholas Berdyaev argues that the communion of one Ego with another which leads to what he calls 'affective knowledge' can include communion with the animal and even the inanimate worlds.[15]

With these reservations we can sum up the implications of the discussion so far in five points:

1.   The consideration of God's creation is intended to lead the mind by grace to repose in the Creator. This repose is a foretaste of the ultimate rest in God which is his purpose for man.

2.   Rest is not mere inactivity which, in the form of sloth, may arise as well from carping dissatisfaction with all actual possibilities as from a deliberate turning away from action, seen as a lesser good, to contemplation, recognized as a greater good.

3.   Self-fulfilment requires the exercise of whatever is best in each individual.

4.  There is an important place in human life for the kind of activity which is an end in itself.
5.  Though we must not deceive ourselves into thinking that we can ever be truly independent of our environment, there is for some men and women a strong psychological appeal in activities which make few demands upon organized society and are relatively easy to undertake in diverse circumstances. For others, there is a sense of achievement in organizing very complex activities.

Aquinas recognized, of course, that there was a place for the active life, of which these complex activities might be seen as the culmination. But he was inhibited by the ecclesiastical structures within which he worked, and trapped by the form of his own dialectical method into supposing that either the active life or the contemplative life must be in the abstract the 'higher' of the two; and that, since a choice must be made, the verdict must go in favour of contemplation. We can use the insights of his theology in discussing what we call leisure without adopting the artificiality of the dialectical method or the self-assessment of the mediaeval clergy. He could not have envisaged the present context of leisure in advanced post-industrial society.

The limitations of his attitude to leisure may be seen in some remarks in his *Commentary on the Nicomachean Ethics of Aristotle*. He writes:

A person is said to have leisure when he has nothing further to do – a condition he finds himself in on arriving at some goal. For this reason the philosopher adds that we are busy in order to have leisure, that is, we are active in working – this is being busy – in order to rest at the end – and this is having leisure.[16]

Leisure is interpreted as inactivity ('nothing further to do'). It is a 'special property' of the happiness which comes from achieving a particular goal. It takes its place as one of the three attributes 'customarily assigned to the happy person: self-sufficiency, leisureliness, and freedom from labour'. Such a description fits the tabby cat basking in the sun. It will hardly do for the week-end of the five-day worker or the fifteen long years of retirement, let alone the thirty years of the prematurely redundant or the long-term unemployment of the victims of economic recession. Happiness in small doses would be within almost everybody's grasp in the Western world if it were compounded of self-sufficiency, leisureliness, and freedom from work. The fact is, however, that for most people most of the time happiness is more likely to be made up of inter-dependence, time well spent and rewarding activity. The problem of leisure as we know it had not arisen in the scholastic period; but if it had, the scholastic mind might have offered a simple solution. 'Let them contemplate.' It brings to mind the legendary (and unhistorical) solution of the problem of hunger offered by Marie Antoinette: 'Let them eat cake.'

It was too exclusive for Aquinas to say that 'it is contemplative happiness to which the whole of political life seems directed', and that 'contemplative activity of the intellect clearly provides for man the attributes customarily assigned to happiness'. The logic that led to such a conclusion had one great fault. It assumed that there was nothing else besides the contemplative life which could be an end in itself; that there was nothing else to which people could apply themselves 'for its own sake' besides contemplation. He decided that everything else belonged to the active life, and that was defined as the realm of moral virtues, which are directed to an end beyond themselves. You are moral, not just for the sake of being moral, but in order to enhance the quality of human life or to offer loving obedience to God. The exercise of the moral virtues does not contain its own 'rest', but through them you come to repose in something else – in the leisureliness which may be filled with contemplation. That was the justification of his division of human life in the way he did. But today, with the development of leisure, we can see that the active life has other departments in which the moral virtues are not in question; there are other things which are 'ends in themselves'. Every ideal leisure activity has no other purpose than its own accomplishment, be it hang-gliding or playing the clarinet or reading a novel. Leisure stretches far beyond the confines of inactivity. Not only does it aspire to equal status alongside the active life and the contemplative life. It grows till even contemplation is in danger of being swallowed up and surviving only as a constituent of leisure itself. We need to criticize the assumptions underlying Aquinas's argument. Yet even if we reject or at least question some of them, there may be elements of truth in them which can throw light on the understanding of leisure. We can try to extract principles of enduring validity and wider relevance from this particular discussion of the contemplative life and reapply them in our present context.

First, the fulfilment of God's intention for man must lie in the use of whatever is best in human nature. That 'best' will vary from one individual to another, at least in proportion. But something in each must be his or her particular best. And though each individual must inevitably spend much time in the exercise of other faculties and the pursuit of other ends, if this 'best' is starved and stunted the individual cannot attain full stature.

Next, there are some human activities which are their own reward, whereas others merely serve other ends – fulfilments or enjoyments extrinsic to themselves. This is a principle which may be none the less true for being very difficult to apply in particular cases. The difficulty often lies in drawing limits around what we choose to treat as the units of activity. Is the arduous training for a race part of the race itself? Is the tedious rehearsal of a play part of the public performance? The sensible answer seems to be that any preparation which is essential to the intended activity should be regarded as part and parcel of it. In work, the job often has no natural connection with the pay which is arbitrarily attached to it. The same wage might be earned in dozens of other ways. In leisure activities the race or the play could be achieved no other way than by training or rehearsal. Training and race, and rehearsal and play, are essentially connected.

Even if there remains room for disagreement about this, it is clear that some types of activity are in no sense their own reward, most obviously in the realm of work as opposed to leisure. There are some kinds of work which no one would do for its own sake. A great deal of the repetitive work common in modern industrial society is done only for the sake of the wage which is its obvious, and perhaps its only, reward. The distinction between the two types of relationship, between an action and its reward, is not always clear. But the principle, that there are some human activities which are their own reward, can still be affirmed. Aquinas says that this is true of contemplation alone. We can claim to extend the category to include other activities, and put them together under the heading of 'leisure'.

That is the very word which he uses to make his sixth point. Contemplation is superior to action, he says, because it consists in leisure (*vacatio*) and rest.[17] The argument does not, of course, mean that contemplation is a 'leisure-time occupation', but that it is not restless, not concerned to achieve something beyond itself. It 'rests' within its own boundaries. Its 'vacancy' consists in its freedom from ulterior objectives. This is the same as saying that contemplation is its own reward; but the point is set out as a separate argument partly because it relies on the quotation of a particular text from the Vulgate: *vacate et videte quoniam ego sum Deus* – be at leisure and see that I am God.[18] There is little enough in the Christian Bible which refers to the contemplative life. This text was important, therefore, as providing what was taken to be explicit justification for the practice of contemplation, a justification less easily extracted from the Hebrew or Greek than the Latin, which imports in translation (probably for alliterative reasons – *vacate et videte*) the idea of the 'vision of God', where the Hebrew and Greek speak of 'knowing' God.

The fourth point in Aquinas's list, that contemplation is superior to action because it is more self-sufficient and less dependent on circumstances, is a further variant on the same general argument. The underlying assumption is that happiness can only be secure if it is liberated from dependence on anything outside the happy individual. It is an assumption which goes back at least as far as the Stoics, with their assertion that the wise man is happy 'even on the rack'. It would be more convincing if it were not true that the practice of contemplation in complex societies and uncongenial climates has usually been made possible only by some kind of social structure which emancipates an élite from the necessity of earning their own bread by the sweat of their brows. Contemplation, like wisdom, comes (as Ben Sirach says) by opportunity of leisure. 'How can he become wise who handles the plow?'[19] Equally, we may ask, how can anyone contemplate, except for the ploughman's work on which we all depend? It is only a narrow view of the case that the contemplative is self-sufficient.

There is some appeal in the argument that activities requiring very complex organization are inherently insecure, and to that extent less desirable. But it obviously appeals in varying degrees to different psychological types. Some people are drawn to activities and experiences precisely because they are complex or risky or fragile. Human beings whose nature and constitution make them so vulnerable and whose temporal existence hurries them from one phase of life to another may well argue that the perfection of humanity is as likely to be achieved through glad acceptance of their own transience as through the attempt to achieve what their creatureliness seems to deny them – stability, security, timelessness. Aquinas, who has denied that human beings can ever rest in themselves as God did on the seventh day of creation, wants to find the next best thing in emancipation from all except God. But no incarnate creature can ever renounce its physical dependence upon the environment which sustains its life. Dependence on God is in fact mediated through the universe of God's creation. Once we have recognized that, there does not seem much point in trying to reduce the number of environmental factors which we choose to utilize, nor much cogency in the argument that there is some principle at stake in choosing the fewest possible, once questions about 'sustainable development' have been answered. The appeal of the argument is psychological, rather than logical; which is to say that it evokes assent only from people with a particular cast of mind.

Dare we then say, as the argument seems to be leading us to say, that these areas of life, though omitted from Aquinas's scheme, are, like contemplation, superior to the active life (the life of morality which embraces all work, all politics, all social concern, all charity) because they use the best in man, they can be more continuously practised, they are more delightful, they are more self-sufficient, they are loved for their own sake, and so on? The argument sounds much more plausible than one might have expected. Many people seem to act on it, even though they might hesitate to avow it as their conviction. But we have already claimed our freedom from the dialectical method. Why should we fall back into the trap, and assume that one form of life is somehow 'superior' to another, when all are parts of the complex fabric of human life? We need not despise one thing merely to enhance the merits of another. Nor is it quite true that we can make clear distinctions between different kinds of activity. The very same activity which is leisure for one person is often work for another. In sport professionalization and commercialization blur distinctions. And what if someone is paid to contemplate? Certainly we can no longer treat as unimportant the things which Aquinas tacitly relegated to the level of triviality because they belonged neither to the active nor the contemplative life. As we watch the expansion of those areas of human life which are devoted neither to the worship of God nor to the service of others we need to consider what it means to be human in a fresh way.

There is one other hint which we may take from Aquinas in searching for a doctrinal approach to the question of leisure. He refers with approval to the assertion of Pope Gregory the Great that the contemplative life offers 'a foretaste of the coming rest'.[20] That 'coming rest' is the rest of paradise, and if there is a likeness between the contemplative life and the life of leisure, then leisure too should offer at its best a foretaste of heaven. Perhaps we can gain some insights into leisure by reasoning back to it from what we believe about the life of heaven. The Johannine teaching that eternal life is a present reality means that heaven is with us now. In that case, eschatology may begin to be realized in leisure.

The problem, of course, is that Christian teaching about heaven is hardly simple or coherent. The conflict of ideas is well represented by Hans Küng.[21] He quotes Augustine:[22] 'There we shall be at leisure (*vacabimus*) and we shall see, we shall see and we shall love, we shall love and we shall praise'. Then he brushes these ideas aside with a rhetorical flourish:

> Does not the narrow outlook of the Neoplatonic become apparent here, individualizing, interiorizing and intellectualizing everything...? What happens to human communication, language, fellowship, love? What about nature, the earth, the cosmos?

Singing alleluias on the clouds is (in that ultimate modern condemnation) boring. We need richer metaphors, while recognizing that they are no more than metaphors. Marriage feast, living water, the new Jerusalem – such are the metaphors of God's kingdom, standing for community, love, clarity, fulness, beauty and harmony.

Küng is here taking sides in a conflict of ideas about heaven which has a long history. The one thing Christian teachers have always felt it was safe to say about heaven was that it was where worship preoccupied the redeemed. It certainly did not seem boring to Richard Baxter.

> A heaven of the knowledge of God and his Christ, and a delightful resting in that mutual love and everlasting fruition of our God, a perpetual singing of his high praises – this is a heaven for a saint, a spiritual rest, suiting a spiritual nature. Then, dear friends, we shall live in our element. Now we are like a fish in a small vessel that contains only as much water as will keep him alive; but what is that compared with the full ocean?[23]

Nature, the earth, the cosmos, all fade before the knowledge of God and his praise. Julian of Norwich, three centuries before Baxter, saw the littleness of all that is made, and that it was sustained from falling suddenly into nothingness only by the love of God. It followed that

> they that are preoccupied wilfully with earthly business and ever more seek after worldly weal are not His in heart and in soul here: they love and seek their rest in this thing that is so little, wherein is no rest, and

know not God who is All-Mighty, All-Wise and All-Good. For He is very rest.[24]

The world of sense must not be a barrier between us and God. But others wanted to stake a claim for pure enjoyment in the life of heaven. It was a repeated theme of Thomas Traherne. Even in heaven, he declared, we shall be 'ravished with sensible pleasures' springing from higher delights.[25] We can hardly begin by assuming that heaven means something less intricate and fascinating than the astonishing cosmos in which we already live. There are these two ways of speaking about heaven. It is where everything falls away except the vision of God. It is also the consummation of earthly experience within the redeemed community, the heavenly city. It is this second opinion which has the greater relevance in any comparison between leisure and heaven.

In reading the varied and often contradictory ideas about heaven which Christian writers have expressed we can see how easy it has been for them to find good reasons for commending what each of them happens to find interesting or congenial. Sometimes we can detect an apologetic purpose. A curious example is that of Karl Barth.[26] He wanted to justify to himself and his readers his extreme admiration for the music of Mozart, which he played to himself every day. But, as John Updike comments, a serious theologian can be somewhat embarrassed by leisure, even his own. Barth imagines people shaking their heads that he, an evangelical Christian, can proclaim the worth of Mozart the Catholic Freemason. But he does not hesitate to say that, although he is not sure whether the angels play only Bach in praising God (would that have bored Küng?), he is confident that '*en famille*' they play Mozart, and that God is delighted to listen to them. (In passing, we may note the problem that music is the form of art most dependent upon time, and heaven is the place of the timeless.) Being Barth, he cannot leave his opinion undefended but has to devise an argument that Mozart has a place in theology, especially in the doctrine of creation, because he knew something about creation in its total goodness which was hidden from the Fathers, the Reformers, the orthodox and the liberals, the exponents of natural theology, the existentialists, and even the musicians (but not, of course, from Barth himself). This secret is the distinction between nothingness (*das Nichtige*), which is opposition to God's will, and the dark, negative, shadowed side of God's creation.

This is not the place to discuss that distinction or the question whether music which expresses it is likely to be part of the experience of eternal life. The example of Barth's claim about Mozart is used here only to illustrate the way in which believers, and even theologians, tend to argue from their own preferences to the description of heaven; that is to say, from leisure to eternal life and not *vice versa*. We expect this to be the case where the idea of heaven is not taken seriously. There is a great range of jokes about 'the next life'. An elaborate example is to be found in Julian Barnes's *A History of the World in 10½ Chapters*, in which the final chapter consists of a 'dream' of another life in which all possible desires can be fulfilled. What Barnes presents is a life of unrestricted food, sport and sex, which is ultimately unfulfilling. It is no surprise that those who pass on to such a life eventually opt to die again. It can be taken as a satire on the kind of wish-fulfilment promised by much commercial entertainment.

The quest for teaching about leisure in doctrine about heaven does not add significantly to what has been said previously in other contexts – about the sabbath or about the contemplative life. Indeed some of the theological discussion about heaven seems all too much like the sort of notion expressed in saying that heaven would not be heaven without one's pets. We want what we like. And yet the comparison is worth bearing in mind; for there may be qualities of life expressed in some kinds of leisure which we find it more difficult to project conceptually into the nearer presence of God than others. We may be grateful to Julian Barnes for his satire more than to theologians who give a religious slant to their dislikes or their hopes and preferences.

The polarization of the Christian life between two alternatives (the active and the contemplative) with the mere possibility of toggling between them (to use a handy metaphor from the digital age) owed much to the story of Mary and Martha in their village house which is found only in St Luke's Gospel (10.38–42). The long history of its interpretation has been set out with exemplary care by Giles Constable.[27] He has shown the great variations in the way the story was used. For those who debated the comparative values of the active and the contemplative forms of life its most obvious application seemed to favour withdrawal from busy activity into sitting at the Lord's feet and hearing his word. But the contrast between the two sisters raised the question whether the two different ways could form parts of a single life or were appropriate separately to two different kinds of Christian within the church.

The interpretation of Mary and Martha as two types of life which were combined and interactive in individuals in this world and fully separated only in the next was still found in the tenth and eleventh centuries, but it was paralleled and to some extent challenged by a tendency to distinguish the two lives, and even to regard them as mutually exclusive, in this life and to identify each with a different category of people.[28] In the 'central Middle Ages' Mary was increasingly seen as representing the life of the monks and hermits and Martha the life of the clergy and laity. But interpretation was complicated by the identification of Mary with Mary Magdalene, who could be seen as the penitent sinner sitting at the Lord's feet and being prepared for the actively charitable life which was already embodied in her sister Martha. So the meaning of the story could be turned upside down, if you wanted to play down the role of contemplation and urge the primacy of the charitable life. Protestant theology, on the other hand, in its attack on 'works', could be led to tip the balance back again and exalt the figure of Mary which had been used by others as the very icon of the monastic life .

Constable sums up his survey of these developments with a charitable verdict on its confusions:

The very variety and ambiguity of these interpretations is evidence for the richness of the text and the ingenuity of its interpreters. To argue that there is one true and correct meaning is to dishonour their efforts and their intelligence. Mary and Martha meant different things to different people, and sometimes to the same person, but the variety of interpretations shows the power of men and women to find in the Bible a message that is true for themselves, and reflects the changing values of Christian thinkers and writers over the centuries.[29]

That looks unhappily like a licence to turn the text to our own purposes. But at least the survey points to some considerations which need to be borne in mind in discussing leisure in the modern world. If there are two kinds of life, the active and the contemplative, they can be seen either as parts of one individual's experience or as characteristics of the whole church embodied in its different members. If there is any comparison to be drawn between the contemplative life and the experience of leisure, the first of these alternatives leads to the traditional teaching that leisure is a short-term expedient to prepare for the strenuous demands of practical life. The second raises the question whether there is an inherent value in leisure as a way of life for some members of the church even when there is no prospect of their returning to the business of active charity.

The division of human life assumed for the purpose of argument in the *Summa* was a simple division into the active and the contemplative life. Thomas must certainly have been aware that there were some human pastimes which did not fit into this scheme, but they did not seem important. We might represent his view of life as having three tiers or storeys. At the top there was the contemplative life; below it was the active life; and at the bottom there was the level of 'things indifferent', neither good nor bad in themselves. Our present situation suggests an alternative division of life into two compartments: the realm of moral virtues (containing work, politics, social responsibility, and so on) and the realm beyond morality (containing contemplation, creativity, play, and so on). The second is the realm of leisure. Of course this schematic representation is inadequate, as all such tidy schemes are likely to be, and even possibly misleading. But it makes an important point; or at least raises an important question. Is it the case that there is a whole area of human life in which the writ of morality does not run, at the very least in the sense that there are no moral criteria governing choice between doing a thing and not doing it? Is the question 'Anyone for tennis?' a moral question?

We may even find some help from Aquinas here. He says of the contemplative life, that the moral virtues do not belong to it essentially, because the end of the contemplative life is the consideration of truth. But they belong to it 'as a predisposition, because the moral virtues curb the impetuosity of the passions and quell the disturbance of outward occupations'. In other words, the contemplative life is 'beyond morality', but the exercise of the moral virtues is a necessary preparation for it. Perhaps that is true, not only of the exercise of contemplation, but also of a much larger area of human life than just contemplation, or playing tennis. There may be whole areas of science and learning, arts and crafts, sports and pastimes, to which the moral virtues are relevant only as a predisposition. If we had to justify them on the lines of Aquinas's argument, we might say that their 'end' is the consideration of truth or beauty, or perhaps just the 'celebration' of life itself. If so, we should be in danger of the same apparent self-contradiction as Thomas himself, who has argued that contemplation is 'for its own sake' and now seems to say that it is for the sake of something else. The contradiction, however, is more apparent than real. He might just as well have said that contemplation *is* the consideration of truth. And we might say that science and learning *are* other ways of considering truth, the arts and crafts *are* ways of considering beauty, sports and pastimes *are* the celebration of life's fecundity.

But the question posed above requires further exploration. Is it the case that there is a whole area of human life in which the writ of morality does not run?

## NOTES

1.   S.Parker, *The Future of Work and Leisure* (London 1972), 37.
2.   Hebrews 10.1.
3.   See, for example, the tortuous argument in Karl Barth, *Church Dogmatics* III (Edinburgh 1961), 52.
4.   See R.T. Beckwith and Wilfrid Stott, *This is the Day: The Biblical Doctrine of the Christian Sunday* (London 1978), 66. Hebrews 4.9–10.
5.   Jeremy Taylor, *Ductor Dubitantium or The Rule of Conscience* (2nd edn London 1671), 273.
6.   Richard Baxter proposed one day a month or one day a fortnight for sports. *The Divine Appointment of the Lord's Day Proved*, quoted in W.B. Whitaker, *Sunday in Tudor and StuartTimes* (London 1938), 183.
7.   Augustine of Hippo, *The City of God*, trans. Marcus Dods (Edinburgh 1872), bk 19, ch. 19.
8.   Thomas Aquinas, *Summa Theologiae*, ed. and trans. Thomas Gilby (London 1964–81) I.73.
9.   Ibid. II.i.100.
10.  Ibid. II.i.100 3 ad 2.
11.  Ibid. II.i.100.5 ad 2.
12.  Taylor, *Ductor Dubitantium*, 273.
13.  Willy Rordorf, *Sunday: The History of the Day of Rest and Worship in he Earliest Centuries of the Christian Church* (London 1968), 1.
14.  *Summa Theologiae*, II.ii.182.1; on Aristotle's *Nicomachean Ethics*, bk X, chs 7–8; Luke 10.42.
15.  Nicholas Berdyaev, *Solitude and Society* (London 1938), 112.
16.  Quotations from Thomas Aquinas, *Commentary on the Nicomachean Ethics*, trs. C.I. Lotzinger OP (Chicago 1964), 912.
17.  *Consistit in quadam vacatione et quiete.*
18.  Ps. 45.11 (Vulgate) = 46.10 AV.
19.  Sirach, 38.25.
20.  *Summa Theologiae*, II.ii.182.2.
21.  Hans Küng, *Eternal Life?* trs. Edward Quinn (London 1982), ch. 8: 'Heaven on Earth', 225ff.
22.  Augustine, *City of God*, bk 27, 30.
23.  Richard Baxter, *The Saints' Everlasting Rest*, ed. C. Pipe (London 1994 [1650]), 151.
24.  *A Shewing of God's Love*, ed. Sister Anna Maria Reynolds, CP (London 1958), 11.
25.  Thomas Traherne, *Christian Ethics*, ed. C.L. Marks and G.R. Guffey (Ithaca NY 1968 [1675]), xliv–xlv, 123.
26.  See *Wolfgang Amadeus Mozart*, trs.C.K. Pott (Grand Rapids, Mich. 1986) with foreword by John Updike; and *How I Changed my Mind* (Edinburgh 1966), 10, 71–2.
27.  Giles Constable, *Three Studies in Mediaeval Religious and Social Thought* (Cambridge 1995): 'The Interpretation of Mary and Martha'.
28.  Ibid. 31.
29.  Ibid. 141.

# 2

# Beyond Morality?

*Does leisure belong to an area of human life which is beyond morality? The idea presents difficulties, because of the strongly moralistic tradition of Western Christianity, and its use by Nietzsche and others who rejected that tradition. Formal games and athletics are examples of non-moral activities, but they are moved into the arena of morality through professionalization and commercialism. Writers such as Josef Pieper show the influence of Aristotle which also affected the monastic ideal of the contemplative life expressed in the works of Thomas Aquinas. This is beyond morality; but it leaves no place for other possibilities in leisure, such as creativity, self-realization and even self-love.*

Thomas Aquinas's broad division of human life into two parts, the active and the contemplative, is inadequate as a basis for forming a critique of leisure in modern industrial society. It was inevitably conditioned by the disciplined structure of the monastic life and too largely influenced by a dialectical method which depended on clear-cut contrasts. An alternative analysis might be to draw a distinction between the realm of moral virtues and a realm 'beyond morality' which would include various activities regarded as 'ends in themselves'. Creativity and play might stand alongside contemplation under the general heading of leisure. For the Christian theologian, however, the very idea of a realm 'beyond morality' presents difficulties. These include the dominance of morals in the prophetic tradition of Hebrew and Christian teaching and the use of similar words in anti-Christian polemic.

The words 'beyond morality' bring to mind the title of one of Nietzsche's books, *Beyond Good and Evil*. The philosophy of self-fulfilment expressed in his writings is one of restless striving, not of anything we recognize as leisure. Nietzsche declares that the morality of the Jewish Old Testament, the book of divine justice, to which Christianity has 'glued' the New Testament, is in ruins. So the emancipated human being has the freedom which lies 'beyond morality'. But even here we cannot escape the ambiguity of the idea. Nietzsche also says that 'what is done out of love always occurs beyond good and evil'.[1] It is a strange echo of the teaching of Paul, learnt of Jesus, that the law is fulfilled in love.[2] How Nietzsche interpreted his freedom to act when he had shaken off the shackles of morality is not the point to consider here, but the meaning of that 'beyond good and evil'. For Nietzsche it meant freedom to be oneself without reference to any external standards. It was like moving into a new, self-created universe. His use of 'beyond good and evil' is not directly relevant to the discussion of leisure as one of three areas of human experience – work, social duty  and leisure – because for Nietzsche the realm beyond good and evil is not a discrete element in a life which admits moral imperatives elsewhere, but a comprehensive description of the complete life of the liberated man.

His attack itself bears witness to the overwhelming importance of morality in post-Reformation Christianity in Europe. This had, at an earlier stage, provoked the response of Schleiermacher (1768–1860) on different lines. He postulated a realm of feeling, which was distinct from, if not 'beyond', morality. 'Piety and morality form each a series by itself and are two different functions of one and the same life.'[3] Morality had its own methods, which did not need the props of religion, though religious feelings should accompany the active life, like a sacred music. He offers something like a three-fold division of human life – piety, morality, and a third area which includes both science and the arts – different from the notional division assumed in the present study (work, social duty and leisure). Leisure did not feature in it as a distinct area of contemporary life, though he looked forward to a time when 'the physical world and the governable part of the mental world may be changed into a fairy-palace ... then every life will be practical and contemplative at once ... and every man will have rest and leisure to reflect on the world in himself.'[4] There is no clear separation of his three divisions, since piety exists at such a profound level of human experience that it cannot be separated from any human activity. No area of life is beyond piety. But for Schleiermacher there are large areas of human life which are beyond morality. In his scheme morality does not underlie either piety (religious feeling) or the fulfilling activities of arts and sciences.

The tenor of Schleiermacher's argument was to restrict severely the role of theology. He was saying, in effect, to the cultured despisers of religion that theological statements might be true or false, but they must not be allowed to negate the reality of religion, which was to be found at a level of experience deeper than rational argument. If we are seeking a theological approach to leisure, we cannot begin here. If leisure is to be equated with a realm beyond morality, there is too much competition, in Schleiermacher's scheme, to occupy that realm; most of human life is found in it. By drawing close boundaries round morality, he seemed to represent the majority of human experience as lying outside its dominance. Perhaps it did not seem as obvious to him as it does now that much of the activity in both arts and sciences is caught up in moral issues. They are not located in a fairy-palace.

In another tradition, which may perhaps be traced back to Kant, the strong emphasis on morality as an all-encompassing characteristic of human life continued to influence Christian thought. When the critical analysis of the Old Testament developed in the nineteenth century it led to the view of the Old Testament as bearing witness to the triumph of moral faith over amoral ritualism, of Yahwism over the cult of heathen deities. This supposed evolutionary pattern was even used to determine the relative dating of different elements in the Old Testament. There followed a reaction when further study broke down the supposed alienation of the prophets from the cultic sanctuaries. 'No fundamental declarations of anti-cultic principles are to be found in the prophets, no matter how diligently scholars persist in their attempts to find them.'[5] The excesses of an evolutionary interpretation, however, should not obscure the fact that the prophetic tradition represented a moral judgement on every aspect of Israelite life. The messages of the prophets set morality above ritual, and the condemnation of ritual enveloped the self-indulgent leisure associated with times of festival.[6] If sacred ritual came under moral judgement, there could be no other aspect of corporate life which could claim to be beyond morality. The repeated destruction of the Temple and the consequent exile and diaspora (both in the sixth century BC and in the first century AD) ensured that ritual ceased to occupy the central place in Judaism and helped to create a form of religion in which legalism was triumphant. When that form of religion faded away in Gentile Christianty, the moral strictures of the prophets were regarded as the treasured inheritance of Christianity from Judaism. The justification of leisure, as beyond morality, would have to be argued in the face of the prophetic inheritance.

If leisure could ever be seen as a realm beyond morality, there had to be a prior recognition that human experience can rightly be divided into areas which are at least relatively autonomous. In the areas of life we call political and social, moral considerations are rightly supreme, but they do not have the same force elsewhere. Perhaps, indeed, 'recognition' is the wrong word, since it implies a truth which has only to be seen to be accepted. That is not the case. Totalitarian regimes of all kinds, whether political or religious, inevitably take a strongly moralistic attitude to every department of life, however much their particular moralities may differ. Nothing escapes the net of censorship. Science, art, literature, drama, and even sport and recreation, become matters of right and wrong in the eyes of the authorities.[7] Ultimately the secret thoughts of the heart, even the concerns of the contemplative life itself, come under moral judgement. It cannot be otherwise, because morality implies the subordination of actions to an end beyond themselves which is seen as the supreme good, and a totalitarian regime is one in which everything without exception is subordinated to a single end, the supreme good as defined by the wielders of authority. The specific type of morality will naturally differ according to the particular definition of that supreme good. It may be embodied in the will of an individual, the destiny of a social class, the mystique of a nation, an economic theory, or a political ideology.

Totalitarianism is not, however, confined to secular life. The mediaeval church, like all such authoritarian regimes, asserted its authority over every area of life and applied moral criteria everywhere, except in the contemplative life. Western Christians, inheriting this tradition, find it hard to acknowledge as possessing inherent value those areas of human experience which have nothing to do with morality. They cannot be wholly ignored, but they are almost inevitably treated as trivial. Recreation which, as re-creation, ought to mean the divine activity of 'making all things new', appears to be just a doodle in the margins of life. The present line of argument is that, as contemplation is beyond morality, being an end in itself, so there may be all kinds of other human activities which qualify in the same way to be regarded as beyond morality. That does not mean that they are lacking in value, but that their value does not consist in leading to some end beyond themselves.

The Reformation has been blamed by its critics for a reversal of values which elevated the life of action above the life of contemplation, and utility above virtue. Work, it has been said, was exalted only because it was not repose. 'Perhaps it is a dislike of leisure which we find at the root of this love of work, a hatred of what is pleasant in the sudden passionate quest for the useful'.[8] There is some truth in this criticism, as well as some error. It is more pertinent to argue that the absence of contemplation accompanying the rejection of monasticism created a void which could most easily be filled by the expansion of an ideal of work.[9] The Puritans did not dislike pleasure in itself, though they were inclined to ask what purpose it could serve.[10] Perhaps we see the transition to utilitarian ethics in Jeremy Taylor, who does not mind coupling together profit and pleasure as possible 'ends' of action, though he says that both are 'under a law'.[11] It is just a question of terminology whether pleasure is said to be the 'end' of an action or to make an action an 'end in itself'.

Even when leisure is being assessed outside the religious context, however, its moral value keeps coming back into focus. The dominance of utilitarian ideas in the eighteenth century meant that leisure, like everything else, had to justify itself as useful, and this habit continued in writers who would reject the name of utilitarian. In his reminiscences of Ruskin, Arthur Severn speaks of his disagreements with 'the Professor' (as he called Ruskin) about recreations.

> Some of our sharpest bouts were about recreation, games, music, rowing, oars, etc. I tried to explain to him that he was quite wrong in thinking all recreation should if possible be useful, that it was too exalted an ideal for people who worked hard, the pleasure of a game of lawn tennis or rackets or backing up a football match was refreshing to the mind.[12]

Matthew Arnold also wanted to claim that culture was socially useful and motivated by the moral and social passion for 'doing good'. But his arguments are hardly self-consistent, for in *Culture and Anarchy* he wanted to commend Hellenism as against Hebraism in the Western inheritance, declaring that Hebraism was 'deaf to the music of freedom and spontaneity, the disinterested love of truth'.[13] Such disinterested love could not be justified by its social utility.

In the Marxist tradition leisure did not really achieve independent status and was always in danger of being assimilated to the notion that human fulfilment will come from work itself when it is freed from the shackles of capitalist organization. In *The German Ideology* Karl Marx imagined a time in the development of society when the distinction between work and leisure would fade away.

> In communist society ... it is possible for me to do one thing today and another tomorrow, to hunt in the morning, fish in the afternoon, rear cattle in the evening, criticize after dinner, in accordance with my inclination, without ever becoming hunter, fisherman, shepherd or critic.[14]

But this kind of vision was bound to lose its importance in view of the struggle to overturn the existing order of society. The notion of work and leisure being indistinguishable survived in the Marxist tradition in William Morris's *News from Nowhere* in which Ellen reproaches the time-traveller for falling into mere dreamy musing, 'no doubt because you are not yet used to our life of repose amidst of energy; of work which is pleasure and pleasure which is work'.[15]

Marx's son-in-law Paul Lafargue actually wrote an extended pamphlet with the title 'The Right to Be Lazy' (*Le Droit à la Paresse*); but it was primarily an attack on capitalist society, and its title was chosen deliberately to shock. As Leslie Derfler has written:

> Rather than a denial of work or an affirmation of leisure as an end in itself, 'The Right to Be Lazy' was a celebration of life, or rather of what life could be: not merely recuperation from labour, but the essence of life itself. Far from advocating a hedonistic philosophy, it condemned only excessive and abusive labour.[16]

It was not easy, perhaps not appropriate, for revolutionary writers to distract attention from the need to change the nature of work by exploring the idea of leisure. In something of the same way Walter Rauschenbusch, the exponent of American social Christianity, in his *Christianity and the Social Crisis* (1913), spares little thought for the possibilities of leisure, and can only say that if 'we had more leisure for the higher pursuits of the mind and the soul, then there might be a chance to live such a life of gentleness and brotherly kindness and tranquillity of heart as Jesus desired for men'. When he wrote *Prayers of the Social Awakening* (1909), he included a prayer 'for the idle' which was mainly in praise of work:

> And to our whole nation do thou grant wisdom to create a world in which none shall be forced to idle in want, and none shall be able to idle in luxury, but in which all shall know the health of wholesome work and the sweetness of well-earned rest.[17]

In sympathy with Marxism the scientist and philosopher J.D. Bernal declared that the mental balance of humanity, to avoid 'distortion', must find an 'activated' leisure. Some leisure time must 'become purposeful and constitute what might be called a second economy beyond the basic economy producing goods and services on a large scale'.[18] Even in a broadly sociological context leisure can be presented as serving society. Stanley Parker proposes three ways: (1) it helps people to learn how to play their part in society; (2) it helps them to achieve societal or collective aims; (3) it helps society to keep together.[19] As soon as leisure is seen as having this kind of function, it ceases to be just an end in itself. In giving it a purpose we subject it to moral criteria, asking how well it does what it is intended to do. This utilitarian interpretation of leisure removes it from a realm beyond morality. It is no longer an end in itself.

There are, however, some twentieth-century writers who offer clues to a theological approach which frees leisure from the need to be justified in these terms, most notably Josef Pieper. But before we proceed to assess this approach, it will be useful to mention a rather simple sense in which leisure might be described as 'beyond morality'. Aquinas has stated that the moral virtues belong to the contemplative life only as a predisposition. As we have seen, he quotes Gregory to the effect that the active life trains men for the contemplative life by teaching them whether they have quelled their passions. This is one way in which leisure may be `beyond morality` – that is to say, it can only be enjoyed properly after the maturing of the personality. The practical working life of human beings constantly poses problems of morality which demand resolution. In the home and the school, at work or in political life, the battle between right and wrong, or at least between better and worse, goes on. In the process people learn, with greater or poorer success, to master their disruptive passions. The hope is that such expertise can be carried into less stressful areas of life. This amounts to a complete reversal of the common attitude which underlies much Christian writing about leisure. It has been common to justify short bursts of leisure because they prepare people for the real business of life, which is work. If we try to extend to leisure Aquinas's argument about contemplation, it would amount to a claim that the active life prepares people for leisure, not simply by giving them the resources leisure requires, but by providing a kind of training course in self-management without which they could not even enjoy leisure activities. For Gregory or Aquinas 'beyond' only meant 'after'. There could be a movement in a lifetime which took the Christian into the contemplative life, carrying a mind trained to self-discipline by the experience of moral conflicts. That kind of description seems unfortunately to speak of a hang-over of moralism, of limits written into the subconscious mind and still constricting freedom. But the experience in some enjoyable moments of leisure, on the contrary, is to feel the complete irrelevance of moral rules. They are not even there to be broken. It is this inward experience of creative freedom which marks leisure at its best.

The phrase 'beyond morality' can have a meaning quite different from the idea of preparatory training. It can indicate a whole area of human experience which is free from moral calculations. But that is a matter of internal attitude, not of outward activity. We may bear in mind a remark of Jeremy Taylor: 'Actions, if they be considered in their physical or natural capacity, are all negatively indifferent, that is, neither good nor bad'.[20] It follows that different intentions put the same action beyond morality or keep it within the moral realm, and in so doing mark it off as play or work or social duty. To make the discussion clearer, we need to look at particular examples, and we can begin with the example of athletics, with its long and revered tradition in Western civilization. Children's races, spontaneous and unorganized ('race you to that lamp-post!') are at one end of a continuum. They are beyond doubt 'play'. They are ends in themselves. They have little or no reference to the rest of life. Athletics for adults organized within a club are also ends in themselves, and again have little or no connection with any other area of life, except perhaps the social life of the club itself, where the constant loser on the track may have a leading role. More obviously extraneous considerations begin to creep in, at first in an innocuous way, when competitions are organized between different groups – schools, 'houses' or clubs – because of the group emotions and spurious antagonisms which they inevitably arouse. These find a curious sort of acceptance from Veblen who manages to descry in them the instinct of 'workmanship', which is 'an instinct more fundamental, of more ancient prescription than the propensity to predatory emulation'.[21] Perhaps a positivist like Veblen cannot allow himself a moral judgement on what is 'predatory'. But the term itself reveals that the type of action under consideration has moved back into the area of morality.

The situation is further altered by the development of supporting groups of non-participants, usually for fundamentally economic reasons. The supporters invest something – time, emotional energy, their own self-esteem, money – in the group they support. Now the athletes are no longer committed to the chosen activity merely for its own sake. Their efforts serve an ulterior purpose – the gratification of the supporting group, or the maintenance of its financial base, or even, in the case of professional sport, the self-preservation of the (now misnamed) 'player' from loss of status and the promotion of his or her personal security and comfort for the future. At that point the 'game' has become for the participant not play but work. Where the supporting group is a national group, especially if the nation is, as in one way or another they mostly are, the exponent of a distinctive political ideology, the action of the athlete may be interpreted in terms of propaganda. This connection is wholly irrational, yet it has a long history going back to the settlement of disputes by appointed champions. It even has the backing of scripture, if we are prepared to rest any weight on David's words to Goliath: 'the Lord saves not with sword and spear; for the battle is the Lord's and he will give you into our hand'.[22] There is no question here of an action which is an end in itself. The physical triumph of a champion is taken to prove the superiority of the god of a particular group.[23] It is easy to see a parallel in the modern world, in which success in international athletics has been absurdly interpreted as validating a particular political regime, whether Nazi or communist or democratic. Any element of propaganda such as this places an athletic performance firmly in the realm of the active life, and invests it with a moral claim which is lacking in pure play. The loser interprets failure in moral terms which would be inappropriate to children's games.

Now we are also in the misty borderlands of professionalism which turns sport into work. There can be endless argument about the precise point at which that border is crossed. Obviously regular sporting activity which provides a livelihood for the performer is by any definition work for him or her. There is also an element of work in any part-time activity which brings financial or exchangeable reward. Further, we must distinguish the different significance of an event for the agent and for the spectator. What is work for one may be leisure for the other. What serves an ulterior purpose for one may be an end in itself for the other. That is the case with much, perhaps all, professional sport. In pure play, however, the nature of the event for participant and spectator is the same, in the sense that it is equally an end in itself for both; though the experience for each is different in quality, as between psycho-physical exertion in the one case and vicarious participation in the other.

In the common cases where the participant is a professional and the spectator is chiefly interested in betting on the event, it is difficult to say whether the category of experience (work or leisure) is the same for both participant and spectator. They may both enjoy the event to a certain extent for its own sake, but each has a further interest. The professional's further interest – the earning of a living, the support of a family, and so forth – puts the event firmly in the sphere of the active life. In the case of the betting spectator, we probably ought to regard the event as merely a necessary preliminary to the outcome of the bet (like the rehearsal for the play, previously mentioned), and so we should say that event plus bet constitute something which is an end in itself. On the other hand, if the betting agent claims or aims to make a living by betting, then clearly the event is returned to the realm of the active life. He or she may still get a kick out of betting, but that is not relevant. There is no reason why work should not be enjoyable as well as leisure. It may even appear as an end in itself. The author Harriet Martineau said of her authorship: 'I have not done it for amusement or for money, or for fame, or for any reason but because I could not help it. Things were pressing to be said.'[24]

It is inappropriate to apply moral criteria to activities which are properly to be regarded as beyond morality. If they are to be compared or evaluated, some other standard of judgement may be applicable, such as the standard implicit in the description of an activity as 'life-enhancing' (which will be considered below). Conversely, that standard is inadequate by itself in judging activities which, though rightly described as play, fall into the realm of morality by serving an end beyond themselves, such as ideological propaganda or commercial profit. It is as absurd for the moralist to refrain from criticizing the perversion of the Olympic ideal, if it is judged to have been contaminated by the importation of political ideologies or medal-counting puerilities, as it would be to bring the heavy guns of morality to bear on a happy game of marbles or a life-enhancing round on the seaside putting green.

Some kinds of leisure are almost solitary, and seem to require little preparation by moral training of the kind which Aquinas and others considered necessary for the contemplative life. Their essence seems to be a total loss of self-awareness rather than self-control, a complete absorption in the interest of the moment, whether it is bird-watching or tuning a motor-bike. In that kind of situation the 'interior passions' are not in evidence. Perhaps they are only sleeping. Other kinds of leisure activity require the co-operation of other people. Are they beyond morality? There should not be any uneasy sense of moral constraint, but there must be an implicit acceptance of the principles of subordination or mutual support which any such activity requires. It would hardly qualify for the name of leisure if it raised serious problems in personal relationships, for the effort to solve the problems would dominate the whole activity. This is a possible effect of commercializing sport and offering huge rewards for competitive achievement. Even in uncommercial contexts, leisure activities must not be allowed to become like types of work-situation in which the problems are relational rather than technical. If the existence of good relationships can be taken for granted, then the leisure activity is, to that extent, beyond morality. A crisis may throw it back into the sphere of the moral virtues. Then some of the participants may be tempted to withdraw, because it no longer offers 'repose'. It is no longer an end in itself. Of course, exactly the same might be said of contemplation. It, too, can be interrupted and the contemplator thrown back into the realm of the moral virtues by some extraneous crisis.

In one sense games of an organized type are governed by a kind of agreed, though artificial, morality embodied in fixed rules. These rules can be described as beyond morality, for they are not open to question so long as a game is being played. They are simply taken for granted and cannot be called in question, like the imagined pre-history of the characters of a novel. It is as though the rules belong to past history, beyond the reach of change. Since they are not based on any moral or rational principles, there is no way of challenging them by appealing to some higher law acknowledged by all the participants. The only criterion is whether they make a good game or not. If all the players agree that a change would produce a better, or just a different, game, there is nothing to stop the rules being changed, unlike the basic rules of morality. Equally, there is no possibility of coercing someone to go on playing the game if he or she thinks the change is a mistake and decides to do something different. It is absurd to make the rules of a game a battleground – not, of course, that this absurdity does not happen. But that is because the game has become entwined in something else – something that belongs to the realm of the moral life, such as individual self-assertion or large-scale organization or, even worse, commercial profitability. Such things remove the game from the category of 'an end in itself'. It is hardly any longer a form of leisure. The game has been thrust out of the sphere of leisure and into the sphere of serious moral conflict.

What can be said, without controversy, about formal games may be applied to the whole area of leisure. It must not become serious. That is to say, although it has its own kind of seriousness (and nothing spoils a game more badly than someone who will not 'take it seriously'), it must not have the seriousness appropriate to the active life, which serves an end beyond itself. There is an important distinction between seriousness and value. This is where the concept 'life-enhancing' comes into play. There are many activities which are not serious, but are certainly valuable. They do not promote human survival or affect the maintenance of a just social life, or preserve and sustain mankind by ensuring peace. But they promote a sense of fulfilment in individual or group life, they extend awareness of the rich environment in which personality develops, or they provide enjoyment at levels ranging from evanescent fun to deep satisfaction. Yet all this can happen without raising a single moral issue or a single explicitly religious feeling.

Theologians, deprived of their most appropriate interests, are in danger of writing such things off; in more enlightened moments they would concede that the heavenly Jerusalem is likely to witness plenty of such 'leisure activities' and none of their own favourite pastimes of doctrinal debate and moral assessment. For theological speculation must come to an end in the presence of truth itself and the perfected saints will no longer face moral issues. It has been natural for theologians to assume that nothing will remain except worship and contemplation. The reasoning behind such an assumption depended on the apparently timeless, discarnate nature of contemplation itself, rather than an assessment of the full potentialities of human nature and the ways in which those potentialities might be realized beyond time and space. If we concede a far larger role to leisure than the scholastic theologians troubled to imagine, the question arises with a new importance: how can our many, unserious activities in this sublunary existence achieve fulfilment in the life of the age to come? Are there, perhaps, 'games of the spirit' (*jeux d'esprit*)? We must take care not to write off so large a part of human potential.

The examples of athletics and sport in general have been discussed at length only because they present in an obvious way the range of possibilities from pure play to straight professionalism. But it would divert us from our proper theme if we assumed that sport was more central to the question of leisure than any other activities which may be ends in themselves. Those certainly include pure science and disinterested learning, arts and crafts, and all kinds of pastimes, such as collecting and exploration, whatever it may be that is explored or collected, so long as it is just for the fun of the thing. The range of these activities is as large as the range of human potentialities. If they are to be arranged in any kind of hierarchy – and it is an open question whether they should be – a significant factor may be the range of their effects. For not all activities pursued as ends in themselves actually end in themselves. They may be entirely self-justifying, and yet have repercussions on a much wider public than the specific 'play community' and produce lasting effects which were very far from the minds of the original participants.

We can take as an obvious example a piece of music written by Schubert for his friends and performed by a quartet at one of the semi-private Schubertiades in Vienna. In the narrowest sense it was an activity of four people; the 'play community' was the quartet. The performance would have been rewarding enough for them, even if no one else had heard it. But in fact participation has spread out in a series of concentric circles ever widening through space and time, and the effects of the original composition have been far greater than he was capable of imagining, tied down as he inevitably was by his own historic circumstances. The thing which was an end in itself turned out to be the beginning of something greater than itself. Or take another example from music, the so-called Kreutzer sonata of Beethoven. Clearly the composer could not foresee the by-product of his composition which took form in Tolstoy's story with the same title. Nor could Tolstoy foresee that his story would inspire the quartet by Janacek called the Kreutzer. No doubt the same thing could be said even of the football team on the Wembley (or Cardiff) turf. The players may succeed in retaining amid the ballyhoo a sense of the 'end in itself' which is of the essence of all games, but there are bound to be results of the game both for themselves and for a host of others which will only begin when the game itself is over.

In their different ways the quartet and the cup final contribute to something larger which might be called 'culture', and this brings us back to a particular work in the tradition of Aquinas. When Josef Pieper wrote his celebrated essay, *Leisure: the Basis of Culture*, he was surely not thinking of professional football as the kind of leisure activity which would give rise to culture. He used the word 'culture' in what is now an old-fashioned sense which has little in common with its meaning in anthropological or sociological contexts. It was something to be defended by a renewed understanding of tradition, by emphasizing our inheritance from classical antiquity, and by fighting to retain the 'academic' character of our universities. For leisure, in his definition, was marked by 'effortlessness, calm and relaxation, and its superiority to all and every function'.[25] At first sight he seems to be hoping to turn more and more of the world's workers into replicas of the scholar in the study, if not the monk in the cell. Certainly he is indebted to the line of thought in the monastic tradition. He writes with great sympathy for the traditional, clerical appraisal of life embodied in Aquinas's *Summa*.

He is not merely restating an outmoded view of life, and it is only fair to stretch his definition of leisure as much as his words will allow. The notion of effortlessness, for instance, is not equivalent to mere idleness. It is the positive opposite of strain and tension. Pieper sees leisure as 'a form of silence' in which 'the soul's power to "answer" to the reality of the world is left undisturbed'. Again, calm and relaxation, which may sound inert, are related to the idea of 'celebration', which he uses to describe the affirmation of man's oneness with himself and with the world. It is not a passive attitude, but involves a deliberate recognition of the intensity of life. Accepting all these glosses on Pieper's short definition of leisure, we can see that the range of its connotations can be extended a long way, provided they all satisfy the requirement of 'superiority to every function'. And that, surely, is just another way of saying that leisure activities must be ends in themselves, undertaken for their own sake. So although Pieper explicitly compares leisure to the contemplative life,[26] it need not be restricted to mental activity. Provided we reject his apparent identification of 'culture' with a particular classical tradition, we can accept the assertion that leisure is its basis. Only it is the increasing breadth of our understanding of leisure which will determine what we come to recognize as culture, and not a ready-made definition of culture which will determine what we can allow ourselves to approve as leisure. Within a particular society those activities which are undertaken as ends in themselves do together create a complex structure which can be called its culture.

If, then, we extend the description of leisure beyond the notions of effortlessness, calm and relaxation, to cover a range of activities of which the common factor is that they are 'ends in themselves', including those which are vigorously active, we come within sight of some recent interpretations of physical exertion which stress the importance of attitudes of mind in achieving maximum bodily efficiency. There may not be a very large gap between Pieper's assertion that 'leisure is only possible when a man is at one with himself, when he acquiesces in his own being'[27] and the assumption of the tennis coach Tim Gallwey in *The Inner Game of Tennis* that we need to trust our own potential, that we should discover what we actually are instead of trying to become what we are not.[28] The concept of 'self-fulfilment' has emerged again. This fits in with the description of the realm of true leisure as 'beyond morality'. But it is not every aspect of our humanity which is capable of fulfilment in this way. In the realm of the moral virtues our fallen humanity leads to the constant attempt to become what we are not. Apart from grace, we strive to assert that we are free, though we are in bondage to sin; after grace, that striving is used by the Holy Spirit to convert us from what we are to what we may become. Outside the realm of the moral virtues, however, we share the condition of the unfallen creation, and our true good consists precisely in self-fulfilment, according to the general definition stated by Aquinas: 'The proper good of any being is that whereby it is brought to perfection'.[29]

To sum up the argument so far, we have seen that despite the lack of any specific consideration of leisure in the *Summa Theologiae*, it is possible to elicit from it some pointers towards a Christian critique. The basis of that critique lies in the fundamental distinction between those human activities which are undertaken solely, or at least primarily, for the sake of ends which lie beyond themselves, and other activities which are undertaken for their own sake, even though they may incidentally fulfil functions which are not the primary concern or intention of the agents. The first of these categories may be distinguished into work in the narrow sense – what we do to earn a living –

and those occupations of our free time which are aimed at a definite object – voluntary social or political activities, or indeed anti-social activities of a deliberate kind, such as vandalism or hooliganism. None of these can rightly be called leisure, and we can therefore leave them on one side. They are all clearly part of the active life. Activities of the second type – those undertaken for their own sake – are again divisible into two kinds. On the one hand there are activities which are explicable only by reference to a transcendent reality, namely worship and contemplation; and on the other there are innumerable types of activity which do not require such a reference, though from a Christian point of view they may seem best explicable on the assumption that man is a creature with an inherent drive towards self-transcendence. It is these activities which constitute 'leisure'.

It has also been observed that activities which are ends in themselves, whether worshipful or leisurely, are not essentially affected by the rules of morality which rightly govern all other areas of life. We can say either that they are 'beyond good and evil' or else that the kind of morality which governs them is concerned only with complete self-realization – a morality (if such it may be called) which brings human beings as close as possible to the non-human creation. There begins to form in our imagination a vision of humankind in leisure moments restored to harmony with all created things through complete understanding and complete acceptance of its own nature. It is a vision which appeals to those chiefly concerned with the contemplative aspect of theology, of whom Thomas Merton may be taken as a good representative. In his *New Seeds of Contemplation* he writes:

> The forms and individual characters of living and growing things, of inanimate beings, of animals and flowers and all nature, constitute their holiness in the sight of God. Their inscape is their sanctity. …With us it is different. … Our vocation is not simply to be, but to work together with God in the creation of our own life, our own identity, our own destiny.[30]

It is an open question whether that vision is a lode-star or a will-o'-the-wisp, and the use of the word 'work' risks a return to the realm of morality.

But is this interpretation of human life distinctively Christian, or has Aquinas led us up an Aristotelian garden-path? Perhaps we have only recovered the truth (if truth it be) which Aristotle expounded in the *Nicomachean Ethics*. We have already noticed that Aquinas bases eight out of his nine arguments for the superiority of the contemplative life on it. Aristotle's case is clinched by the following argument:

> That perfect happiness is a speculative activity will further appear from the following considerations. The gods in our conception of them enjoy the most complete blessedness and felicity. But what kind of actions can we rightly attribute to them? If we say 'just

actions', how absurd it will be to picture them as making contracts and restoring deposits and all that sort of thing! Shall we say 'brave actions' then? Can you imagine the gods seeking glory by facing dangers and alarms? And what of liberal actions? Whom are they to be liberal to? What an odd idea that the gods actually possess coined money or something like it! Then there are temperate actions. But what could temperate actions mean in their case? What a piece of vulgarity to commend the gods for not having flagitious interests! And if we go through the whole list we shall find that all forms of virtuous activity must be paltry for the gods and unworthy of them. Nevertheless men have always thought of them as at least living beings and, if living, then doing something, for we cannot suppose that they are always asleep, like Endymion. But if from a living being there is taken away action, not to mention creation or production, what is left but contemplation? We must conclude that the activity of God, which is blessed above all others, must take the form of contemplation. And from this it follows that among human activities that which is most akin to God's will bring us the greatest happiness. What also goes to show the truth of this is the fact that the lower animals cannot partake of happiness, for they are utterly incapable of contemplation. The life of the gods is altogether happy, that of man is happy so far as it includes something that resembles the divine activity; but none of the other animals can be properly described as happy, because they are in no way capable of speculation or contemplation.[31]

It could certainly be argued that Aquinas has swallowed this argument whole; or nearly so, for obviously he eliminated its polytheism. With that single correction, the argument is taken over for Christian use.

The result is unsatisfactory on two counts. First, in surveying the whole range of divine action the argument curiously brushes aside creativity. Secondly, in surveying the whole range of human action it makes no mention of any other self-sufficient action besides contemplation. These defects were inherent in the Aristotelian world-view. His gods were modelled on the free-born intellectuals of Hellenic society, who were primarily concerned with self-cultivation. Karl Barth has argued that this inheritance infected Christian thought:

In the monastic ideal of the perfect life there was undoubtedly at work an ancient Greek and Stoic view according to which perfect man belongs to the higher classes and has the leisure to fashion himself physically, intellectually and aesthetically into a harmonious being, whereas the rest, the real working classes, exist only to procure for the aristocrat, who is occupied with himself, therefore with real living, the basis of existence.[32]

Substitute for those carefree gods the God of Christian revelation – creative, incarnate, inspiring – and the most godlike activities are no longer restricted to contemplation. Substitute for those carefree intellectuals the measure of the stature of the fulness of Christ, and it follows that the full-grown person of Christian thought must find blessedness in all that humanity is capable of, all the forms of virtuous activity become far from 'paltry', and the very content of 'servile work', once liberated from contempt, can be raised to new significance. So the Christian may be 'god-like' in ways which Aristotle would have found distasteful. Some may even find themselves able to break down one of the barriers which divide us from the 'other animals' by regaining that self-acceptance which animals have without effort.

The question whether we can call distinctively Christian an interpretation of human life which owes so much to Aristotle depends for its answer on the extent of that indebtedness. Perhaps Aquinas was led astray by too great reverence for 'the Philosopher'. We need to give full weight to the distinctiveness of the Christian understanding of God and his relation to the world to guard against a false Hellenization of theology which will impose the values of a slave-owning society upon us in our estimate of work and leisure. The curious thing is that Greek civilization, which is commonly thought to have nurtured the cult of the body, should have been responsible in the person of Aristotle for handing on to Christian theology, as we see it in Aquinas, the belief that human beings could reach perfect happiness only by belittling their bodily nature. That consideration is not irrelevant to our proper subject, for it is clear that the great majority of activities which go to make up leisure, in its common significance, are bodily activities. We cannot hope to reach a just estimate of leisure while accepting, however unconsciously, a false estimate of our bodily nature.

Before leaving this consideration of what might lie beyond morality, there are two further lines of thought suggested by Aristotle's statement that 'among human activities that which is most akin to God's will bring us the greatest happiness'. They concern creativity and love. It is a limitation in Aristotle's understanding of divinity that his gods did nothing but contemplate. The image of God revealed in the Christian scriptures is of one who creates and loves. Both creativity and love transcend morality. We think of them as marks of the active life, and yet they may be regarded as ends in themselves. They do not have to prove their worth by their effects. To take first the revelation of God as Creator, it is surprising that theological writers have been hesitant to embrace the idea that there is an analogy between God's creativity and human creativity. In an earlier generation Alan Richardson argued that creativity in the Old Testament is a divine, and not a human, attribute, and cited Isaiah as witness to the difference, not similarity, between God and a human workman.[33] More recently Moltmann has also emphasized the fact that the Hebrew word used of God's creativity (in Genesis and Isaiah) is never used to describe a human activity.[34] He has built upon this unsteady etymological basis an argument about the difference between 'play' in a divine and a human sense, with which we are not immediately concerned. Conceding the difference, however, does not mean dismissing all similarity. There are many other writers, in a tradition going back at least to Coleridge, for whom creativity is one of the defining characteristics of being human.[35]

Perhaps it is better to listen to those who are themselves creative than to theological commentators. A significant instance is *The Mind of the Maker* by Dorothy L. Sayers, in which she elaborated a belief she had already indicated in her earlier 'war-time essay' *Begin Here*, with specific reference to leisure. She foresaw an age which would do its work by 'electric power' when people would have as much as twenty hours of leisure a day. What would they do with their leisure?

> More and more people would enter the entertaining profession for sheer despair at finding nothing else to do... And the moment we took up the active end of entertainment we should be forced again into thinking and feeling for ourselves; otherwise our entertainment would be very dull stuff. For the truth is, that man is never truly himself except when he is actually creating something. To be merely passive, merely receptive, is a denial of human nature. 'God', says the author of Genesis, 'created man in His own image'; and of the original of that image he tells us one thing only: 'In the beginning, God created.'[36]

It is true that this is yet another instance of the way in which people want to make leisure in their own image; but at least it vindicates a proper place for creativity in leisure.

At the same time it is obvious that work can be the setting for creativity. There can be moments when work loses, for the worker, any sense of its purpose in earning a living, as in the instance of Harriet Martineau quoted above. Then work is done 'for its own sake', and it is activities of this sort which, in the view of T.S. Eliot, create what he calls culture. 'Culture is the one thing we cannot deliberately aim at. It is the product of a variety of more or less harmonious activities, each pursued for its own sake.'[37] The relation of creativity in work and in leisure is a topic on which there is little agreement, some claiming that creative leisure compensates for frustration at work while others argue that leisure-time creativity is only possible to those who are creative at work. But creativity at work, regarded objectively and not as a subjective experience, cannot be beyond morality, for it must have a purpose beyond itself: to earn a living by communicating something to other people.

Here we can turn to Nicholas Berdyaev. The shift from the mere act of creation to the second stage, of bringing its effect to bear on others, has been described by him as a kind of fall from freedom. 'Creative inspiration is the highest form of freedom.' But 'spirit objectifies itself in its creative products' and this implies a compromise with the normal world, with social environment.[38] Somewhere in this transition is the borderline between leisure and work, the contemplative life and the active life. It would be impossibly restrictive to suggest that creativity in leisure must be solitary and private. If so, we could only accept as fully creative something like a Schubert symphony never performed or published in his own lifetime. The truth being expressed here is that in leisure the creative activity has no regard for its reception by others. It is an end in itself. There is room for some self-deceit here. Those who adopt the slogan of 'art for art's sake' may be sincere, but they may also be unhappy if no one takes any notice of them.

In reinterpreting Aristotle's assertion that the greatest happiness derives from those activities which are most akin to God's, we must also take into account the other great declaration of the Christian revelation, that God is love. This also is beyond morality, because love has no ulterior purpose. Our understanding of love is too easily spoilt by interpreting the love of our neighbour as always meaning to do them good. In work or in social duty – the other aspects of life lying outside leisure – this may often be the case, but a world consisting entirely of competitive do-gooders is not an attractive picture. As Kenneth Cragg has said: 'The cynic might respond: "They are in the world to do good to others: but what do they think the others are in the world for?"'[39] In leisure, the love of our neighbour is the simple, restful acceptance of the other person as God's creation and the object of his love. What then does it mean to love ourselves?

The very idea of self-love makes us hesitate. Indeed the word 'self' has been a term of opprobrium in some evangelical quarters in the past.[40] Self-love sounds more like a sin than something commanded, although it is enshrined in the two great commandments ratified by Jesus (Mark 12.31). Commentators so concentrate attention on other aspects of this passage and its synoptic parallels – the question of Jesus' originality or the proper way to define a neighbour – that they pass over the words about loving ourselves. But some theologians have explored the idea of self-love in ways which have a bearing on leisure or free time. We may take as examples in different traditions Augustine of Hippo and Bishop Joseph Butler. To begin with Butler, because his discussion is more superficial: he published in 1726 a collection of sermons, which included some 'upon human nature, or man considered as a moral agent', and two in particular were on the text from Romans 13.9, 'Thou shalt love thy neighbour as thyself.' He argued that in a sense 'everything proceeds from self-love', that is, for the gratification of an inclination. But he made a firm distinction between different kinds of self-love. His terminology is strange to modern ears, for he approves 'cool or settled selfishness' (which is like the natural instinct of self-preservation of all sensible creatures) as opposed to 'passionate or sensual selfishness', which he characterizes by remarking that 'people may love themselves with the most entire and unbounded affection and yet be extremely miserable'. Both are, in Butler's view, within the province of morality; but in another sense the former is an end in itself, while the latter aims at something external, such as honour or power or status in society. Butler is aware that his text requires him to find a positive value in self-love, but it is a careful, rational kind of attitude which no doubt commended itself to his respectable congregation, though hardly offering more than negative guidance, not to take it too far. 'Even from self-love we should endeavour to get over all inordinate regard to, and consideration of, ourselves.'[41]

It is a relief to turn to something more imaginative in Augustine, whose writings have been estimated to have 150 references to self-love. They have been carefully studied in Oliver O'Donovan's *The Problem of Self-Love in St Augustine*.[42] The ambiguity of the term requires that he too, like Butler, needs to distinguish its different meanings, this time under three heads. There is neutral or natural self-love, evil self-love, and good self-love. In an alternative categorization, John Burnaby used the terms instinctive self-love, love of personal pre-eminence, and the self-love which loses itself in the love of God.[43] If we ask whether any of these is 'beyond morality', the answer must be that evil self-love is certainly under moral judgement and therefore not a constituent of freedom in leisure. Both of the other types of self-love may be, in different ways, outside the realm of morality. Instinctive self-love is before, rather than beyond, morality. Good self-love, like love of the neighbour, is not concerned with morality, since it is loving what you or your neighbour will be by the grace of God. It proceeds from a natural self-love which is a trace of unfallen goodness remaining in fallen humanity, and moves towards 'man's created teleology', the realization of human potential. This, in Augustine's theology, is self-love '*propter Deum*' – for God's sake, the fulfilment of God's will in a human being. It is perhaps in place here to refer to a rabbinic saying, quoted by Martin Buber. Rabbi Zusya, shortly before his death, said: 'In the world to come I shall not be asked, "Why were you not Moses?" I shall be asked "Why were you not Zusya?"'[44]

In considering the place of self-love in free time, it may help to turn the command the other way round and work from the love of our neighbour to love of self. Loving a neighbour is an exercise of imagination and will, not of sentiment. It involves appreciating and fostering the uniqueness of the other. This kind of love is clearly appropriate in many leisure activities, no less than in the active life of work and society. It follows that in leisure we may learn to love ourselves; that is, to appreciate and foster our own uniqueness. However far we may be from understanding what is meant by the mutual love of the trinity of persons in the godhead, we may at least try out the possibility of some distant reflection of that love in the process of human self-realization.

Part of the mystery of our humanity is the fact that each of us is both subject and object, both experiencing and being experienced. We watch ourselves; we criticize ourselves; we help ourselves. For this we must exercise the same kind of will and imagination as we do when we love our neighbour. In leisure we have special opportunities for this. This is true recreation, true re-making. Forty years ago, in a powerful article in *The Furrow*, John Foster argued the case for a new theological estimation of leisure. In spiritual direction he wanted penitents to be told to stop confessing sins that they learnt about in the kindergarten and to examine their consciences about the wrong use of leisure.

Mere morality, he said, completely missed the point of human recreation, which was to re-establish people in the contemplation of their own mystery.[45]

> A theology of recreation transcends a mere morality because it is not content with the minimum but with the maximum for the human person. Human maturity is its aim. It desires in restoring man to his origins to put him in contact again with the great creative forces at work in the world, to link him with the whole life of mankind past, present and to come, to lead him to discover the deeper levels of his psychic life, to become one with himself and one with the world. In short, to introduce him to mystery and its unfathomable depths and riches.

Leisure does not have to be a 'doing' in the obvious sense; it can be just a 'being' – being quiet, being aware, being open to the world about us to find these riches.

That is different from the odd times of relaxation, in front of the telly, in the pub, with the daily paper in a deckchair in the garden. That is hardly leisure, if it is simply taking off the pressure. To qualify as leisure it must be something that has value in itself, that somehow makes us more human. It is better to understand 'beyond morality' as pointing to a realm of the spirit. In the words of Berdyaev: 'Spirit is incarnated both really and existentially in the human personality, in its creatively intuitive attitude to life, in a fraternal communion with other men'.[46] Leisure belongs to grace, not to law. No church has quite responded to that vision. Indeed any attempt to make a positive evaluation of leisure in a Christian context needs to recognize the weight of suspicion which has attached to it in the past. To that we turn next.

## NOTES

1.   Friedrich Nietzsche, *Beyond Good and Evil* trs. R.J. Hollingsworth (London 1973), sect. 153, 103.
2.   Romans 13.10.
3.   Friedrich Schleiermacher, *On Religion: Speeches to its Cultured Despisers*, trs. John Oman (NY 1958), second speech, 59.
4.   Quoted by Jürgen Moltmann, *Theology and Joy* (London 1973), 81.
5.   Ivan Engnell, *Critical Essays on the Old Testament*, trs. J.T. Willis (London 1970), 139.
6.   E.g. Amos 6.4.
7.   In the 1930s the governments of both France and Germany aimed to organize leisure: in Germany by the Nazi *Kraft durch Freude* movement; in France by the appointment of a socialist under-secretary of state for leisure.
8.   Etienne Borne and François Henry, *A Philosophy of Work*, trs. F. Jackson (1938), 62.
9.   Ibid. 211.
10.   See e.g. Leland Ryken, *Work and Leisure in Christian Perspective* (Leicester 1989), 100–104.
11.   Jeremy Taylor, *Ductor Dubitantium* (1671), 756.
12.   *The Professor*, Arthur Severn's Memoir of John Ruskin (London 1967), 94.
13.   See Nicholas Murray, *A Life of Matthew Arnold* (1996), 244, 246.
14.   Lloyd D. Easton and Kurt H.Guddat (trs. and ed.), *Writings of the Young Marx on Philosophy and Society* (Garden City, NY 1967), 424–5.
15.   William Morris, *News from Nowhere* (5th Edn London 1897), 230.
16.   Leslie Derfler, *Paul Lafargue and the Founding of French Marxism 1842–1882* (Cambridge, Mass. 1991), 180–81.
17.   Walter Rauschenbusch, *Christianity and the Social Crisis* (NY 1913), 341; *Prayers of the Social Awakening* (Boston, Mass. 1909), 89–90.
18.   J.D. Bernal, *The Social Function of Science* (London 1939), 105, quoted in Stanley Parker, *Leisure and Work* (London 1972), 104.
19.   Stanley Parker, *Leisure and Work*, 33.
20.   Taylor, *Ductor Dubitantium* (1671), 756.
21.   J.P. Diggins, *Thorstein Veblen*, (Princeton, NJ 1999), 78.
22.   1 Samuel 17.45–7.
23.   Cf. also the use of 'play' in group conflict in 2 Samuel 2.12–17.
24.   H. Martineau, *Autobiography* (1855), quoted in Keith Thomas, *The Oxford Book of Work* (Oxford 1999), 178.
25.   Josef Pieper, *Leisure: the Basis of Culture* (London 1952), 60, 71.
26.   Ibid. 56: 'Leisure, like contemplation, is of a higher order than the *vita activa*'.
27.   Ibid. 51.
28.   Cf. H.A. Williams, *True Resurrection* (London 1972), 34–6: 'I bring to the game my total undivided self, and it is that total undivided self which is active while the game is in progress'.

29. Thomas Aquinas, *Compendium of Theology*, trs. C.Voltert (London 1948), III, 9.329–30.
30. Thomas Merton, *New Seeds of Contemplation* (London 1961), 24–6.
31. Aristotle, *Ethics*, trs. J.A.K. Thomson (Harmondsworth 1955), X.7, 307..
32. Karl Barth, *Church Dogmatics*, III. (Edinburgh 1961), 474.
33. Alan Richardson, *The Biblical Doctrine of Work* (London 1952), 20.
34. Moltmann, *Theology and Joy*, 41. But elsewhere Moltmann says that man shares in God's creative activity. See Philip West, 'Cruciform Labour', *Modern Churchman*, XXVIII, no.4 (1986), 9–15.
35. Examples are W.H. Vanstone, *Love's Endeavour, Love's Expense* (London 1977) and H.R. Rookmaaker, *The Creative Gift* (1982). See also Robert Sencourt on Bossuet, *The Consecration of Genius* (London 1947), 283.
36. Dorothy L. Sayers, *Begin Here: A War-time Essay*, (London 1940): 'The Serial Drama of History', 22–3.
37. T.S. Eliot, *Notes towards the Definition of Culture* (1948), 19.
38. Nicholas Berdyaev, *Solitude and Society* (London 1938), 78; *Spirit and Reality* (London 1939), 58.
39. Kenneth Cragg, *Faith and Life Negotiate* (Norwich 1994), 265.
40. E.g. John Kent, *Wesley and the Wesleyans* (Cambridge 2002), 106f.
41. Joseph Butler, *Works*, ed. W.E. Gladstone (Oxford 1896), 21–7; 187–91.
42. Oliver O'Donovan, *The Problem of Self-Love in St Augustine* (New Haven, Conn. 1980), *passim*, esp. 90–91, 137.
43. John Burnaby, *Amor Dei: A Study of the Religion of St Augustine* (London 1938), ch. 5 – 'The Order of Love', 113–37.
44. Martin Buber, *The Way of Man, According to the Teaching of Hasidim* (London 1963), 17.
45. John Foster, 'Recreation', *The Furrow*, XIII, No.2 (Maynooth, Feb. 1962), 82–90.
46. *Spirit and Reality*, 59.

# 3

# The Case Against Leisure

*Criticism of leisure as wasting God's gift of a lifetime can be illustrated from English spiritual writers such as Jeremy Taylor, Richard Baxter and William Law. They are chiefly concerned with the leisured or prosperous people of their age, and express the Reformation teaching that Christian obedience was to be fulfilled in the active life of a man's calling. The same sense of the stewardship of time is present in evangelical writers of the eighteenth and nineteenth centuries – John Newton, Hannah More and William Wilberforce. A deeper criticism of 'diversion' is to be found in Blaise Pascal, who believed that pleasures as well as duties were tainted by the effect of original sin. A contemporary critique of leisure may proceed from a sensitive response of wonder at the long, slow processes of evolution.*

Before we can justify leisure as a necessary, and even a noble, part of the Christian life, we need to consider how strongly the case against leisure has been argued in the past. It would not be difficult to find examples of the attack on leisure, in the form of idleness, in almost any age. To see how persistent are the traditional arguments, we can turn to an extended essay by Brian Vickers entitled 'Leisure and Idleness in the Renaissance: The Ambivalence of O*tium*'.[1] He demonstrates that the discussion of the topic goes back to classical Latin authors, and that they remained influential in the Renaissance through the continued use of classical texts in education. Although it was conceded that there could be a responsible use of leisure (*otium cum dignitate*) for those who retired from public life, by choice or under compulsion, the more usual assessment of *otium* was negatively critical. The Roman ideal of the active life, especially in the quest for military glory, gave rise to repeated warnings of the debilitating effect of leisure. It was the root of evils (*radix malorum*), leading not only to weakening of moral fibre, but to the vices of gluttony and lust. This general distrust of leisure is repeated in English writers of the Renaissance period. 'Many characters in Shakespeare express a truly Roman detestation of *otium*.'[2] In the Christian context, what had been regarded as vices imperilling the state become also sins imperilling the soul.[3] Milton in *Paradise Lost* (610–16) shows work as man's distinctive role, as compared with the beasts, even before the Fall. Its opposite was not ease, but rest – recuperation for work. 'Any writer wishing to use *otium* in the seventeenth century in a positive sense

... would have had to work hard to remove its pejorative meaning, or to cancel out its ambivalence into some innocuous synonym for *quies*.'[4]

This traditional suspicion of the evils of idleness underlies the discussion of the topic in some of the classics of English spiritual writing, such as Jeremy Taylor's *Holy Living*, published in 1650, and William Law's *A Serious Call to a Devout and Holy Life*, published in 1728. To these we may add the more systematic presentations in Jeremy Taylor's *Ductor Dubitantium* (1671) and Richard Baxter's *Christian Directory* (1673). The characters of these writers were formed in different generations and different circumstances, but they all experienced exclusion from the main current of religious life in England at the time of writing their books, one as a royalist during the Commonwealth, another as a persecuted minister after the restoration of the monarchy, and the third as a non-juror after the accession of King George I. All these books, therefore, are the product of a restricted life, Taylor's within the household of Lord Carbery at Golden Grove, near Llanelli, Baxter's during a period of exclusion from public ministry, and Law's within the even more limited household he shared with two well-to-do companions at Kings Cliffe in Northamptonshire. They were not addressing a general or secular society, but those among their fellow Christians who were willing to listen to them, an elect minority. This kind of pluralism put them nearer to the position of the Christian church in its earliest centuries than those who, in the post-Constantinian church, were called to address believers and non-believers alike.

The general attitudes of Taylor and Law have been distinguished as those of lesser and greater rigorism in morals. It is certainly true that Jeremy Taylor projects a more tolerant image. It would not have been quite in character for him to write anything like William Law's *The Unlawfulness of Stage Entertainments*, in which he wrote:

> You go to hear a play. I tell you that you go to hear ribaldry and profaneness; that you entertain your mind with extravagant thoughts, wild rants, blasphemous speeches, wanton amours, profane jests, and impure passions.[5]

Perhaps the stage deserved that kind of censure in the 1720s, whereas theatre-going was not an option for Taylor before the restoration of the monarchy, if it had ever been available in the Welsh countryside. As for Baxter, his huge range of learning tended to prevent him passing unqualified judgements. He was led

> to travel over such an immense field of inquiry, to meddle with so many topics, to dispute with so many men, to make so many distinctions without any difference, at least such as less acute minds can discern, that it is difficult to gather together and harmonize his opinions, and to say on certain points what he believed and what he did not. It is easy for a man of one-sided views to be consistent, but who that loves truth for

truth's sake, and wishes to see as much of it as possible in this world of imperfect knowledge, will value consistency of this kind?[6]

That is a caution to be borne in mind throughout this discussion of leisure. Consistency is sometimes the fruit of over-simplification.

Yet, for all their differences, these writers have much in common. All three were called to give detailed advice on the practical business of living the Christian life. They share a devout seriousness when they write about the Christian's use of time. It is easy to forget how precious a thing time has been to previous generations of believers. Now that all the resources of twentieth-century medicine co-operate with a far healthier environment to make anyone's death at an age below fifty seem sad and shocking, time has expanded for the individual. Time was once a more precious commodity than it seems today. To those who experienced the brutalities of the Civil War death was always at hand, an ever-present reality. The worst of the conflict was almost over when Jeremy Taylor wrote *Holy Living*, but the terrors of disease remained. Of his five sons only one survived to maturity, two dying in the same year (1657) in an epidemic of smallpox, and both he and his patron Lord Carbery were bereaved of their wives at an early age and at much the same time. It was not only the poet and lover in that age who could say

But at my back I always hear
Time's wingèd chariot hurrying near;
And yonder all before us lie
Deserts of vast eternity.[7]

Though the eschatological hope or threat (haven or torture-chamber) did not press upon believers in the same way as upon the apostolic church, with its expectation of an imminent divine intervention to bring all history to a close, its urgency survived in a different form for the individual, with the fear of disease and violent death.

It is in the context of God's gift of a lifetime that these authors pass judgement on careless leisure. So Taylor begins his book, *Holy Living*, with 'Considerations of the general instruments and means serving to a holy life',[8] and the first instrument of holy living which he commends is the care of our time. 'God hath given to man a short time here upon earth, and yet upon this short time eternity depends.' He does not want to make the care of our time an occasion of scruples or fears. Necessary business or charitable actions are 'a doing of God's work'. Every man in his proper calling is a minister of the divine providence. Business itself can be 'hallowed by a holy intention'. The danger of temptation is less likely to arise in work than in idleness. To Taylor idleness is abhorrent, because it is the waste of that which cannot be replaced, time itself: 'Idleness is the greatest prodigality in the world; it throws away that which is invaluable in respect of its present use, and irreparable when it is past, being to be recovered by no power of art or nature.'[9] There follow twenty-three rules for employing time. These are designed to ensure right employment and right company as well as regular acts of devotion.

The rules concerning what we should now call leisure relate to two situations: the proper function of relaxation, and the profitable use of extended periods free from necessary duties. As for the first of these, Taylor writes:

> Let not your recreations be lavish spenders of your time; but choose such which are healthful, short, transient, recreative, and apt to refresh you; but at no hand dwell upon them, or make them your great employment: for he that spends his time in sports, and calls it recreation, is like him whose garment is all made of fringes, and his meat nothing but sauces; they are healthless, chargeable, and useless.[10]

He quotes a familiar tradition about St John the apostle who 'recreated himself with sporting with a tame partridge', to show that recreation is permissible; but warns his reader not to become too attached to sports, 'for to whatsoever thou hast given thy affections, thou wilt not grudge to give thy time'.

The other situation he considers is that of 'persons of great quality, and of no trade', who are to be 'most prudent and curious in their employment and traffic of time'. Those who have received adequate education are to use their free time in ways 'useful in order to arts or arms, to counsel in public, or government in their country'. Those who lack adequate education for these purposes are to 'learn easy and youthful [*sic* = useful] things, read history and the laws of the land, learn the customs of their country' and generally devote themselves to the needs of their families and their tenants; and 'in this glut of leisure' they are to give more time to religious exercises. Women of noble birth and great fortunes are to do 'the same things in their proportions and capacities'. All are to 'cut off all impertinent and useless employments' and 'whatsoever spends much time to no real, civil, religious or charitable purpose'.[11]

Baxter's *Christian Directory* develops the same themes with equal eloquence. For him, 'redeeming the time'[12] is a fruitful text, as indeed it was to many writers of his age. The original meaning, as intended by the biblical writer, may be obscure, but its usual interpretation could look back at least to Jerome.[13] It contrasted good and bad ways of spending time, though the explanation of the contrast varied. The thesis of Max Weber in his *The Protestant Ethic and the Spirit of Capitalism* that the demise of monasticism in Protestant countries diverted energy and time to the sanctification of work and thrift, and so distinguished them from Catholic countries, does not now command general assent. Christians of different traditions were equally concerned with the use of their time.[14] But they believed that time, redeemed from idleness, should be devoted, not to work, but to prayer and spiritual exercises. All time was God's time, and even work must not be allowed to trespass on time which should be given to religious exercises. Even time spent asleep might be seen as stolen from devotion. The records of the Unitarian Chapel in Leicester show that one

Ralph Thoresby resolved 'to redeem more time, particularly to retrench my sleeping time, and getting an Alarm put to the clock' (in 1680!).[15]

To return to Baxter, he declared, 'I am large about *Redeeming Time*, because therein the sum of a holy obedient life is included.'[16] The time, he says, means both the space of this present life and each special opportunity, and time in both senses is to be treated as 'a most precious thing', to be used 'in the way of duty'. In a characteristically painstaking way he sets out, in chapters V and VI, six 'ends or uses' for which time is to be redeemed, thirteen guiding thoughts (or 'directions contemplative') for its redeeming, and twelve 'thieves or time-wasters to be watchfully avoided'. Like Taylor he recognizes the need for relaxation, as enabling better performance of work and duties. 'A mower that hath a good sythe will do more in a day than another that hath a bad one can do in two.' 'Necessary whetting is no letting.'[17] As for more extended periods of freedom from work and other duties, he treats them only in relation to the aged, the sick and infirm and, with an unexpected hint of his own tribulations, to other people who are suffering from forcible constraint, by imprisonment or persecution or poverty or war. He considers that these are among the special situations which can constitute a call to a contemplative life.

The modern reader will be tempted to minimize the relevance or usefulness of this kind of advice on the grounds that it is all conditioned by the particular structure of society in the writer's age and country. Baxter, like many other writers on the use of time, tends to impose the pattern of his own life-style on other people in different circumstances. The 'glut of leisure' of the few was purchased by the denial of leisure to the many. Whether or not this makes the advice of these writers quite irrelevant to a different situation is a question to be borne in mind.

When we turn to William Law, we find the same sense of the great uncertainty of life in a later age. He, too, feels the preciousness of time and stresses the brevity of life in comparison with eternity:

> If a man had five fix'd years to live, he could not possibly think at all without intending to make the best use of them all. When he saw his stay so short in this world, he must needs think that this was not a world for him; and when he saw how near he was to another world that was eternal, he must surely think it very necessary to be very diligent in preparing himself for it.[18]

But Law shares with Baxter the inability to speak to the poor, labouring people of his day. One of the attractive features of Law's *Serious Call* is the range of character sketches with which he enlivens his argument; but they do not include ordinary working people of either sex. In another work, *The Spirit of Love*, his dialogue includes a character who is given the name Rusticus; but, as J.H. Overton observed long ago, his attempt to include an illiterate countryman in his gallery of portraits is singularly unconvincing. Rusticus can neither read nor write, but argues like an accomplished scholar. Shut away in his chosen retreat at Kings Cliffe, he had little contact with the poor except as the recipients of his charity. He simply shares the common assumption that working people must find fulfilment in their work. Addressing an imaginary woman of leisure, he writes:

> Had you, Serena, been obliged by the necessities of life, to wash cloaths for your maintenance, or to wait upon some mistress, that demanded your labour, it would then be your duty to serve and glorify God, by such humility, obedience, and faithfulness, as might adorn that state of life.[19]

The working woman or the working man had been given the one talent of faithful service and would be rewarded by the great Judge for safeguarding it. Today it is not only feminists who find this attitude abhorrent, however truly it may still portray the grim realities of life for multitudes of people.

Law's imaginary characters, like the readers whom Taylor addressed, are people with time to spare, and his message, like Taylor's, is about time and its preciousness. He introduces the social group on whom he intends to focus with the curiously misinformed statement that a 'great part of the world are free from the necessities of labour and employment, and have their time and fortunes in their own disposal'. On the contrary, they were, as they always had been, a small proportion of the human race. We can only find any relevance in what he has to say by extending this leisured class to include those who find themselves, for whatever reason, with time to spare and freedom to choose how to spend it. The modern secularized reader, in such a situation of leisure, may feel something of a shock to be told: 'let your own soul be the object of your daily care and attendance'. Does retirement counselling ever begin from that starting-point? Yet it is not easy for a Christian to reject the basis of Law's argument. It is, he says

> an immutable law of God, that all rational beings should act reasonably in all their actions; not at this time, or in that place, or upon this occasion, or in the use of some particular thing, but at all times, in all places, at all occasions, and in the use of all things. This is a law that is as unchangeable as God.[20]

Law's application of this principle, however, does not suit us today. In the first place, the pastimes he satirizes as major components of the life of the leisured class of his own day may be acceptable as small elements in a life devoted to other ends. But allowing for that, we can sympathize with his criticism of people who spend most of their time in frivolous ways. There is an amusing portrait of 'Flatus', a rich and healthy man, who constantly searches for happiness in a succession of fads, some with a modern resonance – fashionable clothes, gambling, dancing, drinking, hunting, home improvement, horse riding, tourism, the opera, vegetarianism, even jogging – each one quickly palling and being succeeded by another.[21] But it is not any individual activity that necessarily deserves criticism (though some may); it is the succession of fads and the hope of finding happiness in any. In the second place, he fails to consider any creative use of leisure. There is an interesting reference in passing[22] to arts and sciences, which points to a large area of human interests which might surely form an element in a devout and holy life. It is all the more interesting because it occurs in a chapter which deals with the education of women. It must be admitted that much in the *Serious Call* will grate upon the sensitivities of any woman who reads it now. Women are often represented as devoted to dress and fashion. No doubt Law was describing what he observed, and he does at least blame women's triviality on their upbringing, not their nature. They are 'not only educated in pride, but in the silliest and most contemptible part of it'.

> They are not indeed suffer'd to dispute with us the proud prizes of arts and sciences, of learning and eloquence, in which I have much suspicion they would often prove our superiors; but we turn them over to the study of beauty and dress, and the whole world conspires to make them think of nothing else.

Here Law drops a hint about the arts and sciences as proper concerns of anyone's free time, men as well as women, but he passes quickly on, and never picks it up again.

The question whether there is anything to be learned from those who lived and wrote in cultures so different from our own, is complicated by another factor which even this brief discussion of Taylor, Baxter and Law brings into prominence. That is, the personal way of life of each author. Each of these writers was constrained by his own education and vocation. Neither had any significant experience of the 'arts and sciences' which might have given meaning to that part of a human life which is not occupied with work and social responsibilities and worship. They were scholars with a wide reading in classical literature, but that was as far as their experience of the arts went. None of them had much opportunity to assess the function of painting or the plastic arts in enriching the human spirit when practised in times of leisure. Nor did they know the fascination of exploring worlds revealed by the sciences which were opening to the attention of men of leisure and those who made leisure in the midst of a life of work. If we set alongside Jeremy Taylor and Baxter their contemporaries, Sir Thomas Browne, doctor and naturalist, or John Ray 'The Aristotle of England and the Linnaeus of his age', and alongside William Law his younger contemporary, Samuel Johnson, we see how limited was their appreciation of the abundance possible within a devout and holy life.

Here perhaps is the negative side of something which has been claimed as a merit of Anglican moral theology. H.R. McAdoo, in his book *The Structure of Caroline Moral Theology*, has drawn a distinction between Anglican moral theology and that of continental Roman Catholic writers in the same period.[23] It was unfortunate, he argued, that Roman Catholic theologians came to draw a clear distinction between moral and ascetic theology, the one being concerned only with distinguishing what is lawful from what is sinful, leaving to the other the task of showing the way of perfection. Moral theology was seen as the universal responsibility of the priest in the confessional, and ascetic theology was limited to those who sought the counsel of spiritual directors. We may agree that a legalistic approach to moral theology was defective, in emphasizing the directive function of the clergy to the detriment of the proper freedom of the individual consciences of lay people. It also unintentionally fostered the attitude of those who rested satisfied with a minimum level of moral life, the avoidance of actual sin. The intention of Anglican moral theologians was to direct believers on the way to the highest possible standard of Christian living. It was only to be expected that the training and practice of the clergy would lead them to define that highest standard in terms of worship and social responsibility, for such were their own primary concerns. If there was a place for the arts, it could only be as handmaids of worship; if there was a place for the sciences, it could only be to enlarge the worshipper's praise of the Creator. Such uses of the arts and sciences put them in the realm of devotion rather than leisure. Once the boundaries of leisure had been drawn so as to exclude these creative activities, there was nothing left but futile pastimes, and it was easy enough to ridicule them and show that they had no place in the way of perfection.

Our exemplars, then, offer a largely convincing case against something. But that something is not what we mean today, if we speak of leisure. And even if it is admitted that human life on earth is in a pre-eminent sense the preparation for a fuller life in God's nearer presence (and that is not the starting-point of much modern theology), it does not follow that the rewards of the heavenly life depend upon a carefully planned life on earth. In one way or another we should make room in a life of obedience for all that liberates us into personal and communal fulfilment. Baxter indeed, rather self-contradictorily, leaves room for pleasure in his scheme of living. He even calls pleasure a duty. Perhaps that is the only way he can validate it. 'So much pleasing of the flesh as tendeth to its Health and Cheerfulness is a duty.'

> Remember still that God would give you more pleasure, and not less, and that he will give you as much of the Delights of sense, as is truly good for you, so you will take them in their place, in subordination to your heavenly delights.[24]

There is no doubt of his enjoyment of the natural world, at least where it shows the improving result of human work.

> When the sights of prospects, and beauteous buildings, and fields, and countrys, or the use of walks, or gardens, do tend to raise the soul to holy contemplation, to admire the Creator, and to think of the glory of

the life to come (as *Bernard* used his pleasant walks); this Delight is lawful, if not a duty where it may be had.[25]

It is a cautious acceptance of delight. Perhaps we may apply to him a verdict on the English reformers in general, that

> for all that they deplored the stubborn recalcitrance of a people addicted to their own pleasures, [they] ultimately knew better than to attempt the sort of full frontal assault on merrymaking and folk culture that could ultimately only end in disaster.[26]

The reference to gardens is in a long tradition which exempted gardening from some of the criticisms aimed at other leisure pursuits. It goes back as far as St Augustine,[27] and includes Francis Bacon, Lord Verulam: 'God Almighty first planted a garden. And indeed it is the purest of human pleasures.'[28]

Baxter's justification of pleasure found a more attractive exponent in the contemporary Thomas Traherne (*c.*1636–1674). In a much quoted passage of his *Centuries of Meditations* he wrote:

> Your enjoyment of the world is never right, till every morning you awake in Heaven; see yourself in your Father's Palace; and look upon the skies, the earth, and the air as Celestial Joys: having such a reverend esteem of all, as if you were among the Angels. The bride of a monarch, in her husband's chamber, hath no such causes of delight as you.[29]

But with Traherne, as with Baxter, pleasure is never for its own sake, but as a kind of spiritual aid. Without this religious dimension, it fails to match the duty of redeeming the time.

The suspicion of leisure was widespread at that period. Another witness is George Herbert (1599–1633), poet and Anglican divine, who had renounced the life of a courtier for that of a parish priest. He does not go out of his way to write much about leisure, and when he writes about time, it is not so much to warn of its swift passage as to welcome its passing. His poem with the title *Time* is addressed to Time as a scytheman dreaded by others as having too sharp a scythe, but welcomed by Herbert as one who offers a way to another life.

> Christs coming hath made man thy debter,
> Since by thy cutting he grows better.

Time is

> An usher to convey our souls
> Beyond the utmost starres and poles.

There is a hint of warning here, that people should prepare themselves for this event. But this is no preacher's poem. He speaks to and for himself. When he came to write *A Priest to the Temple* the case was different. He turns to the faults of his parishioners and begins with the sin of idleness.

> The great and national sin of this Land [the parson] esteems to be idlenesse, great in itself and great in its consequence; for when men have nothing to do, then they fall to drink, to steal, to whore, to scoffe, to revile, to all sorts of gamings. 'Come,' say they, 'we have nothing to do; let's go to the tavern, or to the stews, or what not.' Wherefore the parson strongly opposeth this sin wheresoever he goes. And because idleness is twofold, the one in having no calling, the other in walking carelessly in our calling, he first represents to every body the necessity of a vocation. The reason of this assertion is taken from the nature of man, wherein God hath placed two great instruments, reason in the soul and a hand in the body, as ingagements of working, so that even in Paradise man had a calling; and how much more out of Paradise, when the evils which he is now subject unto may be prevented or diverted by reasonable imployment! Besides, every gift or ability is a talent to be accounted for, and to be improved to our Master's advantage.[30]

Here is the Reformation doctrine of the 'vocation' of man as his rightful offering, no less to God than to the human community. Here also is the theme of human inability to use 'free time' for anything but the lowest of pleasures. We may call it élitist, if we choose; but Parson Herbert was near enough to his people in the parish, just as he had known at close quarters enough of the life of the court, to give us a true picture of contemporary human behaviour. One point, however, must be noticed: he does not even mention the leisure-time activities of the women of his parish.

If we move on to the eighteenth and nineteenth centuries, we meet others of the great company of those who saw leisure-time occupations from the view-point of the converted. A paradigmatic figure is that of John Newton (1725–1807). During his lifetime he drafted his own epitaph, in which he described himself as 'once an Infidel and Libertine' and (rather curiously) as a 'servant of slaves in Africa'. It was understandable that in his converted life he should attack the vices which had marked his unregenerate life, the vices of social life more than the sins of his slave-trading days. In his violent attacks on the theatre we pick up once again the theme which we have already met in William Law and which was repeated in later writers. Newton's influence contributed to the conversion of Hannah More (1745–1833), chiefly known for her work in the establishment of Sunday Schools. It is not so often remembered that she had previously enjoyed success in fashionable life, being a friend of the actor David Garrick, and the author of a play presented to acclaim at Covent Garden. She, too, turned her criticism on the theatre. In her later life she realized the contrast between its standards and what she now regarded as the true standards of a Christian.

> Passion, jealousy, hatred, ambition, pride, revenge, [were] elevated to the rank of virtues, and formed 'a dazzling system of worldly morality, in direct opposition to the spirit of a religion whose characteristics are charity, meekness, peaceableness, long-suffering and gentleness.'[31]

Newton's influence was also at work in an even better-known critic of contemporary manners, William Wilberforce (1759–1833). He was already a notable Member of Parliament and a close friend of the young Prime Minister, William Pitt, when he consulted Newton on the question whether he should resign from public life or try to maintain Christian standards in the social level to which he had become accustomed. Newton's advice, to bear his witness as a Member of Parliament, led to his long campaign for the ending of the slave trade. Less well known is his long critique of current views of Christianity published as *A Practical View of the Prevailing Religious System* (1797). It is a sustained attack on nominal Christianity and a declaration of the difficulty of leading a life with the marks of 'real Christianity'. Because it is addressed to the people of his own class, it includes the theatre in the range of its anathemas. The theatre, he says, has been called 'a school of morals'. He accepts the description, and attacks the morals.

Wilberforce was not in the least a grim man; his reputation had always been that of a delightful, witty companion. Dorothy Wordsworth said of him, after he had stayed in Rydal for some weeks: 'There never lived on earth, I am sure, a man of sweeter temper than Mr Wilberforce. He is made up of benevolence and loving kindness.'[32] It is to be expected, then, that he would leave the door wide open for other kinds of amusement. The criterion for acceptability, he says, is plain. Whatever directly or indirectly must be likely to injure the welfare of a fellow-creature can scarcely be a suitable recreation for a Christian. Stated positively,

> the Christian relaxes in the temperate use of all the gifts of Providence. Imagination and taste and genius, and the beauties of creation, and the works of art, lie open to him. He relaxes in the feast of reason, in the intercourses of society, in the sweets of friendship, in the endearments of love, in the exercise of hope, of confidence, of joy, of gratitude, of universal goodwill, of all the generous and benevolent affections; which, by the gracious appointment of our Creator, while they disinterestedly intend only happiness to others, are most surely productive of peace and joy to ourselves.[33]

This is an ideal of leisure, clothed perhaps in a form of rhetoric no longer appealing, but not to be dismissed too quickly as the privilege of a particular social class. He draws a distinction between some kinds of leisure and others, which will become a refrain often heard as the industrial revolution began to spread to other classes the hope of what could be called 'free time'.

These writers were not given to much abstract thought. To find a deeper dimension in the critique of leisure, we may turn back to the seventeenth century and to another country, and listen to Blaise Pascal (1623–1662). In different circumstances he, too, like Jeremy Taylor, Baxter and Law, addressed a minority within his own society. The work known as *Pensées*, first published in 1670, is a collection of notes he left towards a vindication of the Christian life against the free-thinkers of his time. Its apologetic arguments are not directly relevant to the discussion of leisure, but it contains an extended section with the title 'Diversion' (*Divertissement*). The title perhaps disguises Pascal's serious intention here. *Divertissement* has been called 'a profound ontological concept',[34] that is, something belonging to the very existence of fallen humanity. Pascal begins his discussion by proposing that the position which we imagine to possess all possible advantages is that of 'royalty'. He then describes the restless search of the king and his entourage for diversions to occupy their time and prevent them actually thinking about themselves – hunting, dancing, gambling, tennis, bear-baiting, and so on. He says that when he had considered all these, he came to the conclusion that none offered the happiness which the participants were looking for. He had often said that the sole cause of man's unhappiness was that he did not know how to stay quietly in his room.

> But, after closer thought, looking for the particular reasons for all our unhappiness now that I knew its general cause, I found one very cogent reason in the natural unhappiness of our feeble mortal condition, so wretched that nothing can console us when we really think about it.[35]

Pascal is carrying his criticism further and deeper than those who simply point to the sins and vices which attend idleness and condemn it for that reason. He believes that even those activities which are not in themselves sinful reveal the dire situation of humanity. A central theme of the *Pensées* is the greatness and littleness of humanity, its glory and its misery. The necessary consequence of the Fall is that even humanity's greatest attributes are corrupted; and yet that corruption itself points to the greatness of what has been corrupted. So when anyone is given the leisure to act freely, he (and here, too, men rather than women are at the centre of the picture) corrupts free action by turning it to a method of setting himself up above others. This obviously infects sport, but he believes that it even infects serious study undertaken in leisure time; and we recall that Pascal was a brilliant mathematician.

> What is his [the sportsman's] object in all this? Just so that he can boast tomorrow to his friends that he played better than someone else. Likewise

others sweat away in their studies to prove to scholars that they have
solved some hitherto insoluble problem in algebra.[36]

The corruption of leisure is, indeed, just a part of the corruption of all human
activity. And yet every activity, however corrupt, if it depends upon the ability
to think, witnesses to the greatness of humanity.

> Man is only a reed, the weakest in nature, but he is a thinking reed...
> But even if the universe were to crush him, man would still be nobler
> than his slayer, because he knows that he is dying, and the advantage the
> universe has over him. The universe knows none of this. Thus all our
> dignity consists in thought.[37]

Pascal has, in a sense, proved too much. Leisure activities show humanity
running away from itself. They are corrupted by their own motivation. But
such, he believes, is the general state of all human life, not just of leisure; and
the logic of this assessment can only be to drive the individual into a penitent
withdrawal from society, and from study no less than from diversions.

We may note also an unusual criticism of the theatre, as one of the popular
leisure activities of the class of people Pascal has chiefly in mind. It is included
in his papers, though there is some doubt whether he himself wrote it. It is
strangely different from the usual attacks on the corrupting effect of licentious
stage-plays. The danger lies, not in temptation to sinful thoughts, but in
encouraging the audience to think too much about love – perhaps we may say,
to be in love with the idea of love.

> All the major forms of diversion are dangerous for the Christian life, but
> among all those which the world has invented none is more to be feared
> than the theatre. It represents passions so naturally and delicately that it
> arouses and engenders them in our heart, especially that of love; above
> all when it is represented as very chaste and virtuous. For the more
> innocent it seems to innocent souls, the more liable they are to be touched
> by it; its violence appeals to our self-esteem, which at once conceives
> the desire to produce the same effects which we see so well represented...
> Thus we leave the theatre with hearts so full of all the beauty and
> sweetness of love, and our mind so convinced of its innocence, that we
> are quite prepared to receive our first impressions. of it, or rather to
> seek the opportunity of arousing them in someone else's heart, so that
> we may enjoy the same pleasures and sacrifices as those which we have
> seen so well depicted in the theatre.[38]

'All the major forms of diversion are dangerous for the Christian life.' The
theatre, then, is but one example of the agencies which distract the believer

from the serious business of working out his own salvation with fear and trembling.

There is much in this which is characteristic of people who have had some kind of conversion experience. Pascal had been living by standards which would have been thought commendably Christian, until in 1654 he had an experience which – although its details are obscure – radically changed his life to one of austerity and self-denial. It was from that changed life that he spoke of the dangers of *divertissement*. Yet he was unlike Hannah More or Wilberforce, who believed that sinful elements could, with the help of God and a certain amount of self-discipline, be eliminated from their daily life and leave them rejoicing in the blessedness of the saints. For Pascal, the effects of original sin contaminated all levels of human activity. The corruption which infected the leisure activities of the well-to-do was simply the working out of the deep self-concern which marred the seed of Adam, from which nothing could release them but God's own grace. He did not so much make a case against the absurdities of leisure, as use them to illustrate his diagnosis of the misery of humankind.

These exemplars from the sixteenth and seventeenth centuries offer powerful arguments against the misuse of free time in their own age. We should listen to them, for they were serious critics of human behaviour, while at the same time recognizing some crucial differences between their societies and ours. First, the tradition which we can trace from Jeremy Taylor to William Wilberforce is one of criticising the wasteful use of time mainly by an élite in a society where leisure was a luxury. Today leisure is part of the normal experience of the great majority of people in Western society. Secondly, the theological basis of Pascal's critique, in the tradition of Jansenism, is in conflict with the general theological assumptions even of conservative evangelicals today. There are few Christians who would now argue that the good gifts of God cannot be enjoyed without being tainted by the entail of original sin. The Bible has even been called as witness in the defence of 'God-centered hedonism'.[39] We may welcome this more tolerant attitude. It would be absurd to pass judgement on all self-pleasing indulgences in a twenty-year period of retirement – the most consolidated kind of leisure now within the reach of increasing numbers of people.

With the increase in leisure in the present age, the stewardship of time is not usually seen as such a weighty responsibility as it once was, but there is another way in which the appreciation of time has changed, with consequences for our understanding of human nature. That is not through the increase of life expectancy but with the discovery of the process of human evolution in the new dimension of cosmic time. There have inevitably been different responses to this discovery. For many people it seems to reduce humanity to comparative insignificance, in the proportions of millions of years. But given a continuing faith in a personal Creator, the process of evolution may speak with an awe-inspiring voice of a patient work, making humanity into a vessel at last able to hold incarnation.

Even before the transformation in time-scale involved in the nineteenth-century scientific revolution, the Bible could be heard to speak of 'the fulness of time'.[40] Christian believers were assured that they were the ones upon whom 'the ends of the ages' had come.[41] This gracious privilege carried with it the responsibility of living worthily of the vocation with which they were called.[42] That meant not only the rejection of sinful activities but also a scrupulous choice among things indifferent, if only to avoid giving offence to those who were weak in faith.[43] This message was conditioned by the imminence of the expected parousia. As the centuries succeeded each other, the cautionary use of this expectation lost its edge, though it could be revived, for example on the eve of the first millennium. In due course, as the Renaissance encouraged the exploration and appreciation of the riches of the contemporary world, the privilege could be seen much more as that of being human than being Christian. The proper response was quite as much to enjoy the world as to censor one's own choice of actions. This is the theme to be found in Traherne's wondering response, not just to the external world, but also to the marvel of his own nature. He expressed that wonder through his description of himself, and every human being, as an heir of the whole world.

> You never enjoy the world aright, till the Sea itself floweth in your veins, till you are clothed with the heavens, and crowned with the stars: and perceive yourself to be the sole heir of the whole world, and more so, because men are in it who are every one sole heirs as well as you.[44]

In the very different context of the nineteenth century the dimension of time once again became important, but in a new way. There was a small company of those who felt the excitement of a new revelation in the work of Darwin and Wallace, of whom perhaps the chief was F.J.A. Hort. For him, *The Origin of Species* was 'a book that one is proud to be a contemporary with'.[45] He was not alone in welcoming the removal of the idea of a Creator who had to keep interfering in his creation. In the new perspectives time had been transformed from a precious commodity, in short supply, to a prodigally expanded resource in creation. It did not follow that humanity alone fulfilled the Creator's purpose, as a kind of pinnacle of his architecture. All creatures were part of that purpose; but humanity, more than any other part of creation, was able to respond with understanding. In the light of evolutionary ideas creation was interpreted as a long travail instead of a simple fiat. Human beings were now, if heirs at all, heirs of a long succession of strange ancestors. The sense of election could become, in minds attuned to the new perspectives, an equal feeling of responsibility. Redeeming the time could mean, not simply buying up the brief years of a human life, but fulfilling the potential so painfully evolved. So in the twentieth century it was possible to speak, even without the usual teleological arguments, about a process from cosmic beginnings to the moment of incarnation.

> The sequence observed and inferred scientifically implies for Christians that both the processes of cosmic evolution and the Incarnation are alike expressions of the creative, self-limiting love of God. ... Man as a person in time can come into relation with the God who is the ground of all being and the Creator of time itself. ... Our destiny is in God's hands but our lives here and now are ours to direct, in his way, if we so choose. ... The working out of this demand placed upon us is a challenge which is perennial – but is here and now.[46]

It is in this new context that leisure may now be criticised – not only as prolonged with the prolongation of the time of human life, but rather as measured against the millennia of time which have gone to the making of humanity. The problem of extended leisure, as opposed to short-term relaxation, is that it is in danger of elevating trivialities, which may properly offer the best method of relaxation, to the status of the chief purpose of living. We can all choose our own illustrations for this assertion – from other people's trivialities, not our own. It is not the intention of this chapter to offer examples. Only it should be recognized that there is a case against leisure in some of its forms which can be based on our present sense of time. Put in a simple way, it is that the travail of creation, which Paul saw as fulfilled in the children of God, is dishonoured when a single human life is given up to unworthy objects. That leaves wide open the question about what is or is not unworthy. Perhaps a guide might be found in what scientists rather than theologians have said about the uniqueness of the human being.

> [W]hen we view man in his evolutionary context, it is necessary to affirm both his 'physical' nature *and* all that which is specific and unique to him as a man, even if rudimentary forms of, for example, his intelligence are to be found in other higher mammals. One could make a long list of these specific and unique characteristics of man: his intelligence; his curiosity; his adaptability; his creativity; his use of language; his ability to form complex personal and social relationships; his self-consciousness; his ability to transcend in thought his environment and survey it as subject; his use of 'I' in a unique way ...[47]

The new dimensions of time revealed by the scientific revolution suggest a re-interpretation of what 'redeeming the time' should mean. In brief moments of relaxation it is enough to exercise a fragment of our humanity. The case looks different when the moment of leisure is prolonged for decades.

Before leaving the religious case against leisure, however, we need to take the measure of other criticisms, made from a sociological stand-point, and consider whether they should be endorsed within a Christian world-view. They do not focus on the use of time or the degree of permissible self-indulgence, but on the servitude of the individual to undesirable social pressures. Judged by the highest standards, failure to resist these forces may count as a sin of omission.

# NOTES

1.  Brian Vickers, 'Leisure and Idleness in the Renaissance', *Renaissance Studies*, IV, no. 1, pt 1 (March 1990), 1–37; pt 2, (June 1990), 107–54.
2.  Ibid. 141. Examples quoted are *Richard II*, 2.1.10; *King John*, 4.3.67ff.; *1 Henry VI*, 1.1.142; *2 Henry VI*, 3.2.198; *Henry V*, 5.2.51; *Hamlet*, 1.5.32ff.; *Othello*, 1.3.328; *All's Well*, 3.1.17ff..
3.  Vickers, 'Leisure and Idleness in the Renaissance', 111.
4.  Ibid. 144.
5.  Quoted in J.H. Overton, *William Law, Non-Juror and Mystic (1686–1761)* (London 1881), 37.
6.  John Strong, *History of Religion in England*, IV (London 1901), 381.
7.  Andrew Marvell (1621–1678), 'To his Coy Mistress'.
8.  *Practical Works* (London 8 vols, 1838), IV, ch. 1,10–12.
9.  Ibid. ch. 1, sect.1, 15.
10. Ibid. sect.1, 16, 21.
11. Ibid. sect.1. 11, 19.
12. Ephesians 5.15; Colossians 4.5.
13. Jerome, PL xxvi. 559f., quoted in James Barr, *Biblical Words for Time* (rev.edn, London 1969), 129: '*dies malos in bonos vertimus, et facimus illos non praesentis saeculi, sed futuri*'.
14. There are several relevant essays relating to this topic in R.N. Swanson (ed.) *The Use and Abuse of Time in Christian History* (Woodbridge and Rochester NY 2002): papers read at the 1999 Summer Meeting and the 2000 Winter Meeting of the Ecclesiastical History Society.
15. David L.Wykes, in ibid. 214.
16. Richard Baxter, *A Christian Directory* (London 1673) 'Advertisements', I.3.
17. Ibid. 267, 276.
18. William Law, *A Serious Call to a Devout and Holy Life* (London 1899), ch. 5, 68ff.
19. Ibid.69–70.
20. Ibid. 76.
21. Ibid. ch.12, 189-90.
22. Ibid. ch. 19, 348.
23. H.R.McAdoo, *The Structure of Caroline Moral Theology* (London 1949), 9, with ref. to J. MacQuarrie, *Three Issues in Ethics* (London 1970) 74–5; see also H.R. McAdoo, *First of its Kind: A Study in the Functioning of a Moral Theory* (Norwich 1994), 25, 33.
24. Baxter, *Christian Directory*, 272.
25. Ibid. 266, 272, 267.
26. A. Pettegree in *History Today*, Dec. 1999.
27. See Carol Harrison 'Augustine and the Art of Gardening' , in Swanson, *The Use and Abuse of Time*, 13–33.
28. Francis Bacon, *Essays, or Counsels, Civil and Moral*, ed. Brian Vickers (London 1996): 'Of Gardens'.
29. Thomas Traherne, *Centuries of Meditations*, ed. Bertram Dobell (London 1948), I.28

30. George Herbert, *A Priest to the Temple* (London 1632) ch. 32: 'The Parson Surveys'.
31. Margaret Cropper, *Sparks among the Stubble* (London 1955) 150.
32. Dorothy Wordsworth, letter to Jane Marshall Oct. 1818.
33. W. Wilberforce, *A Practical View of the Prevailing Religious System* (London 1841), 312–13, 417.
34. Hans Urs von Balthasar, *The Glory of the Lord Vol. III – Studies in Theological Style* (Edinburgh 1986), 213–14.
35. Blaise Pascal, *Pensées* ed. and trs. A.J. Krailsheimer (Harmondsworth 1966) 37–8.
36. Pascal, *Pensées* 40.
37. Ibid. 66.
38. Ibid. 232.
39. Leland Ryken, *Work and Leisure in Christian Perspective* (Leicester 1989), 191.
40. Galatians 4.4.
41. 1 Corinthians 10.11.
42. Ephesians 4.1.
43. Romans 14.
44. Traherne, *Centuries of Meditations* I.29, cf. II.34, IV.90.
45. A.F. Hort, *Life* and *Letters of F.J.A. Hort* (1896) III, 416.
46. J. Dominian and A.H. Peacocke, *From Cosmos to Love: The Meaning of Human Life,* Hulsean Sermons (London 1976), 36–7.
47. Ibid. 27.

# 4

# The Social Frame

*Sociological criticism of leisure in modern Western society since Thorstein Veblen has focused on its use as an expression of class superiority or social subordination. Christian response to the corruption of leisure has varied from the quietist to the politically optimistic. The 1924 COPEC conference marked the acceptance of leisure as a valuable element in human life. A distinction emerged between short-term relaxation and more extended leisure, with an emphasis on creativity and imagination. But the Bible includes prophetic denunciation of class exploitation, and the churches have shown continuous concern about the quality of leisure activities. It is difficult to distinguish between those criticisms which are objective and others which show class bias. Women's leisure is markedly different from men's, and is the subject of lively interest at present.*

Pascal provides a convenient bridge to the consideration of a different form of attack on leisure. His psychological analysis exposed two motives which animate most voluntary activities: 'the flight from being present to oneself; that is, from communion with God',[1] and the urge to show one's superiority over others, whether in sport or in scholarship. The assumptions of sociologists hardly allow them to notice the first of these two, without a great deal of rephrasing. But the second opens a doorway into discussion of the social pressures which create the forms of leisure and the purposes which they serve. It is not the purpose of this study to describe or assess sociological critiques of leisure in any detail, but it is necessary to take account of some of the general lines of criticism, to see what, if anything, a theologian might have to say, in agreement or disagreement.

There are two general lines of attack on the uses of leisure in society. It is described either as a medium for the expression of superiority or, more deplorably, as an instrument of control or actual oppression. We begin, then, with leisure as an expression of superiority. Examples could, no doubt, be found in all ages of human society. There was private indulgence in leisure pursuits among the European aristocracy as early as the tenth or eleventh century, serving 'to differentiate a tiny privileged sector from the rest of society'.[2] But if we are concerned principally with the modern age, the key text is Thorstein Veblen's *The Theory of the Leisure Class*, first published in 1899. Its title is important, because it distinguishes between leisure as an element of almost all human life in any age and a state of society in which, according to Veblen, a distinct class emerges for which leisure does not merely serve the purpose of relaxation or enjoyment, but becomes part of a deliberate strategy to promote self-esteem. Leisure in his argument is not constituted by 'an habitual neglect of work'.[3] It is not 'indolence or quiescence'. It is the 'non-productive consumption of time'.[4] It arises from a sense of the menial nature of productive work, and is used as evidence of sufficient wealth to afford a life of idleness. Mere inactivity, however, would be tedious, and so leisure occupations may have an end in view, so long as they do not leave any material product. Members of the leisure class even need to learn how to live the leisured life in a becoming way. So they may devote themselves to 'quasi-scholarly or quasi-artistic' accomplishments or the acquisition of useless knowledge. These interests include dead languages, occult sciences, domestic music and arts, dress, furniture, games, sports, animals, and other non-productive occupations.[5] We may add (though Veblen does not) the cultivation of religious sensibilities: for example, the patronage of the Gothic revival in English church architecture, of which the 16th Earl of Shrewsbury's patronage of A.W.N. Pugin in the building of St Giles's Church, Cheadle, is a notable specimen.

Veblen was writing in the main about urban society in America. But it is easy to find occupations in the rural life of England in the past which served the same purpose, of differentiating one class from another, and increasing the self-esteem of one group and implicitly subordinating another. A small but intriguing example of this is the institution of games on Dover's Hill in Gloucestershire in the seventeenth century. They were carefully planned to include rough games, such as shin-kicking, for the labourers, while the better classes enjoyed horse-racing at the top of the hill. The later history of these games is instructive. The arrival of the railway in the nineteenth century brought in crowds from Birmingham and the Black Country, who did not respect the control still exercised over the country labourers by their employers. Scenes of fighting and boozing shocked the representatives of the respectable classes, especially the clergy, and the games were abolished. This incidentally enabled the enclosure of some land which had till then been open. But in the twentieth century the earlier kind of social control had largely disappeared, and the land reverted to common use with acquisition by the National Trust. So it was possible for the games to be revived, with attendant commercial exploitation and the growth of tourism.[6]

Another relevant example is given by James Obelkevich. His thesis concerning rural life in part of Lincolnshire in the period 1825–75 argues that the communal spirit of village life there disintegrated into a class-structured society, with the farmers withdrawing their participation in village sports and turning to more genteel pastimes.[7] In this case the differentiation was not so much by conspicuous consumption as by conspicuous abstention which emphasized the distinction between one kind of leisure activity and another. The farmers, resisting the efforts of Methodist preachers and others to raise the self-esteem of the labourers above the level of crude and childish games (climbing greasy poles, jumping in sacks, rolling wheelbarrows blindfold, and so on), might actually encourage their workers to take part while themselves looking on. The wrongfulness of particular leisure habits, in the eye of the secular sociologist, does not consist in wasting God's gifts of time and talents, but in a distortion of social relationships.

Wherever wealthy people aimed to display their difference from the poorer classes, the role of women was of central significance. This is another of Veblen's themes which it is important to notice. At the simplest level, a wife whose husband's income permitted the employment of one or more household servants was set free from housework and displayed that freedom in more or less useless activities. It might look irresponsible, in a traditionally hard-working society, for the husband to waste much time in leisure activities, but there was no equivalent stigma attached to women's free time. This situation would lead, not just to leisure activities, but to conspicuous expenditure by the wife on dress and other luxuries, in her vicarious role as agent of her husband in self-promotion. Veblen criticized women of the leisure class in America for their role as agents of their husbands in displaying their wealth through 'conspicuous consumption', especially in their dress. This, however, leads to a paradox. Women of the leisure class in America have also been in the vanguard of culture,[8] and through their education have come to understand and change their social condition. Veblen himself denounced leisure as wasteful, and yet argued that idleness was the highest state of knowing.[9]

It is only in recent decades that the changing status of women in society has promoted a more general discussion of women's leisure. The examples so far given concern only women of particular classes or as secondary agents of male display. This was not brought out in the seventeenth-century English writers previously quoted, because their main attack was on the foolishness of men. William Law, in his *Serious Call to a Devout and Holy Life*, included the example of Serena among 'persons that are free from the necessity of labour and employments' to teach the need always to choose and do 'the best things', by which he means chiefly the exercises of religion.[10] In general, even where women's activities were noted, as by William Law, they were not seen as agents fulfilling men's need to display their self-esteem, but were held individually responsible, though Law did recognize that their vanities were the outcome of mistaken upbringing. They displayed the characteristics of a particular society which they themselves had not deliberately created. To some extent this anticipates Veblen's analysis, in which women were encouraged by male pressure to display their husbands' wealth. In either case they suffered a kind of alienation from their own individuality.

In many discussions of leisure the distinctive situation of women is inadequately recognized. It is indeed an extraordinary fact that even as recently as 1989 a book of essays on the philosophy of leisure could have been published in which there is no specific consideration of women's leisure as distinctive. All nine contributors were men.[11] The small group of completely leisured women who have received attention form an exception to the general rule. If we turn from the exceptional to the general, there are plausible reasons why women's leisure has been given so much less consideration than men's. It has been easier to investigate men's leisure in industrial society because they can all be treated as normally being employed or occupied with work of some kind. Leisure stands in contrast to work. It consists in the discrete periods of time, shorter or longer, when the demands of work cease and men are free to please themselves how they use that free time. It is not like that with the majority of women. Unless they are without children and live alone, or unless they have full-time jobs (which is to say, unless they are like the male stereotype), their leisure is related to the family, not to work. The lives of many women even in industrial society contain the sort of mingling or alternation of work (housework) and short stretches of leisure which resembles the pattern of an earlier age when many men as well as women worked in or from the home. Even if they have full-time jobs, they generally continue to carry the weight of family responsibilities. 'Full-time working women transfer, rather than abdicate, their work-hour responsibilities for child-care, meeting these by proxy.'[12]

The effect of family responsibilities on the forms of leisure is obvious. The classic study of Lancashire women in the 1950s by Professor Zweig showed a range of activities almost entirely restricted to the home and the local cinema: knitting, reading, the radio, gardening for a few, and for some the television.[13] Hobbies are for men, and are sometimes resented as taking them away from the family. While there are children at home, relaxation best takes the form of things that can be set aside at a moment's notice. That kind of pattern is likely to survive even when there are no longer children at home. If a holiday can be afforded, it is valued not for the change of air or the pleasure of a seaside resort so much as simply for being waited on. All that was fifty years ago, yet some of the restrictions remain. But it is not so much the restrictions which raise a fundamental question, as what people thought then and think now about entitlement to leisure.

It is a common opinion, shared by men and women alike, that men are entitled to some independent leisure in a way that women are not.[14] Even in retirement the idea that leisure is something earned by paid employment continues. One researcher concluded from her study that, whereas a man made a definite move from work to retirement, 'There was no comparable *rite de passage* for the women; that is, at no point in time were they symbolically rewarded for having finished their life-time labour.'[15] There are other aspects of the difference between the common perceptions of men's leisure and women's: characterization of 'hobbies' as male activities, inferior provision of sporting facilities for women as compared with men, even the concern of women to present to society an image of their husbands as enjoying in retirement a 'successful' use of leisure.

Can there be any Christian judgement on this situation and the desire of many – but certainly not all – women to change it? There are few pointers in the Christian tradition to anything that goes beyond making the best and most fulfilling use of the existing social pattern, whatever that may happen to be. Within that pattern the great range of human variability will create different modes of fulfilment in free time for women. Some will surely choose to enjoy the alternation of work and leisure which has so long a tradition behind it. 'The ritual enactment of housekeeping typically links its performer back in time to the company of female ancestors.'[16] Some regard their time with their children as a form of leisure. 'My daughter gives me everything – leisure time, playing about, she's everything.'[17] But also the freedom given in Christ, in whom there is neither male nor female, will enfranchize others to explore ways of leisure which express that proper self-love within the Christian community which must not be lost in loving a family. That, too, will be an exploration of God-given reality.

We referred above to the possibility that the leisure class might not only create wrong relationships with other classes, but also use leisure itself as an instrument of control or exploitation. This is evident in traditional society where patterns which characterize relationships at work may recur in leisure time. A privileged class takes over the organization of leisure for working people, and exploits them. This enables the privileged to combine enjoyment with the exercise of control. An obvious example is an earlier phase of county and country house cricket, where class barriers were firmly maintained; there were gentlemen and players, divided by traditional barriers. The pattern was repeated with variations in industrial society, when large-scale employers provided regulated leisure facilities for employees. The final stage of exploitation, to date, has been reached when mass leisure provision has been undertaken simply for profit, as in the case of the purchase of football teams which are then turned into limited companies with all the trappings of a business enterprise.

This points to other ways in which the general organization of the world of work affects leisure. It is arguable that the invasion of leisure by the standards of business reduces the intrinsic value of leisure time by robbing it of its distinctiveness. Two effects which come within the sociologist's field of interest are commercialization and the cult of competition or efficiency. With commercialization the pressures of the world of work are imported into an area which otherwise would be justified as a different way of living, carefully insulated from considerations of value for money. The negative characteristics of commercialism which are criticized include such things as standardization, exploitation, and passive consumerism. Standardization of leisure habits enables commercial providers to make bigger profits with the loss of variation and originality. Insistent promotion of particular kinds of leisure, or equipment for leisure activities, through the resources of advertisement, exploits vulnerable groups, including children, in the interest of profit, without any clear benefit to the exploited groups. The incessant self-repeating offerings of television engender a kind of passivity unworthy of human nature at its best and create the modern phenomenon of the so-called couch-potato.

These criticisms do not go unanswered. For example, work-based habits of mutual support may themselves be valuable to the individual when carried over into leisure, even if they were initially promoted by an employer for his own benefit. Leisure pursuits have often been closely connected with paid occupations. In many industrial towns football clubs, brass bands, works outings and church-going were all part of a densely woven culture centring on the local pit or factory.[18] So whereas in industrial villages and small towns the development of mass leisure tended to dissolve the older forms of community, in great cities where the older forms had already been eroded these work-based associations created new forms of community. The situation is constantly changing in response to new patterns of employment. Increasing mobility of labour and the virtual disappearance of older industries leave some leisure organizations, such as brass bands, without a base in industrial organization. This creates the need for sponsorship, which again locks leisure into the concurrent patterns of commerce.

Christian opinion has, as usual, been divided in its response. Some Christian theologians, recognizing perhaps with Pascal the reality of original sin, and watching the corruption of leisure no less than the corruption of work, could only look for the ultimate establishment by God himself of the kingdom of heaven, where all is leisure, as in Eden before the Fall. In this world they could expect little more than the creation of moments or oases of right relationship, whether in leisure or at work. On these assumptions the function of the local church community would be to provide some such opportunities for withdrawal. This role was particularly relevant to two types of community: immigrant ethnic groups and sectarian groups professing an exclusive theology which consigned the world to damnation. By contrast, there were those idealists whose political hope on a purely humanistic basis was to remove all forms of exploitation at work with the consequential reform of relationships in leisure as well. William Morris's *News from Nowhere* is one of the best expressions of this kind of idealism. But the fashion for projecting such utopian schemes has been largely swept away with the collapse of Marxism.

There was indeed a time in the earlier part of the twentieth century when Christians within the socialist tradition looked for the remaking of industrial society upon a co-operative rather than a competitive basis. By some Christian thinkers the church was seen as the fore-runner of this new civilization. It was 'God's Co-operative Society'. The Christian Socialists and their sympathizers were, however, a minority in the churches. For the most part, Christian opinion accepted the structure of capitalist society and only came slowly to notice its effect in creating and then exploiting leisure. The process which has made leisure a major factor in social organization had not advanced far enough by the turn of the twentieth century to encourage much thought about the possible effect of any such revolution on the free time of working people. But as the century progressed it was at least recognized that leisure was a right and not merely a luxury.

In England the new Christian attitude to leisure was brought to wider notice in 1924 when the ecumenical Conference on Christian Politics, Economics and Citizenship (COPEC) was held in Birmingham. That has been hailed as a watershed in the development of social thinking in the churches,[19] but it was rather the emergence into public view of a development which can be traced much further back. A more significant turning-point might be identified in the foundation of the Christian Social Union in 1889, which led to the involvement of many Christians (or at least churchpeople) in a new way in the study of social questions. Its leading figures, B.F.Westcott and Charles Gore, were more concerned with study than with political action. When Westcott set out the duties of membership, he wrote, 'The central one is quiet study. It is worse than vain to attempt to "do" anything before you are master of the subject.' That did not prevent local branches from becoming involved in political action.[20]

In the detailed preparatory work which led up to COPEC the other major influence was that of a variety of Social Service Unions which, as their name implies, were more concerned with the practicalities of social reform. The variation in their membership was reflected in their denominational and diocesan origins. According to Maurice Reckitt, it was

> admittedly the example of the C.S.U. which finally induced the non-conformist bodies, as such, to make a move, and when they did so it was by the establishment of quasi-official 'social service unions', which, whatever their limitations, had at least a higher degree of authority in their denominations than the C.S.U. could claim in the Church of England.[21]

The first was founded by the Wesleyan Methodists in 1905 and other denominational social service councils followed. In the Church of England action was taken separately in the dioceses. In 1907 Bishop Percival, who was an enthusiastic supporter of the development, set up a standing Social Service Committee in the diocese of Hereford,[22] and by 1911 it was reported that every diocese had its social service committee.[23] But, as Maurice Reckitt observed, the more clear-sighted of those who promoted these Social Service Unions 'found it difficult to persuade their rank and file that the social problem was something more than a mere amalgam of specific social vices'.[24] Temple recorded that the Hereford diocesan committee produced reports on the wages of farm workers, supply of cottages, rent, drunkenness, gambling and immorality.

When COPEC met, it had inherited this concern for practicalities, and yet it tried to enunciate underlying principles. That is its importance for our present study, although William Temple, looking back from the stand-point of the Malvern Conference in 1941, wanted to stress the theological basis of the later conference, and seems to have had in mind a criticism of COPEC for its paucity of theological thinking.[25] The contrast between the two concerns, for practical action and the establishment of Christian principles for social life, emerges in the report of the Commission on Leisure. It is important, however, to realize that the conference's inclusion of leisure as one of its eleven main topics was forward-looking.

The discussions of the Commission on Leisure were inevitably influenced by the background of its members. Six of them were leaders of work in the London settlements, who were naturally concerned with practical problems.[26] The settlements, once unfairly criticized by H.G. Wells as a sort of 'benevolent picknicking', were not the best preparation for the kind of theoretical criticism which people like Reckitt hoped to hear. Nevertheless it was important that the resolutions included the affirmation that 'Leisure is a part of God's positive purpose for men and women in the development of personality; not only a means of keeping fit for the daily toil.'[27]

The idea of leisure merely as recuperation for further work which had largely dominated Christian thought was at last recognized as inadequate. The Commission's report drew a distinction between recreation and leisure. Recreation meant temporary freedom from the necessity to work. It normally expressed itself in pleasure, laughter, amusements and the restoration of poise. Leisure, on the other hand, meant the deliberate employment of spare time creatively. It could be a growing time of the human spirit.[28] But the Commission could not entirely separate ideas of leisure and work.

> Happy leisure depends to a large extent on happy work, and when work is happy a number of problems connected with leisure today will be found to have disappeared, because there will be greater possibilities for self-realization through work, and consequently people occupied in work that is recognized as worth doing will improve in character and intelligence. The Commission hopes that any suggestion made in this Report will not ignore this standard as its ultimate ideal, but would at the same time point to ways in which leisure may be enlarged and made more satisfying in the world as we know it today.[29]

The Commission did not have space to elaborate exactly how it saw the difference between recreation and leisure, and in fact the distinction fades away as the report develops. It is admitted that they 'merge'.

The attention of the Commission then turned to assessing contrasted kinds of activity in free time. There had long been much unease in Christian circles about degrading types of leisure occupation, such as drinking and betting. For some campaigners this was not a self-righteous attempt to deprive the working man of pleasure or excitement, but the result of observing how the brewers and the betting organizations battened on the gullibility of the poor.[30] The outcome was not only the establishment of temperance societies, but also a desire to promote leisure activities of a more respectable kind. The efforts of Christian denominations went into the provision of two kinds of activities, educational and recreational. The COPEC Report did not include a lengthy discussion of the evils of drinking and gambling, where the abuses were agreed but the remedies contentious, though the resolutions of the Conference inevitably referred to them. Instead the members of the Commission tried to assess alternative free-time occupations, and in doing so revealed their images of a full human life.

The keynotes of their discussion were creativity and imagination, and the way to promote these ideals was seen to be mainly by education. Particular attention was given to drama, fiction and sport, each of which was considered positively. Drama was said to have 'tremendous spiritual importance'. 'Any good play is a religious play.' In particular, amateur drama came in for commendation because it gave scope for aesthetic as well as moral and mental training and was 'an almost ideal use of leisure in fellowship'.[31] Novel-reading had a positive value. Some such reading was a psychological necessity in the lives of most people, particularly those who lived in the country for whom – in the days when cinemas were few and television did not exist – novels were the one avenue to the world of imagination, romance and adventure.[32] It is interesting that the report, recognizing the place of 'phantasy' in human life, declared that it was more safely developed through the reading of fiction (for example, books of travel) than 'in the more self-conscious fictions of our unaided imagination'. That judgement possibly reflected post-Freudian concern with the less pleasant aspects of the human unconscious. It also belonged to an age when formal or informal censorship of published material was still largely accepted, and the darker side of 'imagination' represented by pornography, the cult of violence, and fascination with evil was less in evidence than today. As for sport and games, the report presented a balanced evaluation. Sportsmanship was seen as an asset to the nation, and even, surprisingly, 'akin to Christ-like character'. But games belonged essentially to childhood or youth, and in mature life were likely to 'militate against spiritual progress'. Exaggerated devotion to sport distracted from the great purpose of life. It could amount to 'sheer idolatry'.[33]

The report's approval hardly stretched as far as professional sport. Here the focus properly shifted from participation to spectatorship, since the professionals were obviously not at leisure. The Commission's verdict shows that even in the 1920s it seemed to some critics that professional sport, run purely as a spectacle and a money-making concern, could easily degenerate to resemble the Roman circus, 'as the history of the Football Association proves'. The writers had in mind the unsporting conduct of the players and 'the vast majority of their supporters', the encouragement of foul play, the barracking of opponents, and the savaging of referees. (We may note that racism had not yet come to join other abuses of commercialized sport.) It would be wrong, however, to isolate these critical remarks from the general attitude of approval which permeates the report. Though the love of money, they said, was the one form of idolatry which Jesus saw 'as a constant and immediate danger',[34] perhaps commercialism would shed its vulgarity and learn to follow the example of the Venetian fathers in supporting faith and civic beauty and encouraging the pursuit of scholarship.

The detailed findings of the report were inevitably conditioned by the social situation in which, and for which, they were written. What marks out the report as significant is the conviction that leisure was not merely a time of recuperation for the next bout of work. This conviction found further expression in the writings of individuals. In a notable collection of essays published in

1933 with the title *Christianity and the Crisis*, Dr Maude Royden contributed one which dealt with 'Labour and Leisure', from which two points of interest may be quoted. First, she makes a useful distinction between the leisure of two different kinds of worker, to whom she gives, for want of better terminology, the names 'artist' and 'mechanic'. These are people engaged respectively in creative and repetitive work. The 'artist' does not want less time for work; the 'mechanic' wants more leisure, to be creative. The second point of interest is her reference to a questionnaire on the use of leisure sent to various governments by the International Labour Office. Replies had been received by 1924, and although some governments showed, in her view, 'a rather languid interest', it was evident that the main development in some countries had been the increase in sports clubs and the increase in educational groups. In both cases leisure was given a purposive role: to improve health ('moral and physical hygiene'), and to educate to higher standards of taste and political awareness.[35]

Reckitt himself made a notable contribution to Christian thinking about leisure in his book, *Faith and Society*.[36] He noted the approaching 'universalization of leisure', and presented it as a proper part of human life, not merely a necessary interlude in a life devoted to work.

> The truth is that our conception of leisure is as vague and anachronistic as our conception of work, and equally unworthy. Leisure is not by nature a mere perquisite of economic privilege; still less is it to be identified with a condition of destitute idleness. Its social basis is abundance; its essence is spontaneity; its natural fruits freedom and joy; its discipline responsibility.

He then quoted a contemporary article by W.T. Symonds which declared that it was a necessary act of faith to accept as the norm that part of life in which a man is 'active in his own mode'. The curse of Adam, the writer said, had been worked out and the essential labour of men was to be 'turned inwards upon the inertia of the will'.

The darkening prospects of the late 1930s and the frantic activism of wartime did not encourage much further exploration of the idea of leisure in Christian circles, but by the end of the Second World War it was generally accepted in Christian thinking about society that leisure was not a luxury but a necessity, a proper element in the full human life. One example of this is to be found in an official report to the Church Assembly of the Church of England in 1956 which quoted 'a number of Christian social thinkers' as agreeing that 'the purpose of an economic system is to enable people to provide themselves with livelihood and leisure, not to make work or create new needs'.[37]

Two decades later the Methodist Conference adopted a statement on 'The Christian Use of Leisure' which affirmed that 'life involves a variety of elements which ... include mental and physical effort, play, personal relationships, self-expression, learning, rest and worship – all of which may be associated with work or leisure'.[38] The last clause is rather puzzling, but is presumably an acknowledgement that some people's work may even be to provide rest or worship for others. There had always been an element in Methodism which valued 'self-improvement' in the time free from work and social duties. Although this found justification partly in its results, either in better career prospects or better resources for preaching, it commended itself to the serious-minded for its own sake as a proper use of leisure.[39] The main point, however, is that in an age of greater prosperity for the majority of the population the severities and self-discipline of the Non-conformist tradition gave way to a more comprehensive view of human life under the benevolent eye of the Creator.

The COPEC Report was written at a time when the Christian churches in England were still significant contributors to leisure provision. Since the 1930s the initiatives of the churches in the field of leisure have been progressively superseded in different ways. The need to raise educational standards in an advanced industrial society has driven successive governments to enlarge the opportunities for education; and commercial interest in the profits of large-scale leisure provision has taken many leisure activities out of the hands of voluntary agencies. The general effect of these changes on Christian congregations has been mainly negative. Optimists make a point of welcoming the take-over of church-based initiatives by secular society. But the loss of two kinds of outward-looking activities, education and the provision of leisure, has tended to encourage a more introverted attitude in Christian congregations; and the domination of leisure by secular agencies has tended to remove the sort of moral control which could previously be put in place by the authority of the congregation.

These changes have taken place by gradual stages and without any deliberate declarations of policy. Consequently there has been little attempt to assess the emergent leisure society from a Christian point of view, or even to establish a Christian basis for criticism. Here as elsewhere in questions of social policy any valid criticism must depend upon a general view of God's will for human communities. The COPEC report silently witnesses to the lack of obviously relevant material in the Bible, where the context is normally that of small-scale communities which bear little similarity to modern urban life. The attempt of Leland Ryken to show that 'The Bible provides both a general rationale for leisure and guide-lines for how to pursue leisure' depends upon a doubtful hermeneutical method, which extracts a composite meaning from a varied collection of texts, without regard to their social contexts, in order to re-insert that meaning into alien contexts.[40] A subjective element is always present in choosing a point of comparison between biblical texts and modern situations. The problems of standardization, exploitation and passive consumerism criticized by sociological commentators in modern societies have little in common with the problems of pre-industrial societies in Palestine.

Among these three problems affecting modern leisure, it is tempting to choose for particular application of the biblical evidence the problem of exploitation, since it comes nearest to the kind of corruption the prophets attack. If the modern organization of leisure exploits vulnerable groups – the poor lured into gambling, the young enticed to drink and drugs, children induced to compete with each other in a commercial market – we may call to mind the responses of the prophets, who denounced those who exploit the poor, the needy and the simple-minded.[41] A responsible attitude to the use of increasing leisure opportunities must include awareness of the context of exploitation in which they are frequently set. As for standardization and passive consumerism, it may not be easy to find texts to strengthen our concern about their possible effects. We can say, however, that the kind of society which the prophets envisage and which the writers of the New Testament take for granted is characterized by face-to-face contact. Prophet and priest and king speak to each other, and members of the common people have access to all of them. When crowds gather and the individual loses human identity, then dangers arise. Israel becomes like sheep, led astray or neglected by its shepherds. In the Gospels crowds are almost always a danger and often actively evil. They cheer Jesus for the wrong reasons when he enters Jerusalem, and soon call for his crucifixion. The worshippers of Artemis at Ephesus riot and thirst for blood, encouraged by business leaders, who show that combination of commercial self-interest and outward religiosity which frequently reappears in human history: 'There is a danger not only that this trade of ours may come into disrepute but also that the temple of the great goddess Artemis will be scorned'.[42]

These indications from the Bible do not by themselves determine a Christian response to the emergence of a kind of society in which leisure has become universal and organized; but they stand as a warning against an uncritical acceptance of all kinds of leisure as bestowing a new freedom on those groups which were once condemned to endless labour. We should not ignore the ground-swell of anxiety in the churches for a century and more about the way in which new-found opportunities for leisure among working people might be misused. It would be easy to write this off as evidence of unwanted paternalism or the desire to extend social control from the workplace to the home. No doubt those motives were often at work. But that is not the whole truth of the matter. For one thing, that concern about the working population only carried further the earlier concern of Christian writers who attacked the misuse of leisure by the wealthy. More positively, those who had enjoyed the pleasures and rewards of literature and art and the study of nature were not justly to be criticized if they believed such things should be shared as widely as possible. Perhaps they were enclosed within the limits of their own particular culture and could not appreciate forms of enjoyment which they had never experienced. Certainly the leisure classes themselves often spent a lot of time doing things which had no intrinsic value, except that they provided outlets for surplus energy or opportunities for enjoyable social intercourse. Even so, at its best the desire to share cultural experiences is not to be despised. What was seldom recognized was the difficulty of conveying a set of values across class barriers. Yet it is surprising how often the difficulty was overcome. The success of university extension courses and the vigour of the Workers Educational

Association (WEA), both of them paternalistic in structure, witness to the same appetite for a richer kind of life as the cult of self-improvement in eighteenth-century Methodism.

The relationship between social class and leisure activities is extremely complicated, because it depends upon so many variables. It is affected by time and place, by education, by the structures of employment, by conservatism in social habits, by the rate of change in media of communication, and not least by differences of temperament between individuals. The very existence of distinct social classes is open to question. Nobody seems to know where the boundaries are. Though there is still some truth in Thorstein Veblen's description of conspicuous consumption, it is half a century since J.K. Galbraith declared that the leisure class had disappeared in the United States.[43] It should not be assumed that there are actual entities corresponding to the terms working class and middle class. Each term embraces many varieties of human behaviour, and those include varieties of leisure-time preferences. These may derive from political or religious or educational interests which cut across the boundaries of social class or status at work. That is one reason why it is not satisfactory simply to treat work and leisure as correlatives.

If a Christian critique of different leisure occupations is to be offered, one great difficulty consists in trying to distinguish judgements originating simply from the critic's own cultural background from other judgements which can claim a more objective basis. Separating the rough from the respectable is probably an example of the first kind; separating the cruel from the humane is surely an example of the second. In any age there are examples of social conformity imposed on a weaker by a stronger class or group. But it is not always clear which kind of judgement is at work in a critical response, whether it simply reflects a cultural preference or a principled opposition to what is degrading. A few examples will illustrate some aspects of the difficulty.

In feudal society the common people were excluded from hunting forests. Henry VIII made bowling unlawful for ordinary people, not just on Sunday, but at any time.[44] The leisure industry of Bath, encouraged by the increase in wealth in the national economy, witnessed the gradual refinement of amusements in line with the wishes of the wealthy. Balls and plays and card-playing took the place of such gross diversions as 'jugglers, tumblers, bull-baiting, cock-fighting, grinning through a horse-collar, and swallowing burning-hot frumenty'.[45] Victorian respectability tended to substitute decorous singing round the piano for the joys of the music-hall. In a longer perspective, social pressures have tended to reduce levels of bodily violence regarded as acceptable.[46] There can be no single verdict on all these changes. Of this list, probably only bull-baiting and cock-fighting are likely to meet with universal condemnation by Christians in our present Western society – and not even those in some countries. Nor is it always clear whether the restriction or oppression affected the whole of what we regard as a class today. Not all working people wanted to hunt or play bowls or watch others grinning through a horse-collar or go to the music-hall. Probably those who did came from a variety of class backgrounds. There is a comparable mixture of social backgrounds in those who take part in football hooliganism today.[47]

If it were simply a matter of class preference, Christian belief would be neutral in judgement. Variety in leisure activity is a welcome reflection of the variety of human nature. This is a perception going back as early as Aristotle. But social class can also have a positive role, as even T.S. Eliot recognized. 'Class itself possesses a function, that of maintaining that part of the total culture which pertains to that class.' 'A people should be neither too united nor too divided, if its culture is to flourish.'[48] This does not preclude cross-fertilization between the cultures, and so the leisure habits, of different classes. The self-improving early Methodists and the earnest members of WEA classes were a self-conscious minority among their fellow-workers whose notions of leisure were often far more limited. They had to stand against the pressures of group conformity. And that points us to the problem of the relationship between the individual and the group.

The conduct of human beings in the mass has always had potentialities for good and evil. Mass leisure is just one example of this ambivalence, and is to be seen and assessed against a wider background. The New Testament witnesses to the Pentecostal experience in which the Holy Spirit brings individuals into a deep sense of unity which enriches their lives.[49] But the fellowship of the spirit stands in contrast to 'the world' (in Johannine terminology),[50] which is human society organized apart from God. There is a dark side of the sense of community. It has forced itself on our attention at the highest level with shocking force in recent decades. Those whose hopes were formed in the aftermath of the Second World War looked for something like a growing together of nations in mutual respect. The horrific face of nationalism, seen in the form of Nazism, seemed to have frightened humanity into awareness of the unity of the human race. Christians believed ever more strongly that in Christ there is no longer Jew or Greek, slave or free, male or female.[51] The World Council of Churches was seen by many as a step along the road to a tolerant unity of Christians, which would be the first-fruits of a new world order. By the end of the twentieth century it was obvious that there was no such easy road to utopia. Not only did nationalism revive, but nations themselves were challenged by the assertion of lesser loyalties based on real or imagined historic identities. If denied the outlet of loyalty to a greater cause which patriotism afforded in times of international conflict, men and women (but chiefly men) looked to lose themselves during their leisure time in the role of 'fans'. This could be an uplifting experience; but it could equally well lead to uncontrolled violence. Perhaps the only thing to be learnt from this, in our present context, is that all human beings feel the need to identify themselves with some recognisable group which enhances their sense of identity. It is part of our humanity. Moreover in the complex societies of industrialized nations the individual can find fulfilment at different moments in different groups. For Christians, the only questions of any significance are how individuals relate to each other within a particular group and how the group relates to those outside it.

If the critic is called to make any judgement on particular forms of leisure within its social setting, that judgement will probably depend upon the distinction drawn, for example, by the seventeenth-century writers quoted above, and recognized in the COPEC Report, between leisure as a series of occasional breaks in a life of work, and leisure as a main component in a life within which work is not a significant element, either in retirement or when it is no longer necessary to earn a living. In the one case triviality is to a large extent excusable and commercial organization seems to be merely a convenience. But it is doubtful whether the same excuses are valid within extended leisure.

Even in assessing occasional breaks there may be hesitations. The cult of competitiveness gives leisure the character of training for further conflict which is alien to the inner meaning of leisure itself. And it is irresponsible to keep out of mind the framework within which the individual enjoys freedom of choice – a framework which includes structures of employment for those who provide the facilities necessary for each particular leisure activity or even its equipment. For instance, it is proper to ask what hours of work are demanded in the commercial provision of leisure and at what level of pay. Such questions become more insistent when the setting is seen as global. It becomes necessary to ask how the footballs for the World Cup are made, or what is the social cost of providing 'recreational drugs'. The answers are not always simple to get. The 400 new golf courses constructed in Britain between 1992 and 1996 at first evoke critical comments about the loss of the traditional agricultural landscape or the imposition of urban middle-class values on rural multi-class society. But there is a longer perspective in which that development is seen to be related to a transformation of the landscape through the transformation of agriculture to meet new global competition. It can even be argued that golf courses can be richer in wildlife than the farmland they replace.[52]

The other case, of leisure as a main component of life, is a different matter. Here leisure is unrelated to work, and stands alone as a separate section of the individual's life. Its opportunities and possibilities require more careful thought. The sociological approach to leisure situates what is individual firmly in a corporate context. This is not foreign to the biblical tradition. The tensions evident in the Old Testament between individual and corporate responsibility inevitably take a new form in mass society, but the issue is already addressed, if not resolved, there. It is common to contrast the earlier acceptance of communal guilt with the later stress on the separate responsibility of the individual in Israel. The Ten Commandments continued to be regarded as authoritative in spite of references to penalties which threaten 'the third and fourth generation.'[53] That was strictly in contradiction to the message of the seventh century prophets, who stressed individual responsibility.[54] The position of the individual at leisure may be one of individual innocence in a context of corporate guilt. There is no way to escape this conflict; it is the universal condition of human society.

At its deepest level it is expressed in the story of the cross of Christ: the innocent bearer of the sin of the world. To most people this will seem an absurd thing to say about so trivial a matter as leisure. But it is only to reapply the reported saying of Jesus, that everyone will be judged by his or her lightest word.[55] If for idle words, then also for actions in idleness. The theology of the cross, however, is also a theology of forgiveness. God in Christ bears the sin of humanity, which is thereby released back into the enjoyment of the goodness of the created world, not to waste or exploit it, but to treasure it as a common possession. This perception of the shared bounty of God was a repeated theme of Thomas Traherne: 'Yet further, you never enjoy the world aright, till you so love the beauty of enjoying it, that you are covetous and earnest to persuade others to enjoy it.'[56] Leisure can be interpreted as the union of self-love with the perception of the gifts of creation which are equally owned by others and therefore the ground of mutual love.

# NOTES

1. Hans Urs von Balthasar, *The Glory of the Lord Vol. III – Studies in Theological Style: Lay Styles* (Edinburgh 1986), 213.
2. Michael R. Marrus (ed.), *The Emergence of Leisure* (NY. 1974), 7.
3. Thorstein Veblen, *The Theory of the Leisure Class: An Economic Study of Institutions* (NY 1970 [1899]), 33.
4. Ibid. 46.
5. Ibid. 47.
6. See Percy C. Rusden, *History and Antiquities of Chipping Campden* (London 1911). Dover's purpose is lauded in an epigram of Ben Jonson: 'I can tell thee Dover how thy games / Renew the glories of our blessed Jeames / ....How they advance true love and neighbourhood / And doe both Church and Commonwealth the good ...'.
7. *Religion and Rural Society: South Lindsey 1826-75* (Oxford 1976), 23ff.
8. See J.P. Diggins, *Thorstein Veblen* (Princeton, NJ 1999), xxvii.
9. Ibid. 227.
10. William Law, *A Serious Call to a Devout and Holy Life* (London 1899) ch. 5, 68ff.
11. Tom Winnifrith and Cyril Barrett (eds), *The Philosophy of Leisure* (Basingstoke 1989).
12. Nicole Samuel (ed.), *Women, Leisure and the Family in Contemporary Society* (Wallingford 1996), 157.
13. Ferdynand Zweig, *Women's Life and Labour* (London 1952), esp. ch. 21: 'Hobbies and pleasures'.
14. See Eileen Green and Sandra Hebron, 'Leisure and Male Partners' in Erica Wimbush and Margaret Talbot (eds), *Relative Freedoms – Women and Leisure* (Milton Keynes 1988), 42
15. Jennifer Mason, '"No Peace for the Wicked": Older Married Women and Leisure', in Wimbush and Talbot (eds), *Relative Freedoms*
16. Kathryn Allen Rabuzzi, *The Sacred and the Feminine: Towards a Theology of Housework*, quoted in Keith Thomas (ed.), *The Oxford Book of Work* (Oxford 1999), 283.
17. Tessa Kay, 'Women's leisure and the family in contemporary Britain', in Nicole Samuel (ed.), *Women, Leisure and the Family* , 155.
18. José Harris, *Private Lives, Public Spirit: A Social History of Britain 1870–1914* (Oxford 1993), 138–9.
19. E.g. by Edward Norman, *Church and Society in England 1770–1970* (Oxford 1976).
20. See e.g. for Manchester, Graham Neville, *Radical Churchman* (Oxford 1998), 152–8.
21. M. Reckitt, *Faith and Society* (London 1932), 96.
22. William Temple, *Life of Bishop Percival* (London 1921), 295.
23. Cyril E. Hudson and Maurice Reckitt, *The Church and the World*, III (1940), 155.
24. M. Reckitt, *Faith and Society*, 96–7.

25. See *Malvern 1941: The Life of the Church and the Order of Society* (London 1941), 222. 'The Conference was primarily theological'.
26. See John Wesley Parfitt. 'COPEC: An Interdenominational Movement of Christian Social Thought and Action in Early Twentieth Century Britain' (unpublished PhD thesis, Coventry University, 2000), 153.
27. COPEC Proceedings (1924), 282.
28. COPEC, *Commission Reports, vol. V – Leisure*, 8.
29. Ibid. 16.
30. See e.g. Neville, *Radical Churchman*, ch. 7.
31. COPEC, *Commission Reports, vol.V*, 55–6.
32. Ibid. 29.
33. Ibid. 36–7.
34. Ibid. 78.
35. Percy Dearmer (ed.), *Christianity and the Crisis* (London 1933), 413–27.
36. Reckitt, *Faith and Society*, 359–73.
37. Church Assembly (Social and Industrial Council) *The National Church and the Social Order* (London 1956), 120.
38. 'A Methodist Statement on The Christian Use of Leisure, 1974' in Methodist Church, *Statements on Social Responsibility 1946–1995* (London 1995).
39. For a small example, see Charles Thomas, *Methodism and Self-Improvement in Nineteenth-Century Cornwall*, Cornish Methodist Historical Association, no.9 (Redruth 1965).
40. Leland Ryken, *Work and Leisure in Christian Perspective* (Leicester 1989), esp. 194–204, with references to Leviticus, Psalms, Nehemiah, Esther, Genesis, Hebrews, John, Luke, Proverbs, Psalms again, Zechariah, Jeremiah, Galatians, Ecclesiastes and Amos, in that order.
41. E.g. Amos 4.1.
42. Acts 19.27.
43. J.K. Galbraith, *The Affluent Society* (Harmondsworth1962), 173.
44. W.B. Whitaker, *Sunday in Tudor and Stuart Times* (London 1938), 76.
45. David Selwyn, *Jane Austen and Leisure* (London 1999), 228.
46. L. Haywood (*et al.*), *Understanding Leisure*, 2nd edn (Cheltenham 1995), quoting N. Elias.
47. For a comment, see Rowan Williams, *Lost Icons* (Edinburgh and NY 2000), 62.
48. T.S. Eliot, *Notes towards the Definition of Culture* (London 1948), 35, 50.
49. Acts 4.32.
50. John 14.17; 15.18; 17.14; 1 John 4.5; 5.19.
51. Galatians 3.28.
52. See Bryn Green, 'The Farmed Landscape: The Ecology and Conservation of Diversity', in Jennifer Jenkins (ed.), *Remaking the Landscape* (London 2002), 183–210.
53. Exodus 20.5.
54. Jeremiah 31.29–30; Ezekiel 18.1–4.
55. Matthew 12.36.
56. Thomas Traherne, *Centuries of Meditations*, ed. Bertram Dobell (London 1948), I.29.

# 5

# Reality, Fantasy, Imagination

*Religions point to another kind of reality beyond appearances, hidden, waiting to be acknowledged. There are symbols which guide us to it, such as creativeness and love; but the human spirit is in danger of being dominated by technology, even in leisure. The cult of virtual reality also endangers personal relationships which are fundamental to religion. Leisure allows the apprehension of a reality given by the Creator. This challenges all denials that there is anything there to be revealed and the fascination of the unreal universe of the computer which brings fantasy into the home. In leisure the abundant life given by Christ includes the world of our own imagination as well as the treasure-chest of experiences made possible by the creativity of other people.*

If we accept the division of human life, as suggested above, into the three areas of work, duty and leisure, we can recognize that there is a wealth of experience which belongs distinctively to the third area, that of leisure. This kind of experience is indicated by our use of words such as fantasy and imagination. It is true that they may often have a role in work and social intercourse, but only as means, not ends – to earn a living or create relationships, especially with children. The question of children's fantasy and adult attitudes to it is not here under consideration. The importance of the early period of 'latency' in human development and the way in which it is currently threatened, has been well introduced by Dr Rowan Williams.[1] But it is not the same as adult leisure, where fantasy and imagination may be ends in themselves rather than ways of preparing for the demands of later life. For the adult at leisure the constraints imposed by a work ethic or the demands of conscience are no longer in control. Leisure offers situations in which a human being is free to explore, in thought or word or action, a world exempt, at least in part, from what are regarded as the hard realities of daily life, and to do so without any ulterior purpose. The universal experience of dreaming shows that this release from ordinary realities is part of the essence of human nature. As such, it cannot be a matter of indifference to any theology which takes seriously the whole range of human capabilities.

Here it is important to allow for the distinction, recognized by the COPEC Commission, between recreation and leisure, the short-term winding-down from work or social duties and the longer-term development of an alternative style of life. For although trivial or even ridiculous elements of make-believe may be acceptable in the one, they are more difficult to justify in the other. In an individual life there may be a creeping extension of free time as recreation into the 'year out', the sabbatical, the gap between different jobs, or the period of retirement prolonged from an initial expectation of a year or two to a settled condition of life for fifteen or twenty years. In such cases what was an acceptable triviality may become demeaning or contemptible; in theological terms, soul-destroying. The quest for a theology of leisure requires an understanding of prolonged free time which matches the rich potential of human nature. That theology may, but need not, feed back into short-term relaxation. It will at least create a check-point to prevent triviality becoming the characteristic life-style of the leisured life.

One way of beginning the theological quest is to consider what is meant by 'reality'. It is a term which seems to pass judgement on triviality, and even stands over against fantasy and imagination. There is, however, a problem in determining what we mean by 'reality'. It is not, strictly speaking, an idea familiar to the biblical writers; it belongs in the tradition of Hellenic philosophical thought, with its contrast of appearance and reality. But it is true of all kinds of religion that they tell their adherents that things are not as they seem; that there is another reality which they must find within or apart from the everyday reality they share with non-believers. In the Jewish-Christian tradition that other reality is sometimes called the age to come; sometimes that age is conceived as coexisting with the present age. Reality, like eternal life, is either awaiting or actually present. Eschatology is either futurist or realized

It is only this conviction of another reality which makes sense of some of the language of the New Testament. Jesus says, 'I am the resurrection' – not 'I shall be the resurrection'. Paul says, 'You are dead and your life is hid with Christ in God'.[2] The ultimate reality, then, is not seen or understood by everyone, but it is understood and shared by the whole community of faith. It is no mere individual's fantasy. This reality can be indicated in biblical language in various ways. One is the contrast between that which is temporary and that which is permanent. This is to some extent comparable to the contrasting Hellenic categories of phenomenal and real. It is given classic expression in the prophecies of Isaiah and in the Psalms.[3] God is the enduring reality. The whole universe, which will pass away, only partakes of reality because God has willed it to be.

The apocalyptic hope of the establishment of new heavens and a new earth continues the theme of the transience, and therefore unreality, of everything apart from God, who can withdraw his guarantee from the present universe and provide another to replace it.[4] But within the transient world which God has created, there are, nevertheless, some things which 'cannot be shaken' because it is God's will to sustain them.[5] In the Fourth Gospel in the New Testament this enduring reality is claimed to be present in the incarnate Christ, who existed before Abraham, and in whom grace and truth reside.[6] Those who are Christ's are given a share in his reality, because they belong to him as he belongs to God.[7] This participation in reality, however, is not confined to any separate part of human existence, as though it operated in moments of conscious self-devotion to Christ. It is not a separate 'religious' dimension found in a section of life. Belief in the incarnation of reality in Christ implies that reality was as truly present in his moments of relaxation as in his times of conscious co-operation with the divine will. Reality was not absent when Jesus slept in the boat.[8] So the believer's participation in reality persists in leisure as well as in worship or work or social duties.

This theological understanding of ultimate reality as that which participates in God through the incarnate Christ is not, however, what we usually have in mind when we contrast reality and fantasy even in a theological context. If it has been God's will to sustain humanity through all its history and in all its manifold social forms, then all human life participates to some degree in the reality of the one who sustains it. In our usual discourse, reality is simply that which we share with others, as opposed to that which we cannot share, our dreams and fantasies. Reality is a social experience, and ideally an experience common to all human beings. But because human experience is so varied, people experience different realities according to the groups and communities to which from time to time they relate. In a multi-cultural society someone may think that other people live in a quite different world and experience a different reality. In sociological terms, then, reality is a social construct; or rather, realities are socially constructed, and we may at different times move from one to another. Leisure has been described as offering its participants lesser realities, for example in the experience of drama or sport where they accept temporarily a kind of reality which they know to be artificial. It is not difficult deliberately to adopt some of these conventions, and we can usually return without difficulty to everyday reality. Most of the time we accept as reality the wide-awake, everyday life we share with most people most of the time.[9] This is the reality of work and duty.

Reality, in all its meanings, is something other than appearance. There is a reality hidden, taken for granted, in all kinds of social contexts, in leisure as much as in other areas of human experience. But while accepting lesser realities, that is, the assumptions underlying different kinds of experience, the Christian believer in moments of recollection holds on to the reality of his or her status as a citizen of heaven[10] while participating in these other kinds of experience. Many, if not all, of these lesser realities may be ways of access to the ultimate reality, and Christian writers, when they discuss reality, find it hard to resist the tendency to make great claims for the particular aspect of human life which has captured their closest attention. There is something of this in Aquinas's elevation of the contemplative life above the active life. Again, when Helmut Thielicke introduces his great work on *Theological Ethics*, he claims that ethical enquiry is where we interpret reality.[11] In another vein, Richard Harries looks to some kinds of art as the key to reality. He quotes Graham Howes as saying, 'The icon is a symbol which so participates in the reality which it symbolizes that it is itself worthy of reverence. It is an agent of the real presence.'[12] These varied opinions indicate simply that there are different ways of access to reality for different people. In the context of leisure, contemplation or the response to icons are relevant ways, rather than the way of ethical enquiry.

Against these claims of contact with reality in leisure, we may set the common perception that leisure is just as properly occupied with fantasy as with reality. The question which of the two should predominate in leisure is not an important question to ask if we are thinking of leisure simply as an intermission in work. If it means only a time of relief or refreshment, perhaps fantasy is more useful than reality for relaxing concentration from what are experienced as the hard realities of work. But the case may be different for those who are not committed to work as it is usually understood, and in particular those who are; by choice or chance, retired. If leisure stretches out for a decade or more, perhaps there may be a fundamental choice between reality and fantasy as the dominant element in life. It is at least clear that the scriptures of Old and New Testament set up a number of contrasts between what is worthwhile and what is untrustworthy, and it is possible to take these as prompts for theological enquiry.

One of the concepts that is used in order to alert the servant of God is that of 'vanity'. It occurs in both Old and New Testament: with the Hebrew word *hebel* and with the Greek ματαιοτης. Reality is the opposite of vanity. The most memorable use of *hebel* is in the book of Ecclesiastes, where it occurs over thirty times. 'Vanity of vanities, all is vanity' is like a refrain running through the book. It is found also a number of times in the book of Job, the Psalms and the book of Proverbs. The Greek word ματαιοτης, which is sometimes translated 'vanity', occurs in the New Testament in Romans (8.20), Ephesians (4.17) and 2 Peter (2.18). It cannot be said that these passages give anything like a single or clear definition of what is being held up to criticism. The problem with Ecclesiastes is that 'vanity', which we quite expect to be the label put on 'the laughter of fools' (7.6), is applied at different points in the book to almost every aspect of human life: pleasure and enjoyment, wealth, work, even youth and the dawn of life (11.10). We cannot assume that the word has exactly the same meaning when applied to very different areas of life.[13] But it seems that the author regards the various aspects of human life as vanity, not in being evil but in being transitory, evanescent, unsubstantial, and to that extent worthless. The basic significance of *hebel* is vapour or breath; its metaphorical use indicates something which can be easily blown away, like thistledown. There is an intriguing comparison with another word for breath or wind (*ruach*), which is coupled with *hebel* in the phrase 'all is vanity and a chasing after wind' (1.14). This word, unlike *hebel*, can be used by other biblical writers to describe the action of God which gives new life to what is dead (notably in Ezekiel 37.5). This contrast suggests the idea that reality is a gift of God which, for human beings, is necessary to release them from inert pointlessness. But this is not an idea to be found in Ecclesiastes. There the spirit (*ruach*) returns to God who gave it (12.7). The use of ματαιοτης in Ephesians 4.17–18 is more straightforward, because it is applied to those who are alienated from the life of God and have abandoned themselves to impurity.

But in Romans 8.19–23 Paul writes of the whole creation as subjected to ματαιοτης, and that usage comes nearer to the thought of Ecclesiastes.

This brief consideration of the concept of 'vanity' in the Old and New Testament appears to contribute little to the Christian understanding of reality. But there are kinds of Christian theology which come very close to this train of thought. We have already noted something like it in the Jansenist pietism of Pascal, and we see it more clearly in the Calvinism of John Bunyan. In *The Pilgrim's Progress* Christian and Faithful come to the city called Vanity with its fair set up five thousand years before by Beelzebub, Apollyon and Legion, where all sorts of vanity are sold. Bunyan lists these vanities as 'houses, lands, trades, places, honours, preferments, titles, countries, kingdoms, lusts, pleasures; and delights of all sorts, as harlots, wives, husbands, children, masters, servants, lives, blood, bodies, souls, silver, gold, pearls, precious stones, and what not'. He goes on to mention other things on display which are obviously wrong – cheating, murder, adultery, and so on – but his first list is a mixture of things undeniably evil and things which may be good. It is an exposition of the text, 'Vanity of vanities, all is vanity'. Nothing on offer is of interest to the pilgrims. When they are asked, 'What will ye buy?', they answer, 'We buy the truth', quoting Proverbs 23.23. In other words, truth, or reality, stands in contrast to all ordinary human activity, whether good or bad. Taken to its logical conclusion, this line of thought condemns as worthless all forms of leisure, since nothing but the truth should occupy the thoughts of those on the pilgrim road.

This perception may be appropriate for a prisoner in Bedford gaol, but for everyday purposes there are lesser realities at hand. If vanity is set aside, is it not still possible to find a role for fantasy in human life without the loss of self which may follow total surrender to it? And it is in leisure that fantasy seems most acceptable. Can it be subjected to theological evaluation in spite of the fact that the word, and indeed the idea, is not characteristic of biblical language and thought? Perhaps the universal experience of dreams may be taken as a starting-point for scrutinizing it. For if reality consists partly in being something which we can experience along with other people, then dreams are not part of it. We know that when we wake we may try to tell someone else what we have been dreaming, but at the same time we know that the experience cannot be communicated. It is essentially private, and it is specially elusive because we cannot ourselves entirely understand it. Dreams present an individual with a vivid experience, but they belong to fantasy rather than reality.

If we turn to the Bible, we find that many of its writers value dreams and visions. They are seen as moments of contact with God, and they have a proper place in the prophetic ministry. They may embody a particular message for the prophet to give, or they may direct the dreamer to action according to God's will, and this tradition reappears in the New Testament.[14] But because of the private nature of the original experience, initially it belongs to fantasy, not reality, whatever use the prophet or dreamer may subsequently make of it. The prophet's interpretation of an essentially incommunicable experience could not always claim validity. Its authentication presented an important problem in Old Testament Judaism, to which a variety of answers had been given. There was false prophecy (1 Kings 22.22), and so every prophecy must be tested. Prophecies might be authenticated by orthodoxy (Deut. 13.1–15), or by subsequent fulfilment (Deut. 18.22, Jeremiah 28.9, 17), or by their moral content (Jeremiah 23.14). In the same way, the validity of dreams was to be scrutinized (Deut. 13.1–5). The extended record of a similar kind of experience in the New Testament is the Apocalypse or Revelation of St John the Divine. It shares with our own dreams the characteristic of being only partly intelligible. We may see in it meanings, rather than a meaning. We can only guess how far it had a single meaning even for its author. Because it has this quality of 'fantasy', there are two ways of treating it which are mistaken. One is to claim one's own interpretation of it as the only possible interpretation. The other is to write it off as the misbegotten product of Jewish apocalyptic. It should be understood as offering images and symbols hard to interpret, but evoking profound human responses. It is to be tested by other criteria than its vividness or its psychological appeal: orthodoxy or fulfilment or moral content. In much the same way, our own dreams and visions should neither be ignored nor overvalued, but assessed by their effects on personal life. In leisure they are neither good nor bad, but open to evaluation by their effects. This awareness of the ambivalence of dreams and visions runs through the history of religion from the contest of rival prophets before King Jehoshaphat at Ramoth-gilead (1 Kings 22) to the time when John Wesley still believed in witchcraft, and even to our contemporary experience of serial murderers who have taken their visions for reality and turned their free time into self-bondage.

To sum up so far, both the Bible and everyday life present us with many layers of experience. The deepest level is participation in the ultimate reality of God through Christ. There are social experiences which offer realities shared with others. There are individual experiences, such as those of dreaming, which lack a social frame of reference and cannot claim the status of reality, however vivid they may be. All these levels of experience form part of the nature of human life. It seems self-evident that prolonged leisure should not be surrendered entirely to fantasy; that some priority should be preserved for the structure of reality which religion presents. But since human nature is given to fantasy, it deserves careful evaluation.

The case in favour of fantasy can be traced back to the romantics, such as Schiller. They believed that it was part of the freedom of the artist which was to be exercised seriously. But suppose that such freedom was detached from the notion of seriousness, of responsibility. That is, for many writers and artists, the actual situation today. The realms of fantasy beckon, to be explored without concern for any possible effects on those who read or see. An even worse case would be if the minority who control the media used unreality to keep those whom they exploit in contented subjection, organizing their leisure to distract attention from the worthlessness of their real lives. Seventy years ago Aldous Huxley portrayed this dehumanization in *Brave New World*, with its soma and its 'feelies' and its Malthusian belts. The attractions of drugs and virtual reality and the trivialization of sexual experience which he presented have ceased being fiction and have become part of ordinary life for many people in Western society. But whereas Huxley expected his readers to be appalled by the possibilities he imagined, as yet unrealized, the argument is now wide open. Indeed the 'absurd' can be presented as the proper language in which to represent human experience of the world, since the world itself, without God, has no meaning or rationale. For example, Martin Esslin in *The Theatre of the Absurd* claimed that the watershed between the traditional and the modern is the point at which the dominance of objective reality yields to subjective reality (or, as we might name it, fantasy). For him and others of his way of thinking, inner states of consciousness are no less 'true' than outward reality. What had previously been given the status of objective reality is reckoned to be only a part, and a relatively unimportant part, of the 'real' world.[15] The beginning of this shift may be traced to the work of Freud and his associates who attributed a higher content of reality to the unconscious than to conscious utterance. That case did not go unanswered. There was always an ambiguity in the process of analysis, because it depended upon bringing the rational thought of the analyst to bear upon regions of the mind where rationality did not hold sway.[16] Moreover the arguments of those who revelled in 'the absurd' led logically to a kind of solipsism, with its corollary of the impossibility of love and indeed of any valued human relationships.

In relation to fantasy we must recall the distinction between short-term recreational leisure and the leisure of those who have been released from (or deprived of) work. The Christian is free to think that reality need not, perhaps should not, dominate moments of relaxation. St John and the tame partridge are emblematic; and even Richard Baxter admitted that 'lawful sports exhilarate by a fantasie'. But he was insistent that there must be limits to the proportion of a lifetime which may be devoted to fantasy. The basic reason for mistrusting fantasy is that it is normally the product of some form of frustration. 'Without lies, humanity would perish of despair or boredom'.[17] So it may be a necessary compensation; but that is no justification for the frustration that has caused it.

The history of fantasy might well be traced through recorded time. To go back no further than the last century, it is obvious that since the 1930s or even earlier the cinema offered a fantasy life in compensation for the physical and emotional poverty of mass society. The brutalities of real life in wartime added force to the need for fantasy, and in recent decades the electronic revolution has enriched fantasy with astonishing realism. The result is 'a standardized fantasy life' to be experienced passively.[18] The computer has brought fantasy into the home, emphasizing its separation, not only from the world of work, but even of any actual society.

A Christian assessment of this process must recognize good and bad present in it, perhaps in equal measure. Criticism of fantasy takes a number of different forms in addition to the general unease of the sociologist at the standardization and triviality of mass leisure provision. The encouragement of fantasy, it has been said, turns actors into spectators.[19] Perhaps that verdict is a variant of the morality of St James's Epistle: be doers of the word and not hearers only.[20] Life is real, life is earnest. Fantasy incapacitates people for the discovery of satisfaction in active life. Or again, in the words of Iris Murdoch: 'The chief enemy of excellence in morality (and also in art) is personal fantasy: the tissue of self-aggrandizing and consoling wishes and dreams which prevent one from seeing what there is outside one.'[21]

Then there is the revulsion people feel at the actual content of some fantasy games, in the 'online' world which allows deception, and insulates the participants from the consequences of their choices. In one example 'players spend many months developing their vampire characters and creatively participating in plots of assassination, clan war, kidnapping, and romance'.[22] It is, no doubt, easy to find bad examples like this. But there is another side to the argument. The media can do more than provide an escape through fantasy; they can increase the range of human experience.[23] That was recognized in the COPEC report already quoted. There are different ways of responding to fantasy. An interesting example of the positive use of fantasy was provided by Paul Tillich's 'autobiographical sketch' *On the Boundary*, where he described how his difficulties in coming to terms with reality led to a life of fantasy between the ages of fourteen and seventeen. Imaginary worlds seemed truer than the world outside. In his case the life of fantasy was transformed into the working of the philosophical imagination. Evidently the use to which fantasy is put depends on individual personal factors.

'Virtual reality' is a particular kind of fantasy, not a kind of reality, although it can be shared with other people, at least to some extent. It is a vivid form of fiction. Like all forms of fiction, it originates in human minds and is offered to other people to experience. The ways in which different people react to it will be different. The experience of fear or horror, for example, may give one person an enjoyable *frisson* but induce in another a psychological trauma. In this there lies the potential for destructive psychological effect. It is a particular instance of the increasing dominance of technology over large areas of human experience which leads to the loss of reality.

A contrary case has been argued by Margaret Morse in her book *Virtualities*. She claims that all realities are socially constructed and therefore fictional, and that 'virtuality' is an aspect of that fictionality supported by the television and computer.[24] To those who argue that the status of 'paramount reality' (in Berger and Luckmann's sense) should be given to experiences in which we engage in encounters of the 'I–Thou' kind, Morse does not hesitate to say that the 'Thou' could be the computer. This argument is not convincing, because essential features of personal relationships are the freedom, unpredictability and responsibility of the other person involved in the relationship, and these cannot be guaranteed or simulated in the kind of contacts we are considering. It is notable that another writer, Steven Poole, who is at home in the world of so-called virtualities, recognizes the limits of interaction in cyberspace. He discusses 'the inner life of video-games', and shows that the players' freedom is inevitably limited by what the programmers have allowed.[25] This is very different from proper inter-personal relations. Equally the attempt to produce interactive stories can have only limited success, because stories 'belong to the past', whereas video-games must include repeated choices in the present. Indeed we like stories, he says, just because they are not interactive. All we want in them is an illusion of involvement. Virtual reality is not a pathway to ultimate reality, but only the doorway into an enclosed games-room. To spend prolonged leisure in it would be imprisonment, not freedom. It does not necessarily follow that this experience of unreality cannot have any benefits. It may offer possibilities of fun, of learning, or of therapy which are at worst harmless and at best beneficial: the fun of virtual sky-diving, learning safely how to drive, therapy for phobias. But we need a reminder that behind every kind of technology there is, somewhere or other, a human mind which has laid down the rules and set the limits of interaction.

The contrast between reality and some of the kinds of experience which are distanced from it – vanity, dreams, fantasy – leaves open the question about its true nature and relevance to leisure. In the absence of much previous theological thought in this area, it is worthwhile considering what some Christian writers have said in trying to identify the nature of reality, though not with leisure in mind. One of the most suggestive discussions of this issue is Nicholas Berdyaev's *Spirit and Reality*. His language and his interests are far away from any consideration of the topic of leisure; yet they may lead into paths of thought about it. His basic assumption is that reality is apprehended in the interaction of the creative human spirit and the world which God has created. Spirit is opposed to the material world and yet must take the material world for granted. In its creative activity it introduces something new into that world. Yet in doing so it is forced into compromises.

> The creative act of spirit is both an ascent and a descent. In its creative urge and flight spirit rises above the world and dominates it, but the gravity of the world also pulls it down and makes it conform in its products to the state of the world. Thus spirit objectifies itself in its creative products, and in this way establishes communication with the given state of the plural world. [26]

The originating spirit in doing so creates what Berdyaev calls symbols. These are only related to realities, rather than being realities themselves. The reality of the life of the state, for example, or the life of the church, is expressed through a symbolic hierarchy. 'Titles such as Tsar, general, Pope, metropolitan, bishop are all symbols. In contradistinction to them we have such realities as Saint, prophet, creative genius, social reformer.'

But this kind of contrast, between the outward 'symbol' and the reality to which it relates, permeates all forms of human society, including legalistic morality, social obligations, and even scientific and philosophical knowledge. 'Everything perceptible is a symbol of the imperceptible, everything material a symbol of the spiritual'. Awareness of this relationship has the effect of liberating the human person from slavish dependence on this world, while also revealing purpose underlying an otherwise meaningless world.

The contrast, given above, between titles and realities shows how Berdyaev understood the nature of reality. It has to do with sanctity, prophecy, creativeness and social concern. Or, in another summary statement, the reality of the human subject is in such things as 'holiness, creativeness, freedom, love, fraternity, knowledge, beauty of soul'.[27] With this we may compare a memorable saying of Robert Louis Stevenson: 'Love is so startlingly real that it takes rank upon an equal footing with the consciousness of personal existence'.[28] If we turn back to the language of scripture, we can relate these categories to the use in the Fourth Gospel of words such as way, truth or life. The incarnate Lord is, in Berdyaev's sense, a symbol. What is incarnate in him is reality, not fantasy. But it is important that this reality is in fact incarnated. 'Spirituality affects the whole of life, the whole of man – his body as well as his physical labour.'[29]

It must therefore follow, though Berdyaev is not addressing this question, that spirituality affects what we now experience as leisure. He recognizes its importance only as part of a necessary alternation in daily life. He criticizes forms of Christian asceticism which denied man's need for alleviation, for leisure, for imagination, for laughter. The spiritual life, he says, has a rhythm; its intensity should seek relief in repose, its suffering in joy, its tears in laughter.[30] This leaves unanswered the question how we may relate his definition of reality – or any other such definition – to the prolonged periods of leisure chosen by or forced upon increasing numbers of people in Western society. For them, there is no such rhythm. The intensity, the suffering, the tears do not come to them in a pattern which demands relief in repose, joy and laughter. They will usually plan, in however casual a way, to fill the emptiness of 'free time' with something they enjoy.

Often this will assume a technological form in a technological age. With the encouragement of commercial forces they will turn to the cinema, the radio, the television, the computer, the games console. Even in 1939, when *Spirit and Reality* appeared in English, Berdyaev was thinking about this development – though he uses the word 'technique' where we should now write 'technology'.

> The development of technique and its increasing power over man is of tremendous importance in the destinies of the spiritual life. Technique appears as a despiritualizing force in human life. If incarnation is organic, then technique is not only a despiritualizing but also a disincarnating force. The machine divorces spirit from the organic body... But although technique dehumanizes man, it is a product of the human spirit.[31]

There is, then, a crisis for the human spirit, which is in danger of being dominated by the machine. Man is called to enter a period of more heroic spirituality, and to make technology into an instrument of the spirit.

Whether or not we find Berdyaev's language congenial, the issue which he addresses is clearly important. It affects almost every aspect of human life. In the context of any discussion of extended leisure, which is itself a crisis of the human spirit, it indicates the need to study carefully the effects of technology there also. The criticisms of commercial exploitation, referred to above, suggest a possible distinction between the uses of technology in leisure which subordinate the human spirit to the forces of exploitation and other uses which offer release into freedom. Some of Berdyaev's ways of ascent in the list given above may be most appropriate within the areas of work or active social life: prophecy, social concern, fraternity, knowledge. Others have an affinity with free time: creativity, beauty, holiness, love. These lift the human spirit in such a way as to enable it to 'objectify itself in its products'. Here are possible criteria for the assessment of leisure.

Another possible distinction applicable to leisure is between activities which can be called personal and those which are impersonal. As John Macmurray argued, reality is personal; otherwise religion is an illusion. And personality is essentially mutual.[32] For the Christian these mutual relationships include, indeed culminate in, personal relationship with God. But our industrial society, which endangers personal relationships, endangers also our relationship with God. In his *Theology of Culture* Paul Tillich described the danger of

> the concentration of man's activities upon the methodological investigation and technical transformation of his world, including himself, and the consequent loss of the dimension of depth in his encounter with reality. Reality has lost its inner transcendence, or, in another metaphor, its transparency to the eternal.[33]

The danger implicit in this situation affects not only the world of industrial society, the world of work, but also leisure itself, as it becomes subjected to the same pressures.

The question of virtual reality involving no other actual person, however, is not the same as the question of personal relationships dependent on developing technology. The possibilities of communication have been constantly increasing throughout human history with the development of speech, writing, printing, the telephone, sound recording, television, e-mail and the internet, and with every change there have been new possibilities of understanding and misunderstanding. We may say that every kind of 'Thou' is filtered through some kind of medium. We need critical awareness of the extent to which our appreciation of personal reality is affected and perhaps distorted by the medium through which we meet it. This is just as true in work and duties as it is in leisure. But leisure ought to afford more space, more time, to evaluate the process of communication. Even the internet, which is sometimes presented as facilitating relationships across conventional barriers, has as much capability of generating hate as any other form of interaction. It can release participants from the restraints which face-to-face meetings impose. In her study of *The Psychology of the Internet* Patricia Wallace, accepting the definition of real life as 'everything not on the net', quotes an American writer as describing the world of the internet as 'an unreal universe, a soluble tissue of nothingness', a 'nonplace' in which important aspects of human interaction are relentlessly devalued.[34]

Technology is itself neutral until it is put to use by human agencies. It may open access to reality by enabling personal encounters. But also Macmurray's dictum that reality is personal does not, for the Christian, exclude the reality of things, if it is understood that everything is in some way the outcome of personal action. God is Creator of all things seen and unseen, either directly, or indirectly through the agency of creative humanity. If leisure is to be concerned with reality, much of it will be given to the appreciation of the world of nature and the creativity of human beings. It will be receptive, and through receptivity will open communication both with God who is personal and with humanity which receives its personality from him. As Josef Pieper has written;

> Leisure is a form of silence, of that silence which is the prerequisite of the apprehension of reality: only the silent hear and those who do not remain silent do not hear. Silence, as it is used in this context, does not mean 'dumbness' or 'noiselessness'; it means more nearly that the soul's power to 'answer' to the reality of the world is left undisturbed. For leisure is a receptive attitude of mind, a contemplative attitude, and it is not only the occasion but also the capacity for steeping oneself in the whole of creation.[35]

Rejecting the exclusive ideal of work, Pieper commends an attitude of contemplative celebration. In leisure man gratefully accepts the reality of creation and the 'inner vision that accompanies it', just as Holy Scripture tells us that God rested on the seventh day and saw that it was good.[36] Pieper made this understanding of leisure a launching-pad for an attack on the kind of academic life which had lost its roots in religion and worship. The very word 'academic' had come to mean something sterile, pointless and unreal, offering, in place of reality, 'a world of make-believe, of intellectual *trompe l'oeil*, and cultural tricks and traps and jokes'. That was sixty years ago, and we cannot tell what his verdict on present-day academe might be. But it is hard to resist the temptation to apply precisely those words to the output of commercial television in today's world.

The argument in favour of a quest for reality meets formidable enemies today. Pieper assumed the existence of a reality which was in principle accessible. There is, of course, another type of philosophy, going back at least to Schiller, which exalts fantasy by denying that we have any access to reality, to the 'thing in itself'. Such a view leaves the artist free to create worlds which make no claim to reality. For most Christian believers this seems not only to grant a licence to unfettered individualism which denies the value of community, but actually to make God a deceiver. God has testified to the truth by the revelation made through Jesus Christ.[37] Every human creation reaches out towards a reality given by God and is at the same time subject to judgement by that revelation. There is indeed a place within human experience for creativity, but every creative act points beyond itself to the Creator of creativity. As George Steiner has written, the aesthetic act is a replication on its own scale of the first *fiat* – 'let there be'. Why should there not be *no* poems? There is *poiesis* (the activity of creating) because there is the prior creativity of the Creator. Human creativity suffers 'a fury of secondarity'.[38]

Here we have reached a crucial issue. If leisure is considered as something different from the short-term relief of stress, then it is the point where we ask the essential question about our humanity. What, in fact, is the 'abundant life' which Christ came to give to all? This is a question to which we shall return at the end of our enquiry. Here we can note that the New Testament answers the question in terms which are of lasting relevance but also inevitably related to the particular society its writers were addressing. The abundant life is above all a redeemed life. Christ brings release from burdens: the burden of conscience and the burden of self-justification. Free from sin and from self-concern, the believer enters a life of peace with God and joy in the world.[39] These gifts of grace transformed life in New Testament times for those whose lives were at the same time constricted by the unceasing demands of daily work or the oppressions they suffered in an unjust society. But suppose those demands and oppressions removed, what then? In a different kind of society it is necessary to speak in other terms about 'abundant life'. It must then include all the realms of knowledge and experience which have been disclosed in the centuries which have succeeded the original gift of abundant life through the redemption achieved by the Incarnation. Many of these realms are part of objective reality. Equally, many of them belong, if not to worlds of fantasy, at least to worlds of imagination. There may be an important distinction to be drawn between these two.

The difficulty here is that the two words – fantasy and imagination – are themselves imprecise and have been used in different ways. If we follow Iris Murdoch's example and see fantasy as 'the tissue of self-aggrandizing and consoling wishes and dreams', it can hardly justify for itself a place in the kind of extended life of leisure which is under consideration. Even imagination has not always seemed good in the opinions of Christian writers. Pascal expressed an ambivalent judgement, calling imagination on the one hand the master of error and falsehood, an arrogant force which dominated over reason, but also a faculty which could create beauty and happiness.[40] Perhaps this ambivalence was the result of the secularizing of the imagination which was in process at the time. Writing of Pascal's contemporary, John Milton, Robert Sencourt has said: 'When the great Cathedrals were built ... the task of spirituality had been to master culture and technique. But now culture was escaping from faith, [and] imagination was growing more interested in itself than in worship.'[41]

A more recent writer has contrasted the enjoyment of 'the wide open spaces, the quiet by day and night, the seasonal progress of life' with the abuse of the natural imagination which would supply 'the counterfeit heavens of socialist or commercial fiction'.[42]

There are cautions here which must be borne in mind. The creative imagination may seem to be ignored by the New Testament writers, but it is implicit as one of God's gifts to humanity. It is certainly not mentioned by Paul as one of the gifts of the spirit.[43] But the increase of leisure releases new gifts in a different society. Nor should the scope of imaginative gifts be limited to forms of imagination dependent on language. Lewis Mumford rightly claimed that until modern times the greater part of human thought and imagination flowed through the hands.[44] In any case, our present understanding of the inspiration of scripture allows for the creativity of the evangelists themselves, in fashioning a new kind of literature; and the next generations of Christian believers let their imagination run to the production of those 'apocryphal Acts' (of St Paul and others) which may have some basis in fact but which embroider some truth with much fiction. If we turn back to the Hebrew tradition embodied in the Old Testament, we find there, alongside whatever historical material it may contain, the writings of poets and prophets and wise men. We are used to thinking of their writings in terms of inspiration; but we need to place inspiration itself within the more general category of imagination. Though not all imagination is inspired, all that is inspired must be mediated through the human imagination, whether that flows through the hands or the pen.

No one explored this topic more persistently than Samuel Taylor Coleridge. He rejected the notion, which could trace its origin back to Aristotle, that art somehow held up a mirror to nature; that it was essentially 'mimesis', the product of a mimic faculty. For that kind of activity Coleridge reserved the word 'fancy'. Imagination was something different.

> The artist, trusting more to the imagination than to the memory, abandons the minimal role of holding up a mirror to nature and shapes the world as he experiences it, in metaphor and symbol, his art a self-expression, illuminating and not merely reflecting.[45]

Defenders of Aristotle can make room for this extension of the work of the imagination, by referring to his concession that art can imitate what might be as well as what is. But along one line of thought or the other, we need to assert that the imagination has a creative function. Indeed it has been well argued that this creativity is the essential characteristic of human beings made in the image of God, who is known first and foremost as the Creator.[46]

In trying to relate the fact of extended leisure to ideas of the creative imagination, it looks as if the argument is moving towards the conclusion that true humanity consists in becoming an artist of one kind or another, according to the often quoted saying that 'an artist is not a special kind of person, but every person is a special kind of artist'. But this looks absurd. The ability to be creative, in the restricted sense usually attached to that word, is the privilege of few. What is open and available to everyone in the spaciousness of extended leisure is the co-creation of themselves in union with God. Much of this process can be achieved in being open to the products of the creativity of others, in a hundred varied shapes.

The psalmist could say 'I am fearfully and wonderfully made'.[47] That is doubly evident today. The breath-taking rate of change in Western society, which has brought leisure to millions, has given a new validity to those words by opening a treasure-chest of experiences. Not the devil, but God, has placed human beings on the pinnacle of the temple, to survey and to choose, and human choices are not only about what to do, but also about what kind of person to be. Often among those choices there are moments of division between fantasy and reality. The distinction between short-term and long-term leisure allows us to accept all types of interest in small doses. But for months of leisure or years of retirement a stricter assessment must be made. The Christian believer cannot remain content with fantasy, however alluring. In Christ there is access to the 'paramount reality' of the kingdom of God, for which the words of Berdyaev may be appropriate: 'holiness, creativeness, freedom, love, fraternity, knowledge, beauty of soul'. We can take our search a stage further by choosing from this list the one word which seems almost to sum up the idea of leisure, the word freedom. Where would that lead?

## NOTES

1.   Rowan Williams, *Lost Icons: Reflections on Cultural Bereavement* (Edinburgh and NY 2000), ch. 1: 'Childhood and Choice', 11–52.
2.   John 11.25; Colossians 3.3.
3.   E.g. Psalm 102.24–7.
4.   Revelation 21.1.
5.   Hebrews 12.27.
6.   John 8.58; 1.17. Cf. David Brown, *Discipleship and Imagination* (Oxford 2000), 346: 'The Devil thus does not simply "tell lies"; he is the opposite of eternal reality, just as Christ does not simply speak the truth: he is that reality itself, or, at the very least, the revelation of it.'
7.   1 Corinthians 3.23.
8.   Mark 4.38.
9.   Peter L. Berger, *Redeeming Laughter: The Comic Dimension of Human Experience* (Berlin and NY 1997) 50.
10.  Philippians 3.20.
11.  Helmut Thielicke, *Theological Ethics*, Vol. I – Foundations (English edn 1968), xvii.
12.  Richard Harries, *Art and the Beauty of God: A Christian Understanding* (London 1993), 125.
13.  See R.N. Whybray, *Ecclesiastes* (London and Grand Rapids, Mich. 1989), 34.
14.  E.g. Genesis 31.10–13; Matthew 2.12.
15.  Martin Esslin, *The Theatre of the Absurd* (London 1968), 343.
16.  See Catherine Bates, *Play in a Godless World* (London 1999) 74–5.
17.  Patricia Wallace, *The Psychology of the Internet* (Cambridge 1999), 39, quoting Anatole France.
18.  Harold D. Lehman, *In Praise of Leisure* (Scottdale, Pa. 1974), 69–70.
19.  Henry Durant, *The Problem of Leisure* (London 1938), 30–31.
20.  James 1.22.
21.  Iris Murdoch, *The Sovereignty of Good* (London 1970), quoted in Alan Ecclestone, *Gather the Fragments* (Sheffield 1993), 2.
22.  Wallace, *The Psychology of the Internet*, 38.
23.  J.D. Bernal, *The Social Function of Science*, cited by Stanley Parker, *Leisure and Work* (London 1983), 104.
24.  Margaret Morse, *Virtualities: Television, Media Art, and Cyberculture* (Bloomington, Ind.1998), 10–11.
25.  Steven Poole, *Trigger Happy: The Inner Life of Video-Games* (London 2000), 71.
26.  Nicholas Berdyaev, *Spirit and Reality* (London 1939), 58.
27.  Ibid. 64–7.
28.  R.L. Stevenson, *Essays and Poems*, ed. Clare Harman (London 1992), 56–7.
29.  Berdyaev, *Spirit and Reality*, 43.
30.  Ibid. 125.
31.  Ibid. 69.

32. John Macmurray, *Reason and Emotion* (London 1935), 213.
33. Paul Tillich, *Theology of Culture* (Oxford 1959), 43.
34. Wallace, *The Psychology of the Internet*, 233, quoting Clifford Stoll, *Silicon Snake Oil* (NY 1995).
35. Josef Pieper, *Leisure: The Basis of Culture* (London 1952), 52.
36. Ibid. 55.
37. 1 John 5.10.
38. George Steiner, *Real Presences: Is There Anything in What We Say?* (London 1989), 203.
39. Romans 5.1; Acts 13.52.
40. Blaise Pascal, *Pensées*, ed. and trans. A.J. Krailsheimer (Harmondsworth 1966), 9.
41. Robert Sencourt, *The Consecration of Genius* (London 1947), 246–7.
42. Ulrich Simon, *The Ascent to Heaven* (London 1961), 35.
43. 1 Corinthians 12.4–11.
44. *Technics and Human Development* (1966) quoted in J.P. Diggins, *Thorstein Veblen* (Princeton NJ 1999), 91.
45. David Jasper, *Coleridge as Poet and Religious Thinker,* (London 1985), 76
46. Dorothy L. Sayers, *The Mind of the Maker* (London 1941) ch. 2.
47. Psalm 139.14.

# 6

# Freedom and Boredom

*The church has often upheld authority against freedom; but Christians have also fought against oppression. The Romantic movement championed the freedom of the creative artist. The spread of democracy is parallel to the increase of individual and group freedom, and affluence increases leisure. But that does not by itself bring freedom, for leisure is conditioned by forces making for social conformity and by the fallen state of the human race. The sabbath, reinterpreted in Christianity, should be a joyful celebration, but it may also be a time of boredom if used uncreatively. The nature of boredom, which corresponds to the monastic sin of accidie or sloth, has been analysed extensively by Kierkegaard, who claimed to find ways of exploiting it. Psychoanalytical assumptions remove it from the category of sin. At its best boredom may lead through curiosity to wonder. In retirement restless activity does not overcome boredom, but the loss of power and status may lead to the discovery of a positive value in an attitude of receptivity.*

Anything that might be called a theology of leisure must be a particular aspect of a theology of freedom, because leisure, on any definition, is time freed from external constraints, at work or in social duties. Even in leisure there are still forces at work to limit freedom: the forces of commercial exploitation and social conformity acting from without and the psychological limitations of human personality acting within. But in theory at least, the individual can assert personal liberty against these constraints in a way impossible or inappropriate in the other major areas of daily life. Freedom, nevertheless, can be experienced also as a burden, because it includes responsibility for choice. The lack of the routines of work or social duty may be felt as a waste-land of boredom, not a paradise of possibilities. This suggests a further appraisal, from a theological stand-point, of the alternatives of boredom and curiosity.

First it is necessary to sort out different aspects of freedom. It is useful to bear in mind the distinction between 'freedom from' and 'freedom for'. The mere possibility of leisure depends on the prior establishment of freedom from many kinds of overt oppression. In point of fact, the record of the Christian churches over the centuries, as represented by their moral theologians, does not show an overriding concern for the liberation of human beings from external constraint. Typical categories of moral teaching have had much more to do with inner discipline than with outward freedom. The cardinal virtues (prudence, temperance, justice, fortitude) can be exercised in all kinds of social setting, but seem most at home in a paternalistic and unequal society. This is hardly surprising, when we recall their origin in Plato and the Stoics. The theological virtues (faith, hope, charity) may actually be more evident in individual lives when practised in a repressive society, as indeed the Christian emphasis on them was developed in a society dependent for its functioning on the enslavement of a large proportion of its members. The rough lawlessness of the so-called Dark Ages and the crude struggle for power in the mediaeval period tended to throw the Church's influence into the service of authority, because any authority seemed preferable to none, and there was little scope for the assertion of human rights as opposed to feudal duties.

Even the Reformation, which might have done so much for human liberty, gave back to princes or religious élites the power it had snatched from priests and popes. The revolutionary element was there, of course, in men like the Anabaptists or the Levellers, but by the end of the seventeenth century repressive authority was everywhere dominant once more in the West, with Christian apologists standing beside the seats of power. In England, as Philip Mairet has written,

> The Civil War ... did nothing to change the class structure of society, and the Restoration intensified class consciousness. Religious defenders of social privilege and of inequality of wealth appeal as confidently as before to religious sanctions, but their arguments are not really so religious and are more utilitarian.[1]

The tone is exemplified by Richard Baxter in his *Christian Directory* with its wholehearted acceptance of the stratification of society which makes leisure a class privilege.

In Baxter's work the duties of the poor include their acquiescence in poverty; the duties of the masters do not include any action to elevate the poor out of their poverty. Within the rigidities of a hierarchical social structure it is the intention of Christian moralists such as Baxter to mitigate antagonisms and humanize relationships, as it had been the intention of St Paul, centuries before, to humanize the institution of slavery without passing judgement on it, except obliquely. But any adequate criticism of those who keep their servants in poverty is muted by the argument that the primary concern of Christians is the conquest of sin, and poverty, though unpleasant, is not sinful.

> There is no condition of life so low or poor, but may be sanctified and fruitful, and comfortable to us, if our own misunderstanding, or sin and negligence, do not pollute it or imbitter it to us; If we do the duty of our condition faithfully, we shall have no cause to murmurr [*sic*] at it.

> Therefore I shall here direct the Poor in the special Duties of their condition; and if they will but conscionably perform them, it will prove greater kindness to them, than if I could deliver them from their poverty, and give them as much riches as they desire. Though I doubt this would be more pleasing to the most; and they would give me more thanks for money, than for teaching them how to want it [i.e. do without it].[2]

The logic of the argument seems to require the indefinite postponement of any attempt to conquer poverty, since there will always be the more pressing duty to conquer sin.

It is only fair to Baxter's humanity to notice his slightly whimsical acknowledgement that the poor may find it hard to agree. He was certainly not slow to condemn various kinds of oppression. But the rights of the poor do not, in his scheme of things, extend to anything that could properly be called leisure, unless we are prepared to include under that heading the opportunity to fulfil one's religious duties. The *Christian Directory* contained, however, a section dealing with a particular kind of oppression which was to challenge the Christian conscience with the duty of delivering the oppressed: the oppression of slavery. The condition of slavery may be regarded as the ultimate denial of 'freedom from', which is the pre-requisite of leisure. Baxter condemns the slavery of the innocent, though he admits slavery as a possible punishment for the guilty.[3] A century later William Paley in his *Principles of Morality and Politics* (1785) was still arguing that slavery might arise, consistently with the law of nature, from crimes or captivity or debt. But that did not prevent him from calling the African slave-trade an abominable tyranny and expressing the hope that 'as the knowledge and authority of [Christianity] advance they will banish what remains of this odious institution'.

The same kind of contradiction between theory and practice marked the Evangelical revival. Hannah More might urge the poor to absolute quietism, but her words were not a text for her friend, William Wilberforce, to expound.

> Let us confess, then, that in all the trying circumstances of this changeful scene, there is something infinitely soothing to the feeling of a Christian, something infinitely tranquillizing to the mind, to know that he has nothing to do with events but to submit to them; that he has nothing to do with the revolutions of life but to acquiesce in them as the dispensations of eternal wisdom; that he has not to take the management out of the hands of Providence, but submissively to follow the divine leading; that he has not to contrive for tomorrow but to acquiesce today; not to condition about events yet to come, but to meet those which are present with cheerful resignation.[4]

This kind of teaching, with its implicit limitation of leisure to a privileged class, found favour wherever Christian leaders had been co-opted into the governing class. The established status of the Church of England unbalanced its teaching. It was easier for 'dissenters', who rejected the idea of establishment, to reject also the inequity of such supposedly Christian sentiments. But their struggle for the freedom of the church, the community of believers, did not necessarily involve the freedom of the individual within that community. In fact, 'gathered churches' tend to exercise stricter control over the private lives of their members than churches which aim to embrace entire secular communities. This is a factor contributing to the fissiparous nature of sects. Those who resent control, whether of doctrine or behaviour, are tempted to desert the fold, for good or bad reasons. It is symbolic of this restrictive control, in a trivial instance, that the Primitive Methodists were one of the first denominations to frame a 'no smoking' rule for its preachers, and recommend all its members to be sparing in the smoking of tobacco.[5] Dr David Thompson, commenting on the social concern of the Nonconformists in the nineteenth century, comments that the rather restrictive outlook on leisure which was characteristic of them did not endear them to the mass of the working classes:

> Their agitation against Sunday opening of museums, art galleries and public places, against Sunday rail excursions and Sunday opening of public houses, all hit the working man's day off more than their concern that there should be no Sunday work benefited them.[6]

All this acts as a reminder that freedom is not indivisible. Exponents of different kinds of religion choose which kinds of freedom they demand, partly according to their particular variant of doctrine, but also partly through the unacknowledged particularity of their social context. Evangelicals and their allies who spoke in subordinationist terms to their servants were simultaneously capable of a vigorous and unremitting fight for the abolition of the slave-trade and of slavery in the British empire. But freedom had an irresistible tendency to expand its territories. Once the Christian conscience had been awakened to the duty of liberating the oppressed slaves, it could not ultimately resist the demand for other kinds of liberation. From the Ten Hours' campaign of 1831–47 to the recent development of 'liberation theology', with its call to direct and even violent action, there has developed a strong Christian witness in favour of 'freedom from'.

Concern for liberation, then, has not been anything like unanimous or wholehearted among Christians, and the freedom of leisure has not been high on their agenda. The subordinationist ethic to be found in the New Testament epistles[7] has been invoked in support of a hierarchical view of social relationships, and it has not always been easy to draw the line between subordination and oppression; indeed, it is not self-evident that there is any such line to draw. Christians are not specially enthusiastic about freedom, perhaps because they are rightly impressed with the servant-ideal. The paradox that there is no-one so free as the slave of God could be interpreted as implying unquestioning subjection to the interpreters of God's word or God's authorized hierarchy. But if God's will for all human beings is that they shall fulfil their potential completely, then 'slavery' to God's will is the exact opposite of enslavement to the will of another human being.

The almost universal adoption of democracy as a political ideal, or at least as a political catch-word, has muted some of the traditional apologetic for authoritarianism and set Christian moralists free to espouse the cause of freedom in the last half-century with a vigour they never showed before. The issue has been increasingly forced on the attention of the Western world in recent decades through the development of modern media of communication, which bring into everybody's living room discriminations and oppressions which had gone unnoticed before. In the modern age, freedom has been largely debated in secular rather than religious terms. There is a huge literature dealing with freedom as it is understood in different disciplines. Even a cursory acquaintance with some of the literature reveals that ideas of freedom have always been in process of flux in Western society.[8]

Freedom is usually freedom from some exercise of power seen as restrictive or repressive. The restriction might be a rigid class system, or the regulation of labour under capitalism, or simply the pressure to conform in respectable society. So the ways of escape have been equally varied. In rural England in the eighteenth and nineteenth centuries the Methodist chapels were felt to be islands of freedom for working people; in the industrial revolution some workers found a sense of freedom in trade union organizations; in the consumer society of the twentieth century young people explored the freedom of dropping out of it and repudiating material wealth. Some of these images of freedom relate to work or social duties, but others have a bearing on the idea of leisure.

There is another approach to the idea of freedom which deserves attention in our present context: freedom through artistic activity. It has been argued that the artist, in his or her creativity, finds emancipation from society, from heredity, and finally from reality itself. This conviction has been carefully explored by George Steiner among others.[9] He refers to the claim that in a special sense the artist as poet or novelist exercises freedom in the use of language, because anything can be said and written about anything. Every other human capability has limitations. He quotes the poet Mallarmé as declaring that freedom comes through realizing that words refer only to other words, and that within the language system we possess the boundless, dynamic liberties of construction which are appropriate to the uniqueness of human imagining. By comparison external reality is deprivation. The visual arts and music, though perhaps restrained by technical limits, have their own ways of emancipating the artist from external reality. It is doubtful whether artists, of whatever discipline, see themselves as being at leisure. The writing, the painting, the sculpture, the composition of music – these are their kinds of work, and they will usually feel under an inescapable commitment to it. For them, the gateway to freedom is not their leisure but their work.

Creativity, however, is not confined to those whose art is their full-time occupation. Others are free to be creative in extended leisure or in retirement. Most people are not creative in quite the fashion of the committed artist, but they can enjoy the creativity of others and find a sense of enlargement in doing so. In theory they have the right to choose whether or not to respond to what they are offered. In fact, both freedoms – the freedom of the artist to create and the freedom of the reader or listener or observer to make or refuse a response – are constrained by social factors. The social construction of reality includes the social construction of artistic value. Those who hear the self-justifications of writers and artists when they have produced corrupting novels or plays or works of visual art may be led to consider whether those writers and artists are themselves the product of a corrupt society, as well as whether those who read or watch can possibly be among the pure in heart to whom all things are pure. Walt Whitman once advised the reader to dismiss 'whatever insults his own soul'.[10]

This brief exploration of the idea of freedom in secular terms indicates that it is not confined to the realm of leisure. There can be freedom in work. 'Perfect freedom is reserved for the man who lives by his own work and in that work does what he wants to do.'[11] True freedom is 'the concrete act of work which arouses the sentiment of having mastered a subjugated material.'[12] In contrast to the freedom of chosen work, there may be little true freedom in leisure if it is produced by unsought unemployment. When William Temple, as Archbishop of York, set up a committee on unemployment in the 1930s, its report looked hard for signs of creativity in unemployment, such as a 'little renaissance' of craft work, academic study and discussion, and music and drama, but noted that the whole lives of many unemployed men centred on 'the pools'. The report recognized that curiously enough this represented a desperate desire for freedom. Betting offered the only possibility of making a decision in a life otherwise prescribed in every detail by poverty and necessity, and always the object of other people's decisions.[13] But the conclusion could only be that they were freer when they were in work than in idleness.

Freedom, then, in humanistic terms is another way of describing self-fulfilment. But in work or in leisure the individual is constrained by external forces. In leisure these are most likely to be the forces of social conformity within the existing sub-culture, usually reinforced by the pressures of commercial advertising. For the sociologist freedom is rightly assessed as freedom from conformity to external pressures. That means being professionally, and sometimes painfully, aware that the activities of men and women in the mass are broadly predictable. It is not difficult to forecast within a margin of error how many people will go to football matches or book ski holidays among a given population. They believe they are acting freely, but their apparent freedom seems only to mask a kind of inevitability.

A Christian critique of modern leisure will take account of these secular factors, but will need to set alongside them considerations of a different kind.

The idea of leisure as the area of freedom in human life is open to challenge along theological as well as sociological lines. The theologian is concerned primarily with freedom from sin. The category of 'sin' may be interpreted in more than individual terms. It may be seen to include the corruptions of society which affect leisure as much as work. But it is sin, in one form or another, which deprives human beings of freedom. Christ alone sets a human being free, according to the text: 'For freedom Christ has set us free'.[14] The only freedom worth talking about is the gift of God through Jesus Christ, and it certainly is not available only to the leisured.

When these two kinds of concern, the sociological and the theological, meet in the thought of a single person, the notion of leisure as an important element in human life is very much under question. Just such a thinker is Jacques Ellul, a professor of 'the history and sociology of institutions' no less than a fertile writer on theological themes. He has brought together the two lines of thought which affect our understanding of leisure in *The Ethics of Freedom*. It dates from a time before the collapse of Soviet Communism and the demise of the Marxist hegemony in French intellectual life, and sometimes the arrows of his criticism seem to land in a dead body. But the combination of his sociological understanding with a theology in the Barthian tradition opens a vein of ideas which still need to be taken into account. Whatever reservations Ellul has about the development of Marxism, he accepts Marx's own description of the condition of the worker in capitalist society. That condition is summed up in the idea of 'alienation' or estrangement. The worker is treated as a unit of production. He has no say in the outcome of his labour, and perhaps does not even know what it is. He is estranged, not only from the process or enterprise in which he is involved, but also from his own self-knowledge as a potentially creative agent. If that is his condition, it is clear that he can exercise freedom only within circumscribed limits. But that is not only true of the worker in relation to the world of work; it is also true in whatever may be called culture. There, too, the forces of conditioning are at work. Even religion in its different forms obeys intrinsic necessities such as the formulation of dogma and codes of conduct. So the revelation of God in Jesus Christ is degraded to the level of a religion like all other religions. The only freedom man has is to recognize that he is determined by the 'labyrinthine web' of psychological, sociological and technological conditioning. Some of the effects of these forces may be good, but it is illusory to suppose that we are free to choose those that are good and avoid those that are bad.

Given the validity of this description of the human condition, the Christian understanding of freedom, as set out by Ellul, is inevitably constricted. It turns on the declaration that Christ is the one free man. He alone exercised real freedom to choose, though even he experienced the condition of alienation; that is, he was inevitably subject to the structure of a sinful world. For the fact of alienation was established by the Fall, though its particular form in modern society was due to the nature of capitalism. For the Christian, true freedom is that of the word of God which makes possible the use of this world's goods for different ends. This freedom is a gift which can only be received from outside, from the 'wholly other'. When human beings try to assert their freedom against the determinations inherent in the human condition, which they may do through the use of drugs, for example, or through violent revolution, they merely subject themselves to more stringent determinations.

Even the freedom of the Christian person, bestowed by grace, is not a permanent condition of existence. It has to be lived out, paradoxically through another kind of subordination, through obedience to the will of God. Then obedience ceases to be oppression and becomes freedom, but of a kind which is always in danger of being lost through trying to be free for oneself or even for other human beings. Yet, in the view of Ellul, even grace does not free us from the forces of determination, but only from 'the system', from their systematization. That means the organization of those forces into any kind of system, including even any Christian system. For there is no specific Christian way of life, and there can be no uniformity of behaviour among Christians.

> There is no discrimination between acts, things, professions, commitments, manners, systems, ideas, or philosophies which are Christian and those which are not. Any attitude, opinion, or choice, if it proceeds from freedom in Christ ..., if it is a manifestation at the chosen time of the tension experienced by this free man between the God who frees him and the world which oppresses him, is legitimate.[15]

So the 'ordered universe' of morality is shattered. There are no longer things good and evil in themselves; to be good, they must be sanctified by the word of God and by prayer (as in 1 Tim. 4.4). And acts of freedom do not necessarily liberate others. For other people, they may give rise to enslavement as well as to freedom.

This is a bleak view of the human condition. It is as if we could only try to insert little wedges of free choice into the metaphorical walls of determinism which enclose us, though we knew they would never bring those walls tumbling down. Using a slightly more hopeful simile, Ellul says, 'The yachtsman has to take account of wind and tide. His freedom is the freedom to use determinations... Nothing is worse than a calm.'[16] If we were considering the Christian's involvement in, or detachment from, politics, we should have to discuss how to estimate his advice not to expect anything much from that kind of activity, but still to get alongside secular agents working for change, while being alive to the likelihood that change would make society worse, not better. But our concern is with leisure; and although Ellul is not much interested in it and has little regard for it, the relation of freedom to work and leisure inevitably comes into the picture.

Work, he says is just part of our creatureliness, a battle against hostile nature. He criticizes the overestimate of work as intended for the service of mankind. Work itself is indeterminate. It can be a joyous exercise, but it also stimulates the appetite for material possessions and then easily becomes bondage. The meaning which the Christian tries to put into work is surrounded, in technological society, with a 'swelling ocean of non-meaning'. Work does not belong to the order of grace, but to the order of necessity, which is not abolished in Christ, but conquered. Those given freedom in Christ must struggle to transform the ideological and intellectual milieu of work, for it is a setting for human encounter.

This grim description of the world of work might lead us to expect a positive evaluation of leisure as the realm of freedom. In that we are disappointed. Some ways of escape into freedom, by resort to drugs or violent opposition to established society, lead into even greater bondage. That judgement is not surprising. But even the division of time into hours of work and hours of leisure does not ensure the achievement of freedom outside working time. We are told we must reject 'the seven modern forms of leisure, namely empty leisure, organized leisure, leisure as escape, as conformity, as compensation, as meaninglessness, and as destruction.'[17] The description of these forms of leisure emphasizes the fact that they are themselves subject to social determination. 'The man of leisure is more a slave than the working man.' Society offers the means of imagining freedom, in vacations, sports, television, or even in grandiose political schemes; but in these things, society is actually constraining its members by substituting illusion for reality. Children, in particular, are confronted with the full force of modern society in leisure. They face a void, suffer boredom, and through this traumatic experience try to achieve freedom in catastrophic ways.

There is, however, for Ellul one activity outside work which does offer the promise of real freedom: worship. Here we may turn to Karl Barth. The holy day is an expression of freedom, 'the breaking of daily fetters'. By grace human beings are given a future, to orient their lives. The determining powers are overthrown, and the fruit of grace is in spontaneous obedience to God, which ceases to be oppression and becomes proper freedom. Barth comes to the discussion of freedom in *Church Dogmatics* under the general heading of 'The Doctrine of Creation'.[18] True freedom is expressed in the ordinance of the holy day, which man is to keep as a day of worship, freedom and joy. The freedom which the holy day expresses is freedom for God, and under God for life in fellowship with others. Worship, then, is not a part of leisure, but leisure is a particular form of what worship expresses: the ability to celebrate, rejoice and be free, which is bestowed by grace. The true attitude to Sunday is no different from the true attitude to Monday. So we should ask, 'Will our holy day verify itself or not in the following week, which it should inaugurate as the day of the Lord?'.[19]

Human beings are responsible before God for the ways in which they spend their time on the holy day, in addition to the primary activity of worship. Barth is certain that there are both negative and positive ways of spending time on the holy day. Because one of the characteristics of true freedom is joy, negative ways of spending leisure time are marked by boredom. He has observed human behaviour on Sunday with a sardonic eye.

Is there anything more depressing than the sight of obviously very bored male and female humanity wandering about our streets on a Sunday afternoon around three o'clock all dressed up and pushing prams? What is the point of it? Do we not feel (and from the look of them they themselves above all) that we would like to see them voluntarily put back to some sort of useful activity? But this evidence, and therefore all the fierce or ironical jeremiads which rightly deplore what we nowadays know as the celebration of the day of rest, are wide of the mark to the extent that a day of rest based on merely humanitarian motives cannot as such be a real benefit or fulfil the need and right of resting from work. For what will such a day be used for except what it is actually used for? – various odd jobs and activities, all kinds of necessary and unnecessary meetings and assemblies, 'sporting events' and rapt attendance at the same – enhanced by a lucky win on the tote – and finally and above all a motorized or unmotorized flight to distant scenes, ending up with an escape in alcohol and flirtation. How can it be otherwise? All that we can say against it – and not only against the inevitable 'excrescences' – is true. It is true that a holy day like this relieves man of none of his burdens but only lays new ones on him, that it entails no refreshment but only further toil.[20]

This kind of Sunday is 'alienated from its original and proper purpose', in Barth's judgement, even if it can be given a humanitarian justification. The true significance of the holy day is to be the conscious expression of that self-renouncing faith which ought to characterize the whole of life, weekdays as well as Sunday. It is, of course, easier to criticize negative ways of spending time – negative because ultimately boring – than to give specific prescriptions for its positive use. Barth insists that the use of the holy day should be at God's disposal. He proposes four criteria for its use.

1. It should be liberated and unplanned and therefore refreshing.
2. It should be the joyful celebration of a feast – this is 'the infallible criterion'.
3. It should be spent in relation with our fellows.
4. It should verify itself in the following week. 'Is it well with the Sunday if in the evening we wearily regret that Monday comes again? And is it well with it if we wearily rejoice when it is Monday again?'[21]

Barth's teaching about Sunday has a wider relevance, beyond the holy day, because it focuses attention on the contrast between freedom and boredom. Because both freedom and boredom are inward experiences, we should accept Barth's idiosyncratic description of Sunday afternoons only with considerable reservations. It might actually be true that pushing the pram or running out into the countryside in the car were for particular people quite the opposite of boring activities. Babies in prams can be fascinating; the countryside in spring or autumn can be alive with beauty. Looking back at Ellul's seven modern forms of leisure (empty leisure, organized leisure, leisure as escape, as conformity, as compensation, as meaninglessness, and as destruction) we may judge that he has picked out some forms which are essentially boring (empty or meaningless) and overlooked others which may even be exciting – the very opposite.

Boredom is clearly relevant to the discussion of leisure, as a touchstone of the negative or uncreative use of free time. It is a possible effect of idleness, a topic which has occupied the attention of many Christian moralists. Concern about the vice runs through Christian writings from Clement of Alexandria and Gregory the Great to Thomas Aquinas, who quotes the treatise of the fourth–fifth-century monastic writer John Cassian on 'remedies for the eight principal sins of monks'. Cassian included in his list of sins (*vitia*) something very like boredom to which he gave the name '*acedia*'. As usual when we try to describe states of mind, the meaning of the term is elusive. The Latin expression is simply a transliteration of a Greek word (ακηδια) which was later anglicized as 'accidie' but more often translated as 'sloth'. The basic meaning has to do with the absence of care, or refusal to care. *Acedia* lies over the borderline between what is carefree and what is careless, between the freedom which comes with the absence of obligations and the bondage of being convinced that nothing matters. Ironically it was made possible by the very conditions of life which also made possible the highest reaches of spirituality in contemplation. 'The monk is troubled with *acedia* chiefly about the sixth hour; it is like an intermittent fever, and afflicts the soul of the one it lays low with burning fires at regular and fixed intervals.' Aquinas comments that this affliction has a physical origin: it is the effect of fasting and the sun's heat.[22] Its result is that the sufferer wants to do nothing, and cannot bring himself to begin doing what he knows to be good. It also leads him to think, mistakenly, that his life would be more tolerable in different circumstances or in another monastery. Frustrated, as he thinks, in the pursuit of spiritual good, he indulges himself with thoughts of physical pleasures.

This acute analysis of a particular monastic temptation may be applied to various situations outside monastic walls. Some members of the so-called leisure class in all ages have relapsed into self-indulgence because they could not persuade themselves that anything else was really worth the effort it would take. It was one of the achievements of the Evangelical Revival in England to find work for just such idle hands to do – a notable usurpation of the devil's work. At present the early retired and the haplessly redundant are sitting targets for the attacks of accidie. It is possible that we should relate what we call hooliganism to accidie, at least in arising from frustration of that human nature which we believe to be basically spiritual. This frustration easily leads to indulging in physical activities thought to give pleasure, a desperate search for a way of killing time.

Aquinas makes the important distinction that accidie is the very opposite of that 'rest in God' which is the intention of the observance of the Sabbath.[23] So we are led to distinguish two kinds of inactivity. Accidie is resentful, disgruntled inactivity, in which nothing good is attempted because nothing seems good enough to attempt. The inactivity of the true Sabbath rest is a contented, grateful inactivity in which the mind is wholly given over to the goodness of God, and so there is no time to be concerned about anything else. The wider relevance of Aquinas's description of accidie lies in this distinction. We can apply it to the discussion of leisure, at least to the extent of distinguishing between the attitude to 'free time', whether spent in activity or idleness, which is thankful and therefore restful on the one hand, and the opposite attitude of restless and thankless searching for new experiences and new gratifications, which can alternate with moods of disillusionment in which nothing seems worth doing because something else might be even better, if only one could think of it. The discussion of accidie in the *Summa* is shaped by the specifically clerical and monastic experience of the author. But it corresponds to a reality which can take other forms in lay life and in other social circumstances.

In due course the general Christian assumption that evangelical perfection was available only in the monastic life was challenged by Reformation ideas and the secularization of Western society. The demanding activism which was the very foundation of commercial, and later industrial, society was the antithesis of idleness, and attacks on idleness become more characteristic of Christian thought in the seventeenth century. These carry forward the criticism of boredom as a miserable state of existence, but sometimes without the earlier recognition of the opposite peril of unrestrained materialism. We have already noticed the concern of Jeremy Taylor, Richard Baxter and William Law for that stewardship of time which carries with it the condemnation of idleness. We may add the witness of Robert Burton in *The Anatomy of Melancholy*, who declared that 'the badge of gentry is idlenesse' with 'disports and recreations' to fill their time, with the result that 'this feral disease of melancholy so frequently rageth and now domineeres almost all over Europe amongst our great ones'.[24]

A reaction was to be expected. Even Dr Johnson thought the cult of busy activity overrated. When Boswell said that we grow weary when idle, he evoked the sturdy response: 'That is, Sir, because others being busy, we want company; but if all were idle, there would be no growing weary; we should all entertain one another.' [26 Oct. 1769] It was hardly to be expected that the great conversationalist would be bored when in good company. In due course the unpleasant aspects of bourgeois commercialism led other voices to be raised in praise of idleness. In the late eighteenth century and the early nineteenth century it was part of the attitude of so-called romantic writers to claim that the individual, given the freedom of being idle, could create a world of the imagination. Fichte is quoted as saying, 'One should not so culpably neglect the study of idleness'.[25] Idleness became the mother of invention, though it was always vulnerable to the attacks of boredom. Nietzsche praised the rare examples of men who would rather do nothing than do work which gave them no pleasure, even though they might suffer boredom. In fact artists needed a lot of boredom, he said, if their work was to succeed. It was that 'windless calm' of the soul which preceded a happy voyage and cheerful winds, though those whom Nietzsche said were of 'lesser nature' could not bear it.[26] Later examples of the calm before the creative voyage have been gathered together by Michael Paffard in *The Unattended Moment*. These include the twentieth century poet, C. Day Lewis, who testified to the experience of creativity after the attacks of sloth. He described a miserable teenage experience of black gloom without any gleam of reassurance, and continued:

> I learnt later that theologians knew it as the deadly sin, accidie. But I also learnt by experience that these moods were often fore-runners of a new burst of poetic activity, as though I must go down into the utter darkness before the seeds of light in me could germinate.[27]

The poets did not always have this uplifting experience, but the paradox is that even when they remained dejected, their very dejection might give rise later to creative writing, as witness both Wordsworth and Coleridge.[28] On this evidence accidie, as Paffard says, was rather an affliction than a sin, irresistible and outside the realm of morality.

Christian writers have not found it easy to praise inactivity, let alone the condition of boredom which inactivity often generates. One of the curiosities in this area of thought is the section of Kierkegaard's *Either/Or* with the title 'The Rotation Method – An Essay in the Theory of Social Prudence'. It includes a discussion of boredom, but as usual with Kierkegaard it is virtually impossible to say exactly where he stands. His frequent retreat behind the screen of aliases serves the purpose of allowing him to try out ideas to which he is no more than half committed. In 'The Rotation Method' he handles the idea of boredom from the aesthetic stand-point represented by the first anonymous character, 'A'. He fires off a number of provocative remarks to catch the attention of the reader.

> Boredom is the root of all evil. The history of this can be traced from the beginning of the world. The gods were bored, and so they created man. Adam was bored because he was alone, and so Eve was created. Thus boredom entered the world, and increased in proportion to the increase of population. Adam was bored alone; then Adam and Eve were bored together; then Adam and Eve and Cain and Abel were bored *en famille*; then the population of the world increased, and the peoples were bored en masse.

After a number of asides, he returns to boredom, and the method of handling it. It can be annulled only by enjoying ourselves, and therefore it is a duty to enjoy ourselves. The usual way to do so – 'the vulgar and inartistic method' – is to seek a continuous change of interests.

> One tires of living in the country, and moves to the city; one tires of one's native land, and travels abroad; one is *europamüde* [tired of Europe], and goes to America, and so on; finally one indulges in a sentimental hope of endless journeyings from star to star.[29]

In passing, one must pause to acknowledge this intriguing prophecy of tourism as it would be 150 years later. Millionaires, we are now told, are already queueing up for space travel. Kierkegaard almost seems to know about the Antiques Road Show on the television, as he mocks the collection of porcelain and silver and gold. His own method (or that of his assumed character) is different. He copies the method of the farmer who goes in for a rotation of crops, and uses the same ground over and over again in different ways. Keep doing the same thing again and again, but in different ways. In a typically outrageous example, he says he can even get enjoyment from listening to a bore by watching how he sweats and a drop of perspiration forms at the end of his nose.

Is there anything important to derive from all this semi-serious chatter? That can only be so if it is set in the general framework of *Either/Or*. In Kierkegaard's thought there are three stages, or elements, in human life: the aesthetic, the ethical and the religious. The discussion of boredom belongs in the first of these, the aesthetic, and is represented by the young man 'A', who is also part of Kierkegaard's own personality. This aesthetic character puts on a brave face, but is pushed towards despair. In the second half of *Either/Or* he is addressed by another anonymous person, 'B', a kind of Dutch uncle, as we might say, who points him to the ethical life. The complexity of the book's title begins to appear. It indicates choice; but there are two stages of choice. The first stage is to choose between the aesthetic life and the ethical life. To choose the first, however, is to adopt a life in which choice is not important. One type of activity is as justifiable as another, even though one sort may be 'vulgar and inartistic'. This leads ultimately to despair; indeed the word 'rotation' may suggest to us something like a squirrel in a cage. On the other hand, if the second, the ethical life, is chosen, then choice gains substance. It is the choice between good and evil. There is a 'baptism of the will' which lifts up the choice into the ethical. The difference between the two elements in human life is defined by 'B' like this: 'The aesthetical in a man is that by which he is immediately what he is; the ethical is that whereby he becomes what he becomes.'[30]

Although Kierkegaard could not rest even in the ethical stage but went beyond it into the religious stage, where he committed himself to God by a leap of faith, this did not mean that the other elements were eliminated from the wholeness of his human life. Although he did not say so, we may hesitantly correlate the three stages or elements with the three (not two) directives which can be detected in Jesus' summary of the law. To love God is to fulfil the 'religious'; to love our neighbour is to fulfil the 'ethical'; to love oneself is to fulfil the 'aesthetic'. Each of the later stages in Kierkegaard's trio reflects back on the earlier. As the experience of faith conditions the exercise of ethical judgement, so the experience of ethical judgement conditions the way in which freedom is exercised in the aesthetic life. There is such a thing as 'aesthetic seriousness', and the ethical individual may say with Kierkegaard that 'evil never exercises, perhaps, a more seductive influence than when it makes its appearance in an aesthetic guise'.[31] Kierkegaard considered that the culture of his own age was a predominantly aesthetical culture. We may think that is even truer of our own culture. An important question, then, is whether people live in the aesthetic stage as those who have never discovered anything else, or as people who understand what is meant by 'aesthetic seriousness' because their lives include the ethical and perhaps religious dimensions. A theological understanding of free time requires that leisure, though exempt from conscious awareness of the ethical and religious dimensions of life, can be lived to its fulness only when the personality has been matured by its experience of those dimensions. Or, in terminology employed earlier, leisure is 'beyond' both morality and religion.

When we come to the twentieth century, we pass out of the heyday of romanticism into an age marked by two developments which affect attitudes to idleness and boredom. One is the development of psychiatric interest in the hidden workings of the mind; the other is the growth of the entertainment industry. The former is a specialized area outside the range of this essay. But, to take a single instance, we may refer to an article from the *British Journal of Psychiatry* in 1965. Its title was 'Acedia: Its Evolution from Deadly Sin to Psychiatric Syndrome'. This 'evolution' is seen by the writer as one example of a gradual process by which sins lost their guilt and acquired psychiatric connotations. The writer considered that in the particular case of *acedia* some anticipations of later psychiatric ideas could be found, rather oddly, in the writings of Petrarch. Symptoms mentioned by Petrarch included voluptuous pleasure in one's own emotional sufferings and delight in exhibitionist self-revelation shown in detailed accounts of one's own spiritual sufferings. A Christian moralist must hesitate before accepting the idea that this kind of self-concern contains no element of sin, even if it is no longer characterized as sloth, but as ego-centricity. That, indeed, may be recognized as the main factor in all personal sins, and specially obnoxious in leisure.

The second development characteristic of the twentieth century was the multiplication of the means of entertainment, of which the television is at present the most significant. There are some positive things to be remembered when assessing the impact of television. It has been commended as offering, especially to children, roles and possibilities to play with in the imagination.[32] But it is more usual for critics to warn of its dangers. We find caution even in unlikely quarters. Peter France, discussing the classical Greek attitude to games, turns aside to remark that the experience of encountering actual human suffering as directly presented to us by television cameras is a dehumanizing one because if we reacted with the appropriate human feelings of horror or sympathy we should be disabled from going about our normal lives.[33]

Other criticisms are found in Christian discussion of the effects of television, and they have some relevance to our discussion of boredom. Ellul sees it as one of the means by which society constrains the freedom of the individual, substituting illusion for reality.[34] A recent American writer, Leland Ryken, refers to psychological studies which have documented 'the trancelike fixation of television viewers that destroys the ability to engage in conscious thought'. Studies of brainwave activity show how inactive the brain is while someone is watching television.[35] We hardly need this evidence to recognize that television and other forms of entertainment can fill leisure with a new kind of emptiness, though that is surely not the whole truth.

A critical point is reached when any medium of entertainment either purposely or accidentally stimulates the passive observer into active enquiry or investigation, if that activity is more than group response – laughter, cheering, booing, weeping. That point is the point of transition from boredom to curiosity. Here we may turn to a passage from the writings of Gerald Heard quoted by T.S. Eliot.

Humanity will be bored. The mysterious word which first stole like a grey shadow over the court of le Roi Soleil, and then spread to all places where men of taste lived beyond the struggle for meats and mates, will percolate down from class to class till all are leisured, all are idly rich with a wealth of time on their hands no people have ever possessed, ever been embarrassed with, before. If then mankind is not to weary of its life, to fly to making intentionally the accidents, the strains and anxieties which gave it thrills and spurs and sudden convictions that life is worth while (but which nature no longer makes for it); if it is not, through war, deliberately to break down into anarchy the order it has built up, it must find new interest and excitement. There is only one appetite from which this new stock of interest can spring, and that is curiosity, the finest of the passions.[36]

Eliot went on to quote Herbert Read, who coupled curiosity, the faculty which drives man to seek out the secrets of the universe, with wonder, the faculty which 'dares man to create what has not existed before'. Even so, he was not impressed. Curiosity or wonder, Eliot said, were not ends in themselves, and if elevated to that status they became tedious activities, the restless search for more sensation. They needed to be harnessed to a religious faith. We hear an echo of Pascal, for whom Eliot had much respect. 'Curiosity is only vanity.' But from another point of view it was the very purposelessness of curiosity which was its merit. Rather paradoxically, Thorstein Veblen, renowned for his attack on ostentatious leisure, was also capable of rejecting the praise of purposeful activity as the only proper concern for human beings. He declared that the foundation of intelligence was not in problem-solving, but in pure wonder and innate curiosity.

> Curiosity is a mode of cognition so bereft of functional content that it could not be corrupted by existing institutions, an epistemology so fired by the flame of pure intention that it had no obligation to any other cause than to the canon of curiosity itself.[37]

Two inter-related questions underlie the differences of opinion about curiosity as a proper exercise of freedom in leisure. What is freedom for? What is curiosity about? If freedom is simply to be oneself, then curiosity can be about anything that takes one's fancy, and pleasure or satisfaction is the only criterion. The remedy for boredom is entirely within one's own power. But if freedom is for others, because the self can only be fulfilled in relationships, then the faculty of curiosity is most properly exercised if it ministers to relationships in one way or another. The remedy for boredom is to relate. In practical terms there are two kinds of relationship which enrich leisure. One is sharing interests or discoveries with other people. The other is relating to God, mediately through appreciating the created world or directly through worship in one of its many forms. But in either case, what distinguishes leisure from work or duty is that it has no ulterior purpose. It must be an end in itself. This is obvious in the case of relating to God. Worship is not worship if it has a purpose beyond itself. It is love for love's sake, simply expressed in the hymn attributed to St Francis Xavier: 'My God, I love thee; not because / I hope for heaven thereby.' But the same lack of ulterior motive must apply to the human relationships in leisure, or else they begin to take on some of the characteristics of work or obligation.

Writers on the particular kind of leisure to be found in retirement are tempted to project on to it a pattern derived from their own experience, and that experience can easily take its form from their earlier working lives. When Paul Tournier wrote *Learning to Grow Old* in 1972 he openly advocated a second career in retirement. There is much wisdom in what he says, but his language shows that he carried over into retirement much of the goal-oriented effort of his earlier work. Retirement may be free from social conditioning (contrary to the belief of Ellul) but it must not lack direction. There will be much free time. But free for what?

> To kill time by means of organized hobbies? To be bored? Rather to allow everyone a second career when they are advanced in years, not a professional career, subject to constraint, but a free career. ... leisure activities must retain their imaginative, opportunist, craft-oriented

character. ...The chief motive ... ought not to be for profit, or fashion, or vanity, but pleasure, pure and simple.[38]

There should be a 'reconversion', from earning our living to cultural activity, or to rediscovering spontaneity and originality in order to become oneself. The second career will have no set specifications, no contract, no hierarchy, no age-limit, no routine, no fixed wage tied to an obligation to work. It sounds most attractive – for those with the capacity to be 'craft-oriented'. But in spite of the reference to spontaneity the second career must have 'a goal, a mission, and that implies organization', not in the line of duty, but for the love of people.[39]

Is this consistent? Can love be organized like this? To be sure, freedom without love is very near to boredom. As James Dunn has said, freedom is nothing if it is not freedom to love.[40] But love is much less 'mission' than response, and retirement is above all a time when response becomes more important than initiative. There is often a change of consciousness in that period of life. It is no longer possible to regard one's activity with entire seriousness, if one's well-being depends on what is provided by others. As Vanstone has written, 'It is not necessarily the case that man is most fully human when he is achiever rather than receiver, active rather than passive, subject rather than object.' [41] It is difficult to associate the idea of a second career with this phase of life, now so often prolonged for a period of many years. Boredom cannot be defeated by clinging to the 'sinking ship' of unceasing activism. And something positive is achieved by the attitude of waiting, receiving, and accepting. It is curious that the condition of boredom is often associated in our present society with the two extremes of life, childhood and old age. But they are alike in this, that they are times when responsibilities weigh least but freedom is most constrained by powerlessness, though in different forms. There can be no sovereign remedy for boredom, either in childhood or old age. If freedom is freedom to love, then at both ends of life fellowship sets us free. In childhood, even alone, there may be escape through play. Is that possible or desirable at any age? To that controversial topic we must turn.

## NOTES .

1.  *Philip Mairet, The National Church and the Social Order* (London 1956), 53.
2.  Richard Baxter, *A Christian Directory* (London 1673), II ch. 27.
3.  Ibid. IV, ch. 20.
4.  Hannah More, *Practical Piety, or the Influence of the Heart on the Conduct of Life* (8th edn 1812), II, 230–31.
5.  Minute of the Primitive Methodist Conference, 1823, in D.M. Thompson (ed.), *Nonconformity in the Nineteenth Century* (London 1972), 50.
6.  D.M. Thompson (ed.), *Nonconformity*, 13.
7.  E.g. Titus 3.1.
8.  Ruth Nanda Anschen (ed.) *Freedom: Its Meaning* (London 1942) provides a valuable overview.
9.  George Steiner, *Real Presences: Is There Anything in What We Say?* (London 1989).
10. Quoted in R.L. Stevenson, *Essays and Poems,* ed. Claire Harman (London 1992), 151.
11. R.G. Collingwood, *Speculum Mentis* (1924) quoted in Keith Thomas (ed.)*The Oxford Book of Work* (Oxford 1999), 140.
12. E. Borne and F. Henry, *A Philosophy of Work,* trs. F. Jackson (London 1938), 20.
13. Pilgrim Trust, *Men without Work* (Cambridge 1938), 99.
14. Galatians 5.1.
15. Jacques Ellul, *The Ethics of Freedom*, trs. & ed. G.W. Bromiley (London 1976), 187.
16. Ibid. 233.
17. Ibid. 129–30.
18. Karl Barth, *Church Dogmatics*, III (Edinburgh 1961), 67.
19. Ibid. 71.
20. Ibid. 61–2.
21. Ibid. 66–71.
22. Thomas Aquinas, *Summa Theologiae,* ed. and trs, Thomas Gilby (London 1964–81), II.ii.35 1 ad 2.
23. Ibid. II.ii.35 ad 1
24. Robert Burton, *The Anatomy of Melancholy* (1621), quoted in Thomas, *The Oxford Book of Work*, 39.
25. George Pattison, *Kierkegaard: The Aesthetic and the Religious – From the Magic Theatre to the Crucifixion of the Image* (London 1992), 4.
26. Thomas, *The Oxford Book of Work*, 153.
27. Michael Paffard, *The Unattended Moment* (London 1976) 111–12.
28. William Wordsworth, *The Excursion*, bk III, 'Despondency'; Samuel Taylor Coleridge, 'Dejection, An Ode'.
29. Søren Kierkegaard, *Either/Or* (trs. F.and L.M. Swenson) (NY 1959), 282, 287.
30. Ibid. 173, 182, 229.
31. Ibid. 230–31.

32. E.g. Pattison, *Kierkegaard*, 112.
33. Peter France, *Greek as a Treat* (London 1993), 123.
34. Ellul, *The Ethics of Freedom*, 231.
35. Leland Ryken, *Work and Leisure in Christian Perspective* (Leicester 1989), 54.
36. From Gerald Heard, *Science in the Making* quoted by T.S. Eliot in *Revelation: Essays by Gustav Aulen, et al.* (London 1937), 6–7.
37. Quoted in J.P. Diggins, *Thorstein Veblen* (Princeton, NJ 1999), 81.
38. Paul Tournier, *Learning to Grow Old* (London 1972),129–30.
39. Ibid. 5, 11, 133, 130.
40. J.D.G. Dunn, *Christian Liberty: A New Testament Perspective* (Carlisle 1993), 105.
41. W.H. Vanstone, *The Stature of Waiting* (London 1982), 50.

# Play, Games and Laughter

*In the Christian tradition play has often been denounced. In the twentieth century it was largely reinstated, in reaction against a widely proclaimed gospel of work. Some definitions of play even bring out similarities to ideas of heaven. Huizinga stressed its voluntariness, its distinctiveness from ordinary life, and its orderly rules. In theology play has been re-assessed as a proper image of creation; but this has a shaky scriptural basis, and the argument has been attacked as trivializing creation and even as a device to protect bourgeois enjoyments. Play exists within a separated part of life, and its varieties are too great for it to be treated as a single clear concept. Christian writers reveal their individual preferences in commending different kinds of play within leisure, without always taking adequate account of the pressures of conformity within a consumerist society. Similar difficulties affect the image of dance as an analogy for the divine activity, and the ambiguous ideal of 'eutrapelia' (fun). Laughter, too, is a problematical element in human behaviour – either a 'signal of transcendence' or a sign of the meaningless absurdity of human life. Play, games and laughter are all appropriate to leisure; but they call for a critical awareness of their ambiguity, if they are to lead to abundance of life.*

Play and games have not been given much respect in the Christian tradition. There are obvious reasons for this. In the first age of the church, games in the Roman empire were often degrading spectacles. Whatever nobility there had been in the Olympic ideal, dependent as it had been on civic pride and rivalry, had been forgotten in the mass entertainment of the arenas which were built all over the Roman world. Those who wrote the report of the COPEC Commission on Leisure in 1924 contrasted the 'clean sportsmanship' of the Greek games with the 'bestial passions' of the Roman circus. The fact that some Christians suffered martyrdom in the arena inevitably increased the odium with which the public games were regarded. A further reason for regarding the games with abhorrence was that they still aroused memories of their ritual origins. The emperor Constantine prohibited gladiatorial contests, but other kinds of games flourished, with their attendant excesses. At the turn of the fifth century the behaviour of the crowds in Constantinople at chariot races matched the worst that football hooligans could do in the twentieth. The denunciations of the archbishop, John Chrysostom, rang out. He contrasted the splendour of God's creation with the miserable pleasures of the mob.

> For you the sun rose, the moon lit up the night, choirs of stars spangled the sky; for you the winds blew, and rivers ran, seeds germinated, plants grew, and the whole course of nature kept its proper order; but you, when creation is ministering to your needs, you fulfil the pleasure of the devil.[1]

But Chrysostom could not restrain the fans then; nor has the disapproval of Christian moralists across the centuries. Games and amusements were, to the churchmen of the Reformation period, occasions for sin and pretexts for vice, and needed careful control.

Over the centuries, however, Christian moralists had to accept that the human play instinct would always find some expression. Thomas Aquinas wrote of 'those words and deeds in which nothing is sought but the soul's pleasure' which are called 'playful or humorous' (*ludicra vel iocosa*), and said that they were necessary for the solace of the soul.[2] But he argued that too little playing was less wrong than playing too much. It was necessary to recognize what Caillois called 'the permanence of the insignificant'.[3] More than that, there was a positive tradition about games which contributed to Christian teaching. It had to do with their use in training for battle. A fifteenth-century handbook for the education of boys prescribed stated times for games, and said that they could become more violent as the boys grew up, so that after puberty they should include military drill as well as riding, shooting, slinging, and throwing javelins.[4] The praise of 'muscular Christianity' did not originate in Victorian times, nor did it die then. In 1915 the future archbishop, Cyril Garbett, edited a handbook for parish work in which one of his curates wrote that religion must influence a man's time off as well as his work, and referred with approval to the belief that 'the best test of a man's character is the way he plays his games'. 'There is no more certain criterion of the worth of a man's religion than the way he takes his pleasures.' For boys, that included playing a clean game.[5] The sexism of the times is shown by the author's comparable activity for girls: they would 'romp without coarseness'. It is still true that public attitudes discriminate against equal provision of sporting facilities for women,[6] but so far, at least, women's sport has escaped some of the negative criticisms aimed at male sports in Christian circles.

There has been this double tradition, then, with the emphasis varying from time to time and from writer to writer. The twentieth century seems to have shown an increasingly favourable attitude among Christian commentators, which is no doubt related to the increase in leisure. As early as 1912 the American Baptist theologian, Walter Rauschenbusch wrote:

The real joy of life is in its play. Play is anything we do for the love and joy of doing it, apart from any profit, compulsion, or sense of duty. It is the real living of life with the feeling of freedom and self-expression. Play is the business of childhood, and its continuation in later years is the prolongation of youth. Real civilization should increase the margin of time given to play.[7]

This was a rather unusual attitude, as indeed Rauschenbusch's 'social gospel' was a minority opinion in the American churches. A theology of work was more appropriate to the harder times of the middle decades of the century. But there were other voices to be heard, championing the importance of play in human life. In his autobiographical sketch, *On the Boundary*, Paul Tillich spoke of his early delight in play (games, sports, entertainment) and in 'the playful emotion that accompanies productive moments' which he even called 'the sublimest form of human freedom'.[8] That dates from the early years of the twentieth century. Tillich was born in 1886, but his personal influence extended beyond the Second World War. His *Theology of Culture* was published in 1959. It was in this post-war period that play became a topic for serious discussion in Christian circles.

One of the most sustained attempts to reinstate play in our scale of values was Johan Huizinga's *Homo Ludens*, first published in an English translation in 1949. It concentrates on those activities which conform to his own definition and characterization of play. He defines a game as:

a free activity standing quite consciously outside 'ordinary' life as being 'not serious', but at the same time absorbing the player intensely and utterly. It is an activity connected with no material interest, and no profit can be gained by it. It proceeds within its own proper boundaries of time and space according to fixed rules in an orderly manner. It promotes the formation of social groupings which tend to surround themselves with secrecy and to stress their difference from the common world by disguise or other means.[9]

It is curious that this definition, offered as an objective description of play as we know it, has points of similarity with the Christian understanding of the life of the world to come. It is free from the narrow self-seeking motives of worldly life. It binds the players in fellowship with each other. It is intensely and utterly absorbing. And if we find ourselves thinking that the activity of heaven is traditionally described in musical terms, we have Huizinga to remind us that the verb we use of instrumentalists is precisely 'to play'.

So play, like worship, may be an anticipation of the life of heaven. Does it matter that, unlike worship, it lacks conscious reference to God? 'Thou God seest me' and 'Ever in the great Taskmaster's eye' are clichés of Victorian religion which seem to have an inescapable moralistic connotation, as though

God is on the watch to see whether human beings get up to some naughtiness or take a breather from proper obedience. But even such phrases need not mean that the gaze must constantly be returned. God, it may be thought, does not want his creatures always to be thinking about him consciously here on earth, because it would prevent them concentrating on the task in hand. The eye surgeon, the concert pianist, the athlete at the pole-vault, need all their attention upon what they are doing. Whatever levels of consciousness might belong to another life, the continuation of personal identity would imply some foreground of attention as well as deep awareness of God's glory. The justification of play is precisely that it releases the participants from the demands of work and social duties into a 'world of its own', a lesser reality with its own artificial rules.

In a more extended description of play,[10] Huizinga elaborates three characteristics: its voluntary nature, its distinction from 'ordinary' life, and its orderliness. Each of them may be related to the Christian understanding of humanity. First, voluntariness: 'All play is a voluntary activity ... Play is superfluous ... It is never imposed by physical necessity or moral duty. It is never a task. It is done at leisure, during "free time".' Voluntariness means the exercise of freedom. Here is something which might be part of an answer the question, 'What is freedom for?' The freedom of human beings is for play, as well as for worship and service; they are all essentially voluntary activities. All three can be fitted into Christ's summary of the law. As Coleridge said; 'We must not only love our neighbours as ourselves, but ourselves likewise as our neighbours; and we can do neither unless we love God above both.'[11] The element of self-love (which we have already considered) is assumed in the second great commandment and finds an appropriate outlet in losing oneself in play. It is in losing one's life that one can find it.

The second characteristic of play which Huizinga elaborates is its distinction from ordinary life: 'Play is not "ordinary" or "real" life. It is rather a stepping out of 'real' life into a temporary sphere of activity with a disposition all its own.' It is different because it interrupts the appetitive process. It evokes a special kind of devotion and is satisfying in itself. If we are looking for what Peter L. Berger has called 'signals of transcendence', we can find another such signal here. The 'ordinary' life of the competitive, ambitious world is so little satisfying to human beings that they are driven by their own created and creative nature to invent games; that is, they are driven to invent another world where relationships are different, and even competitiveness is only the limited tension which can be resolved by the final handshake or the drink in the clubhouse. Of course games, like all forms of leisure, can be invaded and corrupted by the 'real' world, and their transcendence thereby destroyed. In their uncorrupt nature, however, they are distinct from ordinary life. But they are also temporary. Like music, all play moves according to artificial rules towards its own opposite – silence, or rest. Perhaps that is another indicator of the life of heaven. 'There remains a sabbath rest for the people of God; for whoever enters God's rest also ceases from his labours as God did from his'.[12] That text refers to the transition from this life to the life of the world to come. What the writer to the Hebrews did not elaborate was how that rest might be more than boring inactivity, when the labours of life were over, or, for that matter, what God might do with his own rest. The analogy with play presents a kind of circular metaphor: from rest through self-forgetful action and back to rest.

It is in terms of the movement of music or of games, through enjoyment to rest, that we can conceptualize a rest that is lively and enjoyable. Huizinga also says that play is secluded in time and space; in time limited but repeated, and in the appointed space of the 'play-ground', where 'an absolute and peculiar order reigns' and where this order creates a community. This sounds rather comic to those who associate the word 'play-ground' with the riotous activities of school breaks; but even there, if we concentrate on particular groups absorbed in their own games, we can see something of the 'peculiar order' and the community which it creates. The play-grounds of this world are a kind of earnest or foretaste of the four-square city of God inhabited by the play-community, God's peculiar people.

It is easy to be carried along by Huizinga's enthusiasm for the play element in culture and to see its relevance to a reinterpretation of the traditional Christian views of the world either as a vale of soul-making or, in the scheme which Aquinas inherited and expounded, as the arena of the active life from which an élite might escape into that life of contemplation which is nearest to the life of heaven itself. He surveys many aspects of human activity which can be called play, especially in the period before the industrial revolution, and offers a varied menu.[13] But there is something unsatisfying about *Homo Ludens* in the end. It is partly, as George Steiner says in an introduction to the English edition of 1970, that it is nostalgic.[14] Huizinga looks back beyond nineteenth-century utilitarianism whose exponents, he says, 'killed the mysteries and acquitted man of guilt and sin. But they had forgotten to free him of folly and myopia, and he seemed only fit to mould the world after the pattern of his own banality.'

In Huizinga's view the real play-spirit is threatened with extinction. Modern developments are either sterile or puerile. The play element has been contaminated and debased by exploitation for ulterior ends, so that it is 'a false seeming, a masking of political purposes behind the illusion of genuine play forms'. But he does not work out the details of this criticism, which might contribute to a positive and theological understanding of leisure. That is not surprising, because Huizinga is not addressing that task. His aim is to argue that civilization, or culture, arises from play 'like a babe detaching itself from the womb'. It 'arises *in* and *as* play and never leaves it'.[15] Neither civilization nor culture is identical with leisure. But if Huizinga's description of play is right, it stands as a permanent critique of the forms of leisure. Those forms need to be judged by the culture which they nourish. Whatever play means in childhood, as an arena of learning, in adulthood its function is to be a continuing witness to the transcendent, to eternal life, to the freedom of heaven.

After the post-war period of austerity, theologians were tempted to jump on the band-wagon of play. There had been so much thought given to the theology of work. Work was a divine ordinance. According to the New Testament, even slaves should see their work as an offering to God, not just to their masters.[16] The rhythm of human life was that of work and worship. Rest from work was either to recuperate for more work or, at best, an opportunity for worship. So, for example, Alan Richardson in his exposition of the teaching of the bible could say:

> There are those who in our day regard progress in history as leading towards a Utopia in which it will hardly be necessary to work at all; from a biblical point of view they are just as much the victims of a mistaken eschatology as were Paul's converts in Thessalonica.[17]

Work had not previously stood on a pedestal for unqualified admiration. A recent essay, aiming to test Weber's thesis in *The Protestant Ethic and the Spirit of Capitalism*, has argued not only that a contrast of Protestant and Catholic cannot be fully sustained, but also that neither tradition surrendered completely to the idea of the sanctification of work and thrift. Work, like idleness, was accused of stealing time that should be reserved for devotion.[18] Perhaps it was the aftermath of the huge destruction during the Second World War which encouraged the emphasis on the supreme worth of labour, when reconstruction was the great priority. But in any case a one-sided stress in Christian teaching had a long history in industrialized society. It has even been suggested that it was as much to blame for the alienation of the working classes from the churches as any other factor. José Harris writes of 'the cumulative impact of several centuries of rationalizing puritanism, that had severed the archaic ties between work, worship, and pleasure', though she also acknowledges that the churches themselves were often to the forefront in promoting many aspects of the new leisure activities in the latter part of the nineteenth century.[19] It is often said that there is a rhythm in human life, alternating between work and rest. Perhaps there is a rhythm, too, in the emphases of theology. In due course the theology of work was succeeded by a theology of play, in which Huizinga was seen as an important ally.

A good example of the theological re-assessment of play is Hugo Rahner's *Man at Play*.[20] Along with others, and indeed with Thomas Aquinas, he refers to the obscure passage in Ecclesiasticus 32.11–12 which seems to say 'play and do what you like'.[21] It is not a passage of great authority, and the fact that writers have to resort to it shows how little else could be found in the Bible to support directly a theology of play. In fact, its immediate context refers to proper behaviour in the company of the great, and its natural meaning is simply advice not to outstay your welcome but to go home and pass the time there in any way you like. Possibly more relevant to the topic of play is the passage in Proverbs 8.27–31 which describes the role of wisdom (*sophia*) in the creation of the world. When God marked out the foundations of the earth, 'I was daily his delight, rejoicing before him always, rejoicing in his inhabited world'. The Vulgate twice translates the word for 'rejoicing' by 'playing' (*ludens*) and this was picked up by later commentators and built into the foundations of a doctrine of creation as the play of the divine wisdom. (This text, too, provides only shaky support for the doctrine, for the original Greek word translated in this way[22] has more to do with inward feelings than outward actions, rejoicing rather than playing.) Rahner offers a catena of references to the idea of play, stretching from Plato and Aristotle through some of the Greek and Latin Fathers to Aquinas. The outcome is to show that the idea of Wisdom or the Word (Logos) 'playing' in the acts of creation has a respectable heredity in Christian thought.

There are a number of obvious problems inherent in this idea. They were evident in the publication of Jürgen Moltmann's essay, 'The First Liberated Men in Creation' under the title *Theology of Play*, together with responses by some 'outstanding representatives of the theology of play' in America. Moltmann had felt free to speak of God's play in creation, and was taken aback to find that the American contributors wanted to extend the idea to include 'the crucifixion as play'. That was going too far in the use of the image of play, and Moltmann had to reply by stating 'the rules of the game this one fellow human feels constrained by'. He quoted Hegel to the effect that 'The divine life and the divine knowing may well also be understood as a play with itself. But this idea deteriorates to mere homily if the seriousness, pain, patience and work of the negative is missing therein.' He then continued:

> Only false prophets speak of peace and of total play when the great play has not even begun. The cross of Christ remains an offense, and Auschwitz remains Auschwitz – until the dead rise and all begin to dance because everything has become new.[23]

For Moltmann play was an eschatological concept.

Apart from any such linking of play with crucifixion, there has been a tendency to focus on the notion of child's play.[24] To equate this with play, games or sport in the adult world puts in question any contrast between experimental play in a period of latency and the proper function of adult recreation. When used as a model for creation it also tends to reduce the dignity of God's creative acts. This led Vanstone to reject the idea of creation as play. His book, *Love's Endeavour, Love's Expense* might be characterized as a thoughtful condemnation of it. The popular image of creation, he said, was of effortless activity, of easy control and limited endeavour, with resources held in reserve, and power unused. It reduced creation to an almost trivial activity and

its ultimate trivialization appears not in popular devotion but in that

school or fashion of contemporary theology which describes the creation
in terms of the activity of 'play' ... an almost explicit repudiation of the
possibility that the creation is the work of authentic love.[25]

Creation is a work of costly joy, not of child's play.

There is certainly some risk of unreal sentimentality in all such invocations
of childhood, excusable perhaps in the light of Jesus' saying, 'It is to such as
these that the kingdom of God belongs',[26] but to be used with great
circumspection. It is instructive to listen to a creative writer who seemed to
have an instinctive sympathy with childhood – as witness *A Child's Garden of
Verses* – Robert Louis Stevenson. He was very clear about the limitations of
child's play. The child, he said, exhibits 'a pedestrian fancy'. There was a
defect in the child's imagination because his experience was incomplete. That
'stage-wardrobe and scene-room that we call memory is so ill-provided' that
he needs some external aid, the wooden sword, or the jointed stick that does
for a doll to represent a baby. So play and conscious art are not the same kind
of thing. Art may be derived from play, but only when it can depend upon
'philosophical interest beyond the scope of childhood'.[27] Imagination belongs
to a later stage of human development than childhood. To quote Coleridge
again, on the maturing personality:

> In Youth and early Manhood the Mind and Nature are, as it were, two
> rival Artists, both potent Magicians, and engaged, like the King's
> Daughter and the rebel Genie in the Arabian Nights Entertainments, in
> sharp conflict of Conjuration – each having for its object to turn the
> other into Canvas to paint on.[28]

Coleridge was the last person to think the act of creation was something easy
or self-regarding. It was hardly play at all; more like heavy work.

The real difficulty, however, of using play as a theological idea is that it is
itself so ambiguous. Along with Huizinga we need to read Roger Caillois to
whom the word 'play' is a trap.[29] He acknowledges fully his debt to Huizinga,
but believes there are 'strange gaps' in his presentation. There is no single
thing called play, but many kinds of play which he sets out to classify. Perhaps
we need not linger over the details of his classification, except to say that he
offers four main categories (competitive games, games of chance, simulation
games, and 'vertigo' or dizzying games); and in each category there are different
examples which range from those which are exuberant or fantastic to those
which have strict rules. Within these categories the common characteristics of
play, according to Caillois, are that it is

1.　Free – not obligatory;
2.　Separate – within certain limits of space and time;
3.　Uncertain – its outcome not determined;

4.      Unproductive – allowing no more than an exchange of property;
5.      Governed by rules, which suspend ordinary laws; and
6.      Make-believe, or a 'free unreality'.

It is worth adding that most types of play involve some kind of interaction with a person of equal status. There are, certainly, some solitary games, but even they (as Pascal said) are often played for the pleasure of boasting how well we played them. They are improved when there is an audience, present or future.

Compare all this with how Hugo Rahner (in his own phrase) begins to 'sketch out a few fundamental ideas' about play.

> Play is a human activity which engages of necessity both soul and body. It is the expression of an inward spiritual skill, successfully realized with the aid of physically visible gesture, audible sound and tangible matter. ... And so we talk of play whenever the mastery of the spirit over the possibilities presented by the body has in some way attained its perfection, a perfection that shows itself in the easy agility, the shimmering elegance of some acquired skill; when word, sound or gesture has been made obedient and pliable to the spirit.[30]

It is clear that Rahner has a special kind of play in mind when he goes on to develop the theological idea of the Logos playing before the face of the Father – there are many kinds of play which do not show 'shimmering elegance'. On the basis of Proverbs 8.27–31 (already quoted) and 2 Samuel 6.5 and 21 (which describes David's dance before the Lord), together with a certain line of thought in some of the Fathers, he feels able to speak of God as engaging in play. This notion then becomes a fact ('since God is a *Deus vere ludens*')[31] and leads to the conclusion that man, too, must be a creature that plays. The best thing for man is to imitate 'the quality of God's own creative power by his lightness of touch, by his regard for beauty, by his wisdom, and by the sober seriousness of his endeavour'.

This line of argument (with its comprehensive spectrum of ideas from lightness of touch to sober seriousness) should only be accepted with many reservations. The scriptural basis is extremely shaky. Wisdom is a feminine noun and its significance in Proverbs 8 is a matter of disagreement among scholars.[32] It is certainly not the Logos in the intention of the original writer. The action described is probably not playing but rejoicing. The idea of the Father introduces an emotive picture of a little child absorbed in some imaginative play while the father watches sympathetically. But the text of verse 30 is uncertain and its meaning obscure. It may simply mean that the personified figure of wisdom was present as an observer and the 'master workman' (if that is the right translation) is not wisdom but the LORD.[33] These reservations do not necessarily invalidate later theological speculations, of course, but they show that in the argument there was a process of reading back into the text ideas which originated elsewhere, probably in Greek philosophy.

Two closely related questions arise which require to be explored further. What kind of play is under consideration? And what is the social context in which play came to the forefront of a particular theologian's attention? First, then, we need to be clear what kind of play may be considered a proper part of divine activity, if we are to accept the idea of the Logos playing before the Father. Huizinga offers us what he intends as an attractive list: 'All poetry is born of play: the sacred play of worship, the festive play of courtship, the martial play of contest, the disputatious play of braggadocio, mockery and invective, the nimble play of wit and readiness.'[34] That has more appeal than Caillois's catalogue, which includes, along with more evidently cultural activities, things like crossword puzzles, wrestling, roulette, children's initiations, and tight-rope walking, not to mention what he calls corruptions such as astrology and drugs.[35] We can hardly include all these as models from which we can extrapolate to the activity of the Logos. In any case, the personification of Wisdom in Proverbs is as much connected with warning against wrong behaviour as with good examples of how to behave. As for the question about the social context in which play was taken to the bosom of theology at a particular time, we have the acerbic remarks of David E. Jenkins, in an introduction to Moltmann's *Theology And Joy*, about

> the possibility that the sudden interest in 'play' ... is largely (and too much) conditioned by the emergence of the space and the need for a 'leisured culture' in the too-affluent and so-called incipiently 'post-industrial' societies ... Talk of 'play' could therefore be a bourgeois device to protect the enjoyment of the bourgeoisie.[36]

It is certainly noticeable that theologians and Christian writers are good at producing reasons to justify the particular forms of leisure activity which they find congenial, and those forms have naturally arisen within their own class cultures. Paul Tournier turned the leisure of retirement into a second career, and wrote as though this should be the general practice. Paul Tillich's task of creating a theology of culture followed from his early experiences, 'the early intoxicated love of literature and the tremendous discovery of art when he sought relief from the horrors of war in a study of painting'.[37] This led in his own particular case to serious academic study, which can hardly count as leisure. But it also validated the enjoyment of literature and art by those who did not have this professional commitment. By other writers the figure of Mozart has been raised to a stature far above mere entertainment, so that he seems almost to be an obligatory object of concern to the Christian believer. Kierkegaard's fascination with him led to an extended analysis of his operas, and in doing so he inevitably justified devoting to his music both time and thought in leisure. An even more curious example is that of Karl Barth. In the study in which he worked two portraits, of Calvin and Mozart, hung side by side and at the same height.[38] He was sure that in heaven (which is often a symbol for leisure), when the angels were not praising God, they played Mozart.[39] This might appear to be just a witticism, if it were not that he devoted some pages of *Church Dogmatics* to a serious claim that Mozart 'has a place in theology'. He knew something about creation in its total goodness which theologians did not know.[40] It would have been intriguing if Barth had attributed theological significance to his other leisure interests: horse-riding and detective novels. Perhaps they could have been subjected to theological inquiry and would have been equally revealing: bonding with non-human creatures or problem-solving as elements in 'abundant life'.

We have here one (but only one) of the difficulties of using the idea of 'play' in a Christian context – the subjective nature of each individual's experience of different kinds of play. Writers have great difficulty in separating their subjective responses from an objective assessment of a particular form of play. If music is regarded as a form of playing, there are so many layers which go to make up its reality: the composer's personality and experience, the performers' interpretation and the listeners' response. There is no single thing that is a piece of music. Barth may enthuse over Mozart, but, as George Steiner has said, he risks the whole gamut of muddle and embarrassment. 'Springs are licensed to murmur and gush; not adults.'[41] The human experience of watching a production of Mozart's *Don Giovanni* will range from the sophisticated reflections of Kierkegaard to something of a merely sensual nature. A theologian may use any experience of play he chooses as a starting-point for his theologizing and some of his readers may find it a helpful way of thinking. But that process by itself does not establish that particular kind of play, or any other, as generally commendable. The theology comes from the theologian not from the example of play.

Perhaps it seems churlish to respond coolly to the enthusiasm, properly so called, of the advocates of play as a key to the mystical understanding of the world. But consider the following extract from *Man at Play*.[42]

> To play is to yield oneself to a kind of magic, to enact to oneself the absolutely other, to pre-empt the future, to give the lie to the inconvenient world of fact. In play earthly realities become, of a sudden, things of the transient moment, presently left behind, then disposed of and buried in the past; the mind is prepared to accept the unimagined and incredible, to enter a world where different laws apply, to be relieved of all the weights that bear down, to be free, kingly, unfettered and divine. Man at play is reaching out – as has already been said – for that superlative ease, in which even the body, freed from its earthly burden, moves to the effortless measures of a heavenly dance.

It is hard to resist putting alongside this idyllic picture another scene which reminds us what 'play' means to other people.

One of the most dreadful sights in the country of the old is that of long rows of women playing the Las Vegas fruit machines. Had Dante heard of it he would have cleared a space for it in Hell.[43]

But the difficulty presented by the mystical view of play lies much deeper than the contrast of surface images and the impossibility of applying Rahner's description to most of the types of play practised in our consumerist society. It lies in the assumption that emancipation from 'earthly realities' (a strange objective in the context of an incarnational religion) is the way to the divine. That was a notion that belonged to the romantic movement, but in an age of deconstruction it may be seen as only one of a number of excusable delusions. Indeed its rejection goes back at least to Nietzsche, for whom play was the highest of human activities precisely because there was nothing beyond it, no eternal realm to which it gave access. It was its own justification.[44]

On the basis of Christian belief there is also another difficulty to be considered, if human play is to be given significance by seeing it as a kind of reflection of the activity of the divine wisdom in creation. It arises from the description of play as something which exists within deliberately drawn limits, and therefore only a part of the totality of experience. It is 'a finite province of meaning to which individuals can emigrate from the reality of everyday life'.[45] More than that, each kind of play represents only one of a number of coexistent provinces of meaning, inhabited by its own defined community of voluntary players. None of them by itself corresponds to the totality of the created order; nor do all of them together. It might just be possible to develop the analogy between the divine creation and our experience of play by suggesting that our particular world, or even our particular universe, is only one of a number of games which God plays. It has certainly been proposed that Jesus Christ is to be understood as God's particular word for this world, and that God has other words for other worlds.[46] As our image of the universe expands through scientific exploration, this line of thought has a certain appeal. Unfortunately the words 'play' and 'games' connote activities which are not serious, not real. They exist as enclaves within reality. We cannot escape the contradiction between unserious playfulness and serious creativity.

Are there, nevertheless, any kinds of playful activity that can be regarded as creatively expressive? Only activities of that sort seem suitable for the divine wisdom before the face of the Father. Other kinds seem derogatory to the act of creation which has produced the wonder and the terror of our universe. Those kinds of play which have arbitrary rules of a competitive kind are not appropriate. Perhaps that is why one particular kind of 'play' has appealed to the religious imagination: the dance. Jürgen Moltmann, in discussing 'the world as dance' has compared the Hindu conception of Shiva as the Lord of the Dance with Christian traditions of the Logos as the leader of the heavenly dance.[47] Here again we face the ambiguity of the significant word, as we do with 'play'. There are innumerable kinds of dance, and many of them are useless as analogies for the divine acts of creation. The war-dance is designed to rouse valour for conflict. Other kinds of dance aim to bond groups of people together so that the individuals lose their identity,[48] or to arouse sexual energies to promote fertility. Yet other kinds of dance tell stories, in order to maintain traditions or simply to provide the enjoyment of story-telling. Moltmann notes that Shiva represents the whole cycle of creation and destruction and creation again, whereas the Christian story cannot be represented by such a circular dance. The best that can be done is to tell the Christian story in terms of an original dancing chorus which has been disorganized by the Fall and is to regain its rhythm and harmony through Christ as the leader of the dance. This kind of image clearly has an appeal to those whose experience of dance has been one of joy and fulfilment. Here we have, perhaps, the relevance of play and dance to the consideration of leisure. It is the mood or frame of mind which is significant, rather than the specific activity. Play or dance can only be seen as a foretaste of heaven if they unite the participants in a joyful self-offering under the loving gaze of the Creator.

It is relevant to notice that the full title of Hugo Rahner's book is *Man at Play, or Did You Ever Practise Eutrapelia?* The position of the final chapter, on 'Eutrapelia: a Forgotten Virtue' (originally a separate essay), at the end of his discussion of play suggests that it is an important part of the message of the book. In it Rahner sets out to reinstate *eutrapelia* as a Greek virtue baptized in Christ. Here again ambiguity attends the word, as it does in different ways 'play' and 'dance'. This time it is not the difficulty of choosing among many possible varieties within the same comprehensive class. It is simply that the word eutrapelia has been used in different contexts to mean almost contradictory things. If we start again with biblical usage, as in the case of playing, there is only one occurrence of eutrapelia in the New Testament, and it does not help with its reinstatement as a virtue. 'Let there be no filthiness, nor silly talk, nor levity, which are not convenient', we read in Ephesians 5.4 (RSV), and the third of these shameful things (levity) is *eutrapelia*. Its earlier Greek usage was less derogatory, and carried some of the force of its etymology, which has to do with turning or flexibility. So it was used of verbal ability – something like 'wit'. It is easy to see how this meaning teeters on a knife-edge between a kind of happy amusement at the oddities of human existence and a sort of smartness which makes a mockery even of sacred things. In the latter sense the writer of Ephesians warns his readers against it. It had not seemed a bad thing to Aristotle, and so when Thomas Aquinas dipped his bucket in the Aristotelian well he came up with a defence of it.

We see the progress of an idea in the changed meaning of the word. Attic wit which had been good at exposing illogicality or hypocrisy could overreach itself (as the writer to the Ephesians knew) in debunking genuine religion or true morality. It was inevitable that the primitive church and the early Fathers would see the bad side of it. In due course the church became responsible for society as a whole and gained confidence from its enhanced status. Then the official attitude to pleasure began to change. It has been argued[49] that 'a new psychological principle of play' became operative in Christianity. 'Whereas a pagan resorted to pleasure as to a drug and anodyne dulling the ugly and gnawing horrors of life's mysteries, the Christian, essentially serious, could give rein to a light-hearted gaiety.' Whether or not this was the case, the change in status of the church from an endangered minority sect to an authoritative power in society enabled it to tolerate amusements which it had once been inclined to condemn, when they had been cleared of their grosser elements. With this change came the rehabilitation of *eutrapelia*. It occupied, in the judgement of Thomas Aquinas, the favoured middle position between a kind of gloomy seriousness on the one hand and scurrilous buffoonery (*bomolochia*) on the other. It acquired the virtuous meaning of moderate light-heartedness – in Latin, *urbanitas*.[50] In Aquinas's praise of *eutrapelia* we can perhaps catch a glimpse of the society he knew best, the enclosed community of a religious order. For it is a common experience that any single-sex group held together by a shared purpose, however serious or earnest they may be in general, will occasionally become childishly hilarious – officers in a regiment, or clergy, or lawyers, or business men or a sorority. They may easily cross the borderline between *eutrapelia* and *bomolochia*, comedy and boorishness.

The evolution of the idea, if not the word, did not stop with Aquinas, as we can see from recent writings in favour of 'play'. The nearest modern equivalent for *eutrapelia* is probably the word 'fun', which has just the same kind of ambiguous meaning. A phrase such as 'just a bit of harmless fun' alerts us to the possibility that fun may be harmful, may be malicious. Here we see the problem of coupling *eutrapelia* with the theology of play. The exalted quality of play indicated by speaking of 'that superlative ease, in which even the body, freed from its earthly burden, moves to the effortless measures of a heavenly dance' is not well described as *eutrapelia*. It is too graceful, too significant, to be fun. The development of the leisure society, however, magnifies the role of fun. It is no longer merely an occasional interruption of the serious concerns of work and social duties, much to be desired in order to relax mind and body. It comes to characterize longer and longer periods of holiday or retirement, and from there it can spread. Leisure is in danger of being taken over by what has been called a 'fun morality', when the justifiable amusements which served a good purpose in a life dominated by work are allowed (in a curious variant of 'Parkinson's Law') to expand to fill the time available for their completion.

One of the difficulties inherent in the use of ambiguous words like *eutrapelia* or fun is that they raise questions of moral judgement which are an incubus in times of leisure. There is a long tradition of amusement derived from deceiving gullible people which exists on a knife-edge between fun and cruelty. Its most evident example at present is a sort of television programme, much in vogue and easy to make with concealed cameras. Going back a few generations, the picture of village life captured by A.L. Rowse in his description of his Cornish childhood is one in which the chief form of amusement was deceiving, and sometimes frightening, each other. 'The great point was to "have" somebody, never to be "had" yourself'.[51] The tradition is fully represented in Shakespeare's plays, where we see the whole range of deceptions from fun to horror. It is easy to laugh at Falstaff in *The Merry Wives of Windsor*, not so easy to laugh at the cruelty practised on Malvolio in *Twelfth Night*, and impossible to find it funny when deception leads to tragedy in *Othello*. In stage presentations other factors are involved, for 'suspension of disbelief' is never total, and we are aware that the deception we are watching does not deceive the actors. But we may be sure that Shakespeare was putting on the stage what he knew to be paralleled in daily life. Because fun can be cruel as well as joyful, we need to hesitate before agreeing with Leland Ryken, that 'we might even speak of the fun impulse evident in Jesus' humor, and we know that a main purpose of leisure is simply to have fun'.[52] Certainly there is no record of Jesus 'having people on'. Those who put a high value on a sense of humour get needlessly worried when they fail to find it, and so have to imagine it, in the gospels. George Tyrrell once teased his friend von Hügel for not having any 'protective vices', and went on, perhaps not very seriously, 'The lack of a play-instinct in Christ is no doubt due to Docetan suppressions, and represents a blemished and imperfect humanity'.[53] Here we have moved far away from the exaltation of play as equivalent to the divine act of creation, and are back in the proper realm of leisure.

The ambiguity which is inherent in the idea of fun also infects laughter. Laughter is a topic of endless fascination for writers in a number of different disciplines,[54] because it seems to be an exclusively human characteristic, and because it is so difficult to explain. Indeed the very notion of explaining it is almost self-contradictory. Explanation is the one thing that is sure to kill laughter. But at least we can try to sort out some of the different kinds of laughter. It does not help our appreciation of the nuances of the word that sometimes writers fail to distinguish between laughter and smiles. For example, Evelyn Underhill says that Dante in *The Divine Comedy* sees the whole universe laugh as it glorifies God, though his meaning is more likely to be something less explosive and short-lived than laughter.[55] A great deal of laughter is cruel, and this is borne out by its commonest meaning in the scriptures. The psalmist often complains that he suffers from the mocking laughter of other people when he is in misery (e.g. 22.7). Such scornful laughter has been a constant feature of human behaviour across the centuries. It is not altogether surprising, therefore, that the same attitude is attributed to God in the Old Testament (e.g. Psalm 2.4; 37.13; 59.8). God has the last laugh. It is an unattractive image of the supreme reality. We can try to come to terms with this kind of language by claiming that in Christian belief God was incarnate, and is always present alongside those who are mocked and derided. The pattern of the sufferer being mocked is repeated in the story of the passion of Jesus. He is mocked by the soldiers before the crucifixion and jeered at on the cross.

In the Gospels there are two different words of related origin with very distinct meanings,[56] and English versions cannot easily bring out the contrast. For example, in Luke 8.53 the laughter is derisive ('they laughed at him'), but in Luke 6.21 it is the laughter of happiness ('Blessed are you who weep now, for you will laugh'). This kind of happy laughter is closely related to the mood of joy which is represented as characteristic of the redeemed, and in one passage is attributed to Jesus himself, when he 'rejoiced in the Holy Spirit' (Luke 10.21). It is a relief to turn from mocking laughter to the laughter which lights up daily life. Even in the Old Testament we can see one kind of laughter being transformed into the other in the story of Abraham and Sarah in Genesis 17.17–21.[57] When they are promised a son in their old age, they laugh with incredulity. When the promise is realized, Sarah laughs with joy. In his own name the patriarch Isaac carries into the future of the chosen people a remembrance of happy laughter. That future was to contain much suffering, but there would always be spaces for laughter. As Vanstone has said,[58]

> In many a concrete situation there is something to spare of triumph and of joy which cannot possibly be expended for the redeeming of tragedy: there is a measure of freedom, of 'leisure', which is unchallenged by the needs and distresses of the surrounding world.

Another testimony is in the writings of Berdyaev, already quoted. He criticizes some kinds of asceticism for denying the human need for leisure, for imagination, for laughter.[59]

> Laughter has a liberating quality which exalts man above his daily worries and oppressive suffering. It must take its place in the spiritual life and help to liberate man from his instincts of masochism and sadism.

This theme of the liberating effect of laughter has recently been developed at greater length by Peter Berger, in the book which has the significant title, *Redeeming Laughter*. For him, the comic is a signal of transcendence, suggesting a world made whole, a world without pain, in which the tragic facts of daily reality are redeemed.[60] The clown, that great maker of laughter, has painlessness imputed to him. Whatever happens to him, he always comes up smiling.

To see laughter like this is, of course, an act of faith. There are others who see it as self-deception, and think it belongs to the dignity of our human status to laugh in the face of meaninglessness. That attitude underlies what has been called 'the theatre of the absurd'. For its exponents there is no objective reality other than the inner reality of our own consciousness. When that inner consciousness is set free from logic, the result may be comic or brutal. Where there is laughter, it is 'liberating laughter at the recognition of the absurdity of the universe'.[61] The writers in this tradition take absurdity as proof of pointlessness, of atheism. This legitimates for them the representation of brutality without moral comment, for brutality is simply one part of a pointless world. But there is another way of responding to absurdity, nowhere better shown than by G.K. Chesterton. He loved paradox and praised nonsense. This attitude which marked much of his writing is concisely expressed in his essay, 'A Defence of Nonsense'.[62] For Chesterton nonsense is the nurturer of wonder, for a thing 'cannot be completely wonderful so long as it remains sensible'. In the Book of Job, he says, the argument which convinces the infidel is not a picture of the ordered beneficence of the creation, but a picture of the huge and undecipherable unreason of it. 'Hast thou sent the rain upon the desert where no man is?' The simple sense of wonder is the basis of spirituality as it is the basis of nonsense. Nonsense and faith

> are the two supreme symbolic assertions of the truth that to draw out the soul of things with a syllogism is as impossible as to draw out Leviathan with a hook. The well-meaning person who, by merely studying the logical side of things, has decided that 'faith is nonsense', does not know how truly he speaks; later it may come back to him in the form that nonsense is faith.

If we feel inclined to write off this kind of thing as mere witticism, we may recall that absurdity, or nonsense, has a place in the recorded teaching of Jesus. The first shall be last. Life is to be found by giving it away. A mite is of more value than many shekels.

Laughter can point to a choice by making the hearer respond to absurdity. Humanity does not seem able to avoid thinking of other possible worlds – the world of the clown in which disaster is never final, or the world of comedy where men and women live happily ever after, or the world of nonsense where 'Every one knows / That a Pobble is better without his toes'. The hearer either thinks that human beings endlessly deceive themselves with imaginations of another reality which does not exist, or becomes committed to the belief that this other paramount reality is sending signals. Then the laughter of joy is understood as just such a signal. Leisure ensures time to take in the signals.

The topics of play, games and laughter are good examples of the difficulty of thinking theologically about leisure. Not only are the words themselves highly ambiguous, but any enquiry into the way they have been used by theological writers shows that theology itself, far from being timeless, is dependent on personal and social factors. The Christian theologian always sees play and games, and hears laughter – and participates in them – in two frames of reference. They are set in a particular social context; and they are under the cross of Christ. So the individual is not free to choose or act even in leisure without being subject to, and contributing towards, forces of conformity or opposition which derive from past history and present conflicts of interest. Equally, the Christian believer stands under the judgement and receives the liberation which the cross bestows. That means, on the one hand, that the believer is, as Luther declared, *simul iustus et peccator*, at one and the same time saved and a sinner. The cross sets individuals free from self-concern; and that is the essence of leisure. Yet it also passes judgement on the root of that self-concern which remains deep in human nature, as Pascal could not forget; and that is something which threatens to throw leisure back into the state of competitiveness and anxiety characteristic of the worlds of work and social responsibility.

Children's play itself illustrates this duality: the child wholly absorbed in 'being' a bird (or, more likely these days, an aeroplane), and no less the child trying to cheat to win a game. This contrast makes it difficult to interpret Jesus' saying that his followers must become like little children because the kingdom belongs to such as they are. Moltmann (along with many others) does not hesitate to interpret the likeness as consisting in playing, as taking a game seriously, yet transcending it.[63] But Jesus was well aware of the refractory behaviour of children who refuse to join in a game other children have chosen.[64] There is only this one recorded comment by him explicitly about children's play, and it is one of criticism. The call for all disciples to become like children must refer to some other element in childhood. Perhaps Jesus was remembering his own childhood, from which he had grown up into the full understanding of the blessings and the challenges of the kingdom,[65] and meant that it was this very process of risky exploration, intrinsic to childhood, that entitled anyone to be a member of the kingdom. It must remain the characteristic of a disciple to be open to the future, not tied to the past. But no interpretation can command confident acceptance. In any case, childhood today is not what it was in first-century Palestine. It has become contaminated by the forces which make for premature adult choice. The boundaries of childhood are blurred.[66]

In our own age and society, we may include in our assessment of play the idea of 'latency' discussed by Rowan Williams.[67] He sees a tension between the protracted latency of human childhood (as compared with early maturity in other creatures) and the pressure in a consumerist society to use children as proxy consumers. This blurs the distinction between childhood and adulthood. In other societies childhood could be a time of experiment without commitment, allowing children to move towards adult choice. That would be the nature and justification of 'child's play'. It could not, however, be the model for adult life beyond the period of latency. If play is to have significance in maturity it must have another dimension. Games certainly afford a refuge from the particular stresses of work and social duty, but that is not enough for extended free time, and certainly not for a decade or more of retirement. The kind of play which offers some sort of model in these circumstances is suggested by Williams's use of the term 'charity' (derived from John Bossy[68]). It stands for what is enacted in rituals of acceptance, in contrast to the structured inequalities of common life. These rituals are not necessarily religious in any overt sense. They might include carnivals or village fêtes, as in the past they included fraternities with regular celebratory meals. Games can only qualify as proper adult play if the reward they bring is simply the recognition of the ability to play well. Laughter can only qualify as a proper constituent of leisure if its effect is to bond people together, not to set them at odds with each other. Such a rule would mark out the duality of human nature, leaving huge possibilities for free time, while indicating the threat of its corruption.

Casuistical theology has in the past been described as a game – *lusus theologiae*.[69] In that case it is a serious game and, unlike other games, it cannot simply be suspended because there are better things to do. The paradox about leisure is that the more seriously it is taken, the less it looks like leisure. In the same way, the more seriously games are taken, the less like play they become. It might seem that a theology of leisure, if such a thing is even possible, must not take itself too seriously. But we have seen that when the creative possibilities of leisure are compared to child's play, the comparison is in danger of reducing the universe to triviality. St Paul knew better than that. The whole creation was groaning in labour pains.[70]

As the domination of work lessens through the impact of technology, we come to a parting of the ways. One path leads to the multiplication of intentionally pointless activities, in an arcade of enjoyments. The other is a path to the kind of abundant life which was always God's purpose for humanity. One is a path to bondage of the will. The other reveals the true meaning of free time. It is impossible to be specific about the two paths in leisure, in view of the amazing complexity of human nature. But the traditions of Judaism and Christianity have always stressed the coexistence of alternative ways or paths. In Judaism, that coexistence is a recurrent theme of the Psalms, hammered home from the very beginning. 'The LORD knoweth the way of the righteous; but the way of the wicked shall perish.' In the New Testament, from the parables of Jesus to the visions of the Apocalypse, there are sheep and goats, the righteous and the filthy. Choice is real, and eternally significant. But not every choice has this eschatological weight, and it can be the function of free time to provide moments, of whatever duration, for human beings to be, to live, without looking before or after. But that is not all there is to be said about free time.

The first calls upon human energies are undeniably made by the demands of work and social life; but when those calls have been answered there may be some superfluity of vital energy, some overflow. The language of the New Testament offers three formally related terms, translated 'what is lacking' ($\upsilon\sigma\tau\epsilon\rho\eta\mu\alpha$), 'fulness' ($\pi\lambda\eta\rho\omega\mu\alpha$), and abundance ($\pi\epsilon\rho\iota\sigma\sigma\epsilon\upsilon\mu\alpha$). This last means something more than just fulness – a superabundance, overflowing the vessel which cannot contain it. These terms are characteristic of the Pauline rhetoric, not the Johannine literature; but in John 10.10, where we find the promise of having life abundantly through Christ, the writer unusually resorts to the related adverb ($\pi\epsilon\rho\iota\sigma\sigma\omega\varsigma$). 'Abundant life' is life overflowing. Without question, the meaning in John 10 refers immediately to spiritual life, to love, joy, peace, and all the gifts of the spirit made available in Christ. It clearly does not refer to the realms of work or social responsibility. But in a society increasingly occupied with leisure, perhaps it must now be referred to that realm, as well as to what is generally acknowledged as the realm of spiritual life. Free time may be one (but only one) of the possible locations of this overflow. But what overflows is fed from the wells of the spirit and takes its character from that source. So although leisure is not itself concerned with moral choices, its forms are determined by previous acts of choice. It is 'beyond morality' in two senses:

developing out of a pattern of behaviour controlled by some form of implicit morality, and yet not itself an area of moral choices. What may come under judgement is the dominant, if unarticulated, form of morality expressed in someone's life outside the realm of leisure, not the particular activities adopted in leisure itself, though they are its fruit.

As usual with questions of morality, there is seldom such a clear-cut division as between sheep and goats, between righteous and filthy. But extremes are distinguishable. In the present situation of Western society, two critical questions are those which concern an individual's relationship to other people, and to the environment. The extremes in both cases may be characterized as the attitudes of selfish exploitation (of other kinds of people or the earth's resources) on the one hand, and imaginative understanding (of human inter-dependence or the independent validity of all that is not human) on the other. Each attitude can determine action at work and in social duties. Hesitantly, one may suspect that chosen forms of leisure, even of play, games and laughter, reveal an underlying morality which is not being consciously applied, but is nevertheless operating below the level of consciousness. It is, of course, virtually impossible for even the most sensitive and self-critical person to escape involvement in patterns of leisure which are morally objectionable at some level. To belong to a society which is proudly competitive and exploitative, of persons and of the environment, means to share its guilt. To recognize that is to rediscover some of the meaning of the doctrine of humanity's fallen status, which Pascal saw as infecting and corrupting even *divertissement*. It remains possible that a pre-conditioning life-choice of imaginative understanding may lead to uses of free time which are creative, celebratory and joyful. Leisure is not the basis of a single culture, but of many variants of culture. We can add T.S. Eliot's defence of multiplicity to Pieper's general rule that leisure is the cradle of culture and hope for a multi-cultural kaleidoscope. We need not think all its elements are equally enriching.

## NOTES

1.  John Chrysostom, *Contra Ludos*, quoted in W.R. Stephens, *Saint Chrysostom* (London 1872), 234.
2.  Thomas Aquinas, *Summa Theologiae*, ed. and trs. Thomas Gilby (London 1964–81), II, ii art. 2.
3.  Roger Caillois, *Man Play and Games* (Eng edn 1962 [1958]), 81.
4.  Mafeo Vegio of Lodi, *De Liberorum Eruditione*, quoted in Bede Jarrett, *Social Theories of the Middle Ages 1200–1500* (London 1968 [1926]), 63–4.
5.  W.M. Pryke, 'The Social Life of the Parish' in G.F. Garbett (ed.), *The Work of a Great Parish* (London 1915), 266–7.
6.  See Margaret Talbot, 'Their Own Worst Enemy? Women and Leisure Provision' in E.Wimbush and M.Talbot (ed.), *Relative Freedoms: Women and Leisure* (Milton Keynes 1988), 161–76.
7.  *Christianizing the Social Order* (NY 1912), 248, quoted in Robert Lee, *Religion and Leisure in America* (Nashville, Tenn 1964), 90.
8.  Paul Tillich, *On The Boundary: An Autobiographical Sketch* (London 1967), 25.
9.  Johan Huizinga, *Homo Ludens: A Study of the Play Element in Culture* (London 1970 [1949]), 32
10. Ibid. 26–7.
11. S.T. Coleridge, *Biographia Literaria* (London 1956 [1817]), ch. 24.
12. Hebrews 4.9.
13. See below, page 129.
14. Huizinga *Homo Ludens*, 13
15. Ibid. 12.
16. Ephesians 6.6; Colossians 3.23.
17. Alan Richardson, *The Biblical Doctrine of Work* (London 1952), 39. The reference is to 2 Thessalonians 3.6–12.
18. Michael A. Mullett, 'Catholic and Quaker attitudes to work, rest and play in seventeenth and eighteenth century England', in Swanson (ed.), *The Use and abuse of Time in Christian History* (Woodbidge and Rchester N Y, 2002), 185–209.
19. José Harris, *Private Lives, Public Spirit: A Social History of Britain 1870–1914* (Oxford 1993), 160.
20. Hugo Rahner, *Man at Play, or, Did You Ever Practise Eutrapelia?* trs. B. Battershaw and E. Quinn (London 1965)
21. Vulgate 32.15–16: *illic lude, et age conceptiones tuas.*
22. ευφραινεσθαι.
23. Jürgen Moltmann, *Theology of Play*, trs. R. Ulrich (NY 1972), 111.
24. The Greek words for play-thing and playing (παιγνιον and παιςειν) are connected with 'child' (παις).
25. W.H. Vanstone, *Love's Endeavour, Love's Expense: The Response of Being to the Love of God* (London 1977), 60–61
26. Mark 10.14.

27. 'Child's Play', *Cornhill Magazine* (Sept. 1877) reprinted in *Essays and Poems*, ed. Claire Harman (1992).
28. Letters, 9 Oct. 1825, to James Gillman in *Collected Letters of Samuel Taylor Coleridge*, ed. E.L. Griggs (Oxford 1971), V, 496..
29. Caillois, *Man Play and Games*.
30. Rahner, *Man at Play*, 6–7
31. Ibid. 25.
32. See e.g. R.N. Whybray, *Proverbs*, New Century Bible Commentary (London 1994), 26–30
33. Ibid. 134–6
34. Huizinga, *Homo Ludens* 151.
35. Ibid. 54, 36
36. Jürgen Moltmann, *Theology and Joy*, with an extended introduction by David E. Jenkins (London 1973), 20
37. Tillich, *On the Boundary*, viii.
38. Karl Barth, *How I Changed My Mind* (Edinburgh 1966), 25
39. Ibid. 10
40. Karl Barth, *Church Dogmatics*, III.3 (Edinburgh 1961), 295 ff.
41. George Steiner, *Real Presences: Is There Anything in What We Say?* (London 1989), 178
42. Rahner, *Man At Play*, 65–6.
43. Ronald Blythe, *The View in Winter: Reflections on Old Age* (London 1979), 36.
44. See Catherine Bates, *Play in a Godless World* (London 1999), ch. 2: 'Of the Death of God, Deconstruction, and Play', 42 ff.
45. Peter L. Berger, *Redeeming Laughter* (Berlin and NY 1997), 13.
46. E.g. Alice Meynell, 'Christ in the Universe': 'O, be prepared, my soul! / To read the inconceivable, to scan / The million forms of God those stars unroll / When, in our turn, we show to them a Man.' In *An Anthology of Modern Verse*, ed. A. Methuen (28th edn London 1934).
47. Jürgen Moltmann, *God in Creation: An Ecological Doctrine of Creation*, Gifford Lectures 1984–5, trs. Margaret Kohl (London 1985), 304–7
48. See Rowan Williams on 'raves' in *Lost Icons* (Edinburgh and NY 2000), 66–7.
49. See F. Gavin, 'The Catholic Doctrine of Work and Play', in *Theology*, XXI (July 1930), esp. pp.33–4
50. See M.A. Screech, *Laughter at the Foot of the Cross* (London 1997) 13–40.
51. A.L. Rowse, *A Cornish Childhood* (London 1983 [1942]), 49–50.
52. Leland Ryken, *Work and Leisure in Christian Perspective* (Leicester 1989), 200
53. Nicholas Sagovsky, *'On God's Side': A Life of George Tyrrell* (Oxford 1990), 245.
54. Peter L. Berger mentions philosophy, physiology, psychology and the social sciences: *Redeeming Laughter: The Comic Dimension of Human Experience* (Berlin 1997), xi.
55. Evelyn Underhill, *Mysticism* (Rev. edn London 1930 [1911]), 438. *Paradiso*, xvii, 4: *un riso / Dell' universo*.

56. γελαω and καταγελαω.
57. See Screech, *Laughter at the Foot of the Cross*, ix–xi.
58. Vanstone, *Love's Endeavour*, 104–5.
59. N. Berdyaev, *Spirit and Reality* (London 1939), 125.
60. Berger, *Redeeming Laughter*, 204, 210
61. Martin Esslin, *The Theatre of the Absurd*, (rev. edn London 1968), 404.
62. G.K. Chesterton, *Stories, Essays and Poems* (London 1935), 123–7.
63. Moltmann, *Theology and Joy*,  41.
64. Matthew 11.17.
65. Luke 2.52.
66. Williams, *Lost Icons*, 28.
67. Ibid., 11ff.
68. John Bossy, *Christianity and the West 1400–1700* (Oxford 1985).
69. Blaise Pascal quoted in H.R. McAdoo, *The Structure of Caroline Moral Theology* (London 1949), 11.
70. Romans 8.22.

# Postscript: Concerning Worship

The relationship between leisure and worship is not at all clear. Sociological writers, who inevitably concentrate on observable practice, include church attendance among leisure activities, often with special reference to women's leisure. In previous generations pubs and clubs were almost exclusively places for men, and the church or chapel provided the only respectable places where women could spend their free time. What they did there included worship along with general social activities. There was a close relationship between worship and leisure. This situation gradually changed after the First World War with the foundation of secular organizations for women, such as the Women's Institutes and the Women's Co-operative Guild. The separation of social and religious activities has gone on, in different ways, in organizations for men and for young people. Public worship today in Western society is clearly reserved for free time, except where it survives in schools. But from a committed religious point of view it is marked off from other activities in free time both by its explicit reference to the transcendent and by the element of duty or obligation which it entails.

Outside the sociological context the meaning of worship cannot be restricted to overt religious practice. Because it is essentially inward and spiritual, it can penetrate and transform the other main areas of human life beside leisure – work and social obligations. The witness of Brother Lawrence in the seventeenth century represents a widely held perception:

> You must find joy in God's company and make it a life-time habit to speak with him humbly and lovingly throughout the day. ... We must not work with an undisciplined spirit, but work in God's presence quietly, placidly and lovingly. Pray to God that he will approve of your work.[1]

Nor was it only work which could be permeated by the attitude of worship. Leisure itself might be penetrated by prayer.

> Among the actions which count as prayer, I include visits of courtesy and kindness, also necessary recreations of body and mind, so long as

these be innocent and kept within the bounds of Christian conduct. None of these things is incompatible with unceasing prayer, and except those which are evil, unsuitable, or useless, none which the Holy Spirit cannot justify, find means to sanctify, and include in the Kingdom of Prayer.[2]

Worship transcends any artificial analysis of the complex richness of human experience into the different areas of work, social obligation and leisure.

That has not prevented different writers from seeing a particular affinity between leisure and worship, perhaps with the intention of raising leisure from triviality to greater significance in the Christian life. Ryken, for example, argues that there is a 'kinship between worship and leisure'. This is reasonable enough. The two have features in common, and it is valuable to emphasize that the purpose of 're-creation' which is central to leisure is also the heart of the gospel. 'The person in Christ has an identity towards which we aspire'.[3] If we avoid the Pelagianism which this might unintentionally suggest, this is a valuable insight into the meaning of leisure. But in line with the general intention of his book Ryken approves the idea that both leisure and worship 'call a temporary halt to our work and active duties'. They should not be seen as interruptions of something else. That would be to assume that work is the real business of life and, in doing so, to place both leisure and worship on a lower plane. Neither leisure nor worship is then allowed to be truly 'an end in itself'.

There are also important elements in worship which have no obvious 'kinship' with leisure. These include confession and intercession, but much else beside. There are

> the solemn rites which hallow the achievement of adolescence, the blessings of ruler, traveller, bride and bridegroom, the churching of women, ceremonial care for the dead. All these, together with the benediction of house, fields, food, instruments of labour, or badges of service, are to be regarded as acts of worship: for they refer to God as a distinct yet present Reality, and acknowledge His hallowing action and unlimited claim.[4]

These are woven into those parts of human life which are most active, most purposive, and so least like leisure.

In relating leisure to worship, a key word commonly used is 'celebration', which is seen as characteristic of both. The best exponent of this idea is Josef Pieper. He contrasts leisure with the exclusive ideal of work as unremitting activity, first as an attitude of inward calm, and then as an attitude of contemplative 'celebration'. He refers to the statement in Genesis that God rested from creation and saw that it was good. 'In the same way man celebrates and gratefully accepts the reality of creation in leisure, and the inner vision that accompanies it.' Pieper declares that leisure had its very origin in feasts, which were celebrations. So it is not just a break in work for the sake of returning to work. Unlike Ryken, he says that the point of leisure is not to be a restorative, a pick-me-up, whether mental or physical, or even spiritual – though it may incidentally have that kind of effect. The real point is rather 'that he should continue to be capable of seeing life as a whole; that he should fulfil himself, and come to full possession of his faculties, face to face with being as a whole.'[5] It is difficult to give a precise meaning to this idea of celebration. It seems to stretch far beyond the limits of anything like an organized activity, which its stated origin in feasts would seem to imply.

This corporate dimension is stressed by Karl Barth in discussing the Sabbath commandment in the context of freedom before God. He declares that 'observance does not simply mean resting but, positively, the celebrating of a festival'. This involves 'participation in the praise and worship and witness and proclamation of God in His congregation, in common thanksgiving and intercession.'[6] In the Reformation period the Puritans wanted to make a clear distinction between the celebration of the Sabbath and the enjoyment of leisure. The proper arrangement would be to keep the Sabbath entirely for worship and devotional exercises, and to designate one day a month for leisure of a secular kind.[7] In that pattern it would not have made sense to describe secular leisure as a kind of celebration, which strictly belonged in the religious context. They would have noted that festivals in the Old Testament celebrated God's mighty works for Israel, and reapplied the same understanding to God's work of salvation in the new dispensation.

The meaning of celebration has changed with the increased secularization of Western society. Nowadays we celebrate all kinds of anniversaries in individual and community life. Our communal feasts and festivals have little to do with salvation history. They are more characteristically national or seasonal, and have sometimes become entirely detached from their origins – as with 'bonfire night' on 5 November. Even in the church the celebration of Christ's birth merges into a general celebration of the family. That is why it seems to come more easily than the celebration of Christ's resurrection, because it touches a universal human experience. There are other changes in the temper of worship now widely accepted, which may be indicated in the shift from penitence to eucharist. In the Reformation era, suffering and disaster were usually interpreted as divine punishment for human sin, the sin of disobedience to God. Celebration then was celebration of God's loving-kindness in redeeming fallen humankind. Now penitence is inclined to be perfunctory, and the worshippers' awareness of suffering, being directed by the media to the four quarters of the earth beyond the reach of practical action, takes the form of petition, as though to say to God, 'What are you going to do about it?' Tradition ensures that the eucharistic prayers still celebrate the wonder of God's redemptive action, but the canon is often prefaced with blessings of God for the gifts, not of salvation, but of creation and human labour.

These changes are not necessarily to be decried. It is natural enough to celebrate the gifts of God to humankind in the form of skills and abilities.

Even in the seventeenth century Thomas Traherne was ready in his *Meditations* to celebrate the gifts of other people.

> In every soul whom Thou hast created, Thou hast given me the Similitude of Thyself to enjoy! Could my desires have aspired unto such treasures? Could my wisdom have devised such sublime enjoyments? Oh! Thou hast done more for us than we could ask or think. I praise and admire, and rejoice in Thee: who art infinitely infinite in all Thy doings.[8]

This is part of loving our neighbour. Leisure, at its best, also gives individuals an opportunity to celebrate their own abilities as gifts of God. 'Leisure is only possible when a man is at one with himself, when he acquiesces in his own being.'[9] In that sense, and not in any other, it is right to love ourselves as we love our neighbour. It is hard to say whether this belongs to worship as usually understood. There is a tradition, represented by the story of the Jongleur de Notre Dame, who did his tumbling tricks before a statue of Our Lady, that apparently trivial gifts can properly be offered in worship. The gifts of God are in a sense reciprocal: to be received with thanksgiving and offered back in celebration. It is possible to see leisure in this way, too.

But there is a significant difference in common perception. Most people, apart from the assertively 'self-made man', are ready to acknowledge that their abilities are not their own creation: they are 'received' from genetic inheritance, from their nurturing in family and society and nation, from education, from their experience of corporate life in the church, and so on. But leisure is regarded as something earned, deserved, possessed as due reward for work. That was the firm belief, not only of the men, but also of the women of Lancashire, as recorded by Professor Zweig in the 1950s. It even obstructed the enjoyment of leisure on equal terms by husband and wife, except on the annual holiday. Leisure was earned, and if you earn something, you have the right to do with it what you choose – to waste it or throw it away, if you like.

If this is how people understand leisure, it makes it harder for them to relate it to worship, or even to think that it is of interest to God. There are other things which can be offered, that is, consecrated, to God – talents, and the money which work yields. It is not difficult to see how they can be used somehow or other in the service of God and one's neighbour. The idea of stewardship covers both kinds of offering. They can be directed to purposes which are seen as having divine approval. But it is of the nature of leisure that it cannot have any purpose beyond itself, or it ceases to be leisure. Free time becomes dedicated time. It exists in its own time and space, insulated from purposive activity.

The relation of leisure to worship, therefore, can only be in thanksgiving. The blessing of God for his gifts, which is prominent in the worship of Judaism and is beginning to be recovered in Christianity, must include blessing for the gift of free time. It will still seem incongruous to some worshippers to bless

God for a darts match or the visit to a theme park. Certainly the act itself may not be very significant. Its meaning lies in the self-realization of the participant. 'Blessed art thou, Lord of the universe, that thou hast made me even such as I am.' Leisure is a way of knowing God, knowing what he has made me to be, and knowing, in the silence which follows when competitiveness is shut out, the God who has given free time as a gracious gift. We go back to Psalm 46.10: 'Be still and know that I am God'; or perhaps to the Latin version: *vacate et videte quoniam ego sum Deus*: Have leisure, and see that I am God.

## NOTES

1. Brother Lawrence, *The Practice of the Presence of God*, trs. D. Attwater (London 1926).
2. J.N. Grou, *The School of Jesus Christ*, 37th lesson, quoted in Evelyn Underhill, *Worship* (London 1936), 187.
3. Leland Ryken, *Work and Leisure in Christian Perspective* (Leicester 1989), 204.
4. Underhill, *Worship*, 12.
5. Josef Pieper, *Leisure the Basis of Culture* (London 1952), 54–7.
6. Karl Barth, *Church Dogmatics* (Edinburgh 1961), III, 62.
7. Possibly the second Tuesday. See W.B. Whitaker, *Sunday in Tudor and Stuart Times* (London 1938) 156–7.
8. Thomas Traherne, *Centuries of Meditations*, ed. Bertram Dobell (London 1948), I.69.
9. Pieper, *Leisure*, 51.

# Select Bibliography

*(Place of publication is London, unless otherwise noted)*

ABSE, Joan, *John Ruskin, The Passionate Moralist* (1980).
ALTSCHULE, M.D., 'Acedia: Its Evolution from Deadly Sin to Psychiatric Syndrome', *British Journal of Psychiatry* III (1965), 117–19.
AMIEL, Henri-Frédéric, *Journal Intime*, trs. Mrs Humphry Ward (1889).
ANSCHEN, Ruth Nanda (ed.) *Freedom: Its Meaning* (1942).
AQUINAS, Thomas, *Commentary on the Nicomachean Ethics*, trs.C.I. Litzinger (Chicago 1964).
AQUINAS, Thomas, *Summa Theologiae,* ed. and trs. Thomas Gilby (1964–81).
ARISTOTLE, *Ethics*, trs. J.A.K. Thomson (Harmondsworth 1955).
ARNOLD, Matthew, *Culture and Anarchy* (1869).
AUGUSTINE of Hippo, *City of God,* trs. Marcus Dods (Edinburgh 1872).

BARR, James, *Biblical Words for Time* (rev. edn 1969).
BARTH, Karl, *Church Dogmatics*, vol. III (Edinburgh 1961).
BARTH, Karl, *Ethics*, ed. Dietrich Braun, trs. G.W. Bromiley (Edinburgh 1981 [1928]).
BARTH, Karl, *How I Changed My Mind*, (Edinburgh 1966).
BARTH, Karl, *Wolfgang Amadeus Mozart*, trs C.K. Pott (Grand Rapids 1986).
BATES, Catherine, *Play in a Godless World* (1999).
BAXTER, Richard, *A Christian Directory* (1673).
BAXTER, Richard, *The Saints' Everlasting Rest*, ed. C.Pipe (1994 [1650]).
BECKWITH, R.T. and STOTT, W., *This is the Day: The Biblical Doctrine of the Christian Sunday* (1978).
BEGBIE, Jeremy, *Voicing Creation's Praise: Towards a Theology of the Arts* (Edinburgh 1991).
BERDYAEV, Nicholas, *Solitude and Society* (1938).
BERDYAEV, Nicholas, *Spirit and Reality* (1939).
BERGER, Peter, *Redeeming Laughter: The Comic Dimension of Human Experience* (Berlin and NY 1997).
BERGER, Peter, *The Social Reality of Religion* (1969).
BLYTHE, Ronald, *The View in Winter: Reflections on Old Age* (1979).
BORNE, E. and HENRY, F., *A Philosophy of Work*, trs. F.Jackson (1938).
BRANSON, N. and HEINEMANN, M., *Britain in the 1930s* (1971).
BRETT, R.L., *Faith and Doubt: Religion and Secularization in Literature from Wordsworth to Larkin* (Cambridge 1997).
BRIDGE, David, *Looking at Leisure* (1978).
BRIGHTBILL, C.K., *The Challenge of Leisure* (New Jersey 1960).
BURNABY, John, *Amor Dei: A Study of the Religion of St Augustine* (1938).

CAILLOIS, Roger, *Man, Play and Games* (1962 [French edn 1958]).
CAREY, John, *The Faber Book of Utopias* (1999).

CHURCH ASSEMBLY (Social and Industrial Council) *The National Church and the Social Order* (1956).
CLAYRE, Alasdair, *Work and Play: Ideas and Experience of Work and Leisure* (1974).
COLERIDGE, S.T., *Lay Sermons*, ed.R.J. White (Princeton 1972).
CONSTABLE, Giles, *Three Studies in Mediaeval Religious and Social Thought* (Cambridge 1995).
COPEC (Conference on Christian Politics, Economics and Citizenship), *Commission Reports Vol.V – Leisure* (1924).
CROPPER, Margaret, *Sparks among the Stubble* (1955).

DAVIES, E.T., *Religion in the Industrial Revolution in South Wales* (Cardiff 1965).
DERFLER, Leslie, *Paul Lafargue and the Founding of French Marxism 1842–1882* (Cambridge Mass. 1991).
DIGGINS, J.P., *Thorstein Veblen* (Princeton, NJ 1999).
DOMINIAN, J. and PEACOCKE, A.H., *From Cosmos to Love: The Meaning of Human Life* (1976).
DUNN, J.D.G., *Christian Liberty: A New Testament Perspective* (Carlisle 1993).
DURANT, Henry, *The Problem of Leisure* (1938).

ELIOT, T.S., 'Essay' in *Revelation: Essays by Gustav Aulen* et al. (1937).
ELIOT, T.S., *Notes towards The Definition of Culture* (1948).
ELLUL, Jacques, *The Ethics of Freedom*, trs. G.W. Bromiley (1976).
EMPSON, William, *Milton's God* (1961).
ESSLIN, Martin, *The Theatre of the Absurd* (rev. edn 1968).

FOSTER, John, 'Recreation' in *The Furrow* (Maynooth, Feb. 1962).
FRANCIS, Julian, 'And Off to work', *Crucible* (Jan.–March 1984).
FRASER, Ronald (ed.), *Work: Twenty Personal Accounts* (1965).
FRIENDS, Society of, *Christian Faith and Practice in the Experience of the Society of Friends* (1960).

GALBRAITH, J.K., *The Affluent Society* (Harmondsworth 1962).
GALLWEY, Tim, *The Inner Game of Tennis* (1997).
GARBETT, C.F. (ed.), *The Work of a Great Parish* (1915).
GAVIN, F., 'The Catholic Doctrine of Work and Play', *Theology*, XXI (1930), 14–40.
GELLNER, E., *Plough, Sword and Book: The Structure of Human History* (1991).

HARRIES, Richard, *Art and the Beauty of God: A Christian Understanding* (1993).
HARRIS, José, *Private Lives, Public Spirit: A Social History of Britain, 1870–1914* (Oxford 1993).
HAYWOOD, Les *et al.*, *Understanding Leisure* (2nd edn Cheltenham 1995).
*HISTORISCHES WÖRTERBUCH DER PHILOSOPHIE* (Basel 1971) –'Musse'.
HODGKINS, William, *Sunday: Christian and Social Significance* (1960).
HOPKINSON, A.W., *About William Law* (1948).
HUGHES, Richard, *Fiction as Truth – Select Literary Writings*, ed.R.Poole(Bridgend 1983).
HUIZINGA, Johan, *Homo Ludens: A Study of the Play Element in Culture* (1970 [1949]).

JARRETT, Bede, *Social Theories of the Middle Ages 1200–1500* (1968 [1926]),

JASPER, David, *The Study of Literature and Religion: An Introduction* (1989).
JOUSSELIN, Jean, Article: 'A World of Leisure' in *Student World* Vol.LIX (1966) 36–40.

KIERKEGARD, Søren, *Either / Or*, trs. F. and L.M. Swenson (NY 1959).
KRAILSHEIMER, Alban, *Pascal* (Oxford 1980).
KÜNG, Hans, *Art and the Question of Meaning* (1980).
KÜNG, Hans, *Eternal Life?* trs.E.Quinn (1982).
KÜNG, Hans, *Mozart – Traces of Transcendence*, trs.J.Bowden (1992).

LAMBETH CONFERENCE REPORT 1920.
LANGHAMER, Claire, *Women's Leisure in England 1920–1960* (Manchester and NY 2000).
LAW, William, *A Serious Call to a Devout and Holy Life* (1899).
LEE, Robert, *Religion and Leisure in America: A Study in Four Dimensions* (Nashville, Tenn. 1964)
LEHMAN, Harold D., *In Praise of Leisure* (Scottdale, Pa. 1974).
LOWERSON, J. and MYERCOUGH, J., *Time to Spare in Victorian England* (Hassocks 1977).

McADOO, H.R., *First of its Kind: A Study in the Functioning of a Moral Theory* (Norwich 1994).
McADOO, H.R., *The Structure of Caroline Moral Theology* (1949).
MACINTYRE, Alasdair, *Secularization and Moral Change*, (1967).
MACMURRAY, John, *Reason and Emotion* (1935).
MARRUS, Michael R. (ed.) *The Emergence of Leisure*, (NY 1974).
METHODIST CHURCH, *Statements on Social Responsibility 1946–1995* (1995).
MISSEN, L.R., *The Employment of Leisure* (Exeter 1935).
MOLTMANN, Jürgen, *God in Cration: An Ecological Doctrine of Creation*, Gifford Lectures, 1984–5, trs. Margaret Kohl.
MOLTMANN, Jürgen, *Theology and Joy*, with an extended Introduction by David E. Jenkins (1973).
MOLTMANN, Jürgen, *Theology of Play*, trs.R.Ulrich (NY 1972).
MOORE, Robert, *Pitmen Preachers and Politics* (Cambridge 1974).
MORSE, Margaret, *Virtualities: Television, Media Art, and Cyberculture* (Bloomington, Ind. 1998).
MURRAY, Nicholas, *A Life of Matthew Arnold* (1996).

NEALE, Robert E., *In Praise of Play*, (NY and London 1969).

OATES, Wayne, *Confessions of a Workaholic* (1979).
OBELKEVICH, James, *Religion and Rural Society: South Lindsey 1825–1875* (Oxford 1976).
O'DONOVAN, Oliver, *The Problem of Self-love in St Augustine* (New Haven, Conn. 1980).
OVERTON, J.H., *William Law, Non-juror and Mystic (1686–1761)* (1881).

PAFFARD, Michael, *The Unattended Moment* (1976).
PARKER, Stanley, *Leisure and Work* (1983).
PASCAL, Blaise, *Pensées*, ed. and trs. A.J.Krailsheimer (Harmondsworth 1966).

PATTISON, George, *Kierkegaard: The Aesthetic and the Religious – From the Magic Theatre to the Crucifixion of the Image* (1992).

PIEPER, Josef, *Leisure: The Basis of Culture* (1952).

PILGRIM TRUST, *Men Without Work* (Cambridge 1938).

POOLE, Steven, *Trigger Happy: The Inner Life of Video-Games* (2000).

QUINTON, Anthony, 'Wodehouse and the Tradition of Comedy' in *From Wodehouse to Wittgenstein* (Manchester 1998), 318–34.

RAHNER, Hugo, *Man at Play or Did You Ever Practise Eutrapelia?* trs. B.Battershaw and E.Quinn (1965).

RICHARDSON, Alan, *The Biblical Doctrine of Work* (1952).

ROOKMAAKER, H.R., *The Creative Gift: Arts and the Christian Life* (Leicester 1982).

RORDORF, Willy, *Sunday: The History of the Day of Rest and Worship in the Earliest Centuries of the Christian Church* (Eng. trans. 1968 [1962]).

RUSKIN, John, *Munera Pulveris*, in *Works* (London 1903–12), XVI .

RYKEN, Leland, *Work and Leisure in Christian Perspective* (Leicester 1989).

SAMUEL, Nicole (ed.) *Women, Leisure and the Family in Contemporary Society: A Multinational Perspective* (Wallingford 1996).

SAYERS, Dorothy L., *Begin Here: A War-time Essay* (1940).

SCHLEIERMACHER, Friedrich, *On Religion: Speeches to its Cultured Despisers*, trs. J.Oman (NY 1958).

SCREECH, M.A., *Laughter at the Foot of the Cross* (1997).

SEABROOK, Jeremy, *The Everlasting Feast* (1974).

SEABROOK, Jeremy, *The Leisure Society* (Oxford 1988).

SEABROOK, Jeremy, *What Went Wrong? Working People and the Ideals of the Labour Movement* (1978).

SELWYN, David, *Jane Austen and Leisure* (1999).

SENCOURT, Robert, *The Consecration of Genius* (1947).

SIMON, Ulrich, *The Ascent to Heaven* (1961).

STEINER, George, *Real Presences: Is There Anything in What We Say?* (1989).

STEVENSON, J. and COOK, C., *The Slump* (1977).

STEVENSON, R.L., *Essays and Poems*, ed.Claire Harman (1992).

STOPFORD, J. *Pilgrimage Explored* (York 1999).

SWANSON, R.N. (ed.), *The Use and Abuse of Time in Christian History* Studies in Church History (Woodbridge and Rochester, NY, 2002).

TAYLOR, Jeremy, *Ductor Dubitantium or The Rule of Conscience* (2nd edn 1671).

TAYLOR, Jeremy, *The Practical Works* ed.G. Croly (8 vols, 1838).

TEMPLE, William, *Christianity and Social Order* (1942).

THIELICKE, Helmut, *Theological Ethics: Vol. I. Foundations* (English edn 1968).

THOMAS, Keith (ed.) *The Oxford Book of Work* (Oxford 1999).

THOMPSON, E.P., *Customs in Common* (1991).

THOMPSON, E.P., *William Morris, Romantic and Revolutionary*, (1977). ,

TILLICH, Paul, *On the Boundary – An Autobiographical Sketch*, with an Introduction by J. HeywoodThomas (1967).

TILLICH, Paul, *Theology of Culture* (Oxford 1959).

TOMPKINS, Jane P. (ed.) *Reader-Response Criticism: From Formalism to Post-Structuralism* (1990).

TOURAINE, Alain, *The Post-industrial Society: Tomorrow's Social History* trs. L.F.X. Mayhew (NY 1971).
TOURNIER, Paul, *Learning to Grow Old* (1972).
TRAHERNE, Thomas, *Centuries of Meditations*, ed. Bertram Dobell (1948).
TRAHERNE, Thomas, *Christian Ethics*, ed. C.L. Marks and G.R. Guffey (Ithaca, NY, 1968 [1675]).

UNDERHILL, Evelyn, *Mysticism* (rev. edn 1930 [1911]).

VANSTONE, W.H., *Love's Endeavour, Love's Expense: The Response of Being to the Love of God* (1977).
VANSTONE, W.H., *The Stature of Waiting*, (1982).
VEBLEN, Thorstein, *The Theory of the Leisure Class: An Economic Study of Institutions* (NY 1970 [1899]).
VICKERS, Brian, 'Leisure and idleness in the Renaissance: The Ambivalence of *Otium*', *Renaissance Studies*, IV (1990), no. 1, pt 1, 1–37; pt 2, 107–54.
Von BALTHASAR, Hans Urs, *The Glory of the Lord: A Theological Aesthetics, Vol.III – Studies in Theological Style: Lay Styles* (Edinburgh 1986).

WALKER, A.K., *William Law:His Life and Thought* (1973).
WALLACE, Patricia, *The Psychology of the Internet* (Cambridge 1999).
WALZER, Michael, *Spheres of Justice* (1984).
WEST, Philip, 'Cruciform Labour?', *Theology*, XXVIII, no. 4 (1986), 9–15.
WHEELER, Michael, *Ruskin's God* (Cambridge 1999).
WHITAKER, W.B., *The Eighteenth-Century English Sunday* (1940).
WHITAKER, W.B., *Sunday in Tudor and Stuart Times* (1938).
WHYBRAY, R.N., *Ecclesiastes* (London and Grand Rapids, Mich. 1989).
WILLEY, Basil, *The Seventeenth Century Background* (1949).
WILLIAMS, H.A., *True Resurrection* (1972).
WILLIAMS, Rowan, *Lost Icons: Reflections on Cultural Bereavement* (Edinburgh and NY 2000).
WILSON, John (ed.) *The Faith of an Artist* (1962).
WIMBUSH, Erica and TALBOT, Margaret (eds) *Relative Freedoms: Women and Leisure* (Milton Keynes 1988).
WINNIFRITH, T. and BARRETT, C. (eds) *The Philosophy of Leisure* (Basingstoke 1989).
WOOD, Thomas, *English Casuistical Divinity during the Seventeenth Century* (1952).

ZWEIG, Ferdynand, *Women's Life and Labour* (1952).

# Index of Biblical References

**Old Testament**

**Apocrypha**

**New Testament**

# Index

*Index*

Printed in the United Kingdom
by Lightning Source UK Ltd.
100783UKS00001B/238-441